Roger Delgado:

I Am Usually Referred To As The Master

Roger Delgado:
I Am Usually Referred To As
THE MASTER

A biography
by Marcus K. Harmes

First published in 2017 by Fantom Films
fantomfilms.co.uk

A catalogue record for this book is available from the British Library.

Hardback edition ISBN: 978-1-78196-300-5

Typeset by Phil Reynolds Media Services, Leamington Spa
Printed and bound by CPI Group (UK) Ltd, Croydon, CR0 4YY

Jacket design by Will Brooks

In memory of Roger Delgado (1918-1973)

Universally referred to as the Master

Contents

Acknowledgements

T HROUGHOUT THE RESEARCH and writing for this biography I have been overwhelmed by the generosity of so many people who have shared with me their memories of Roger Delgado and given me their time and expertise.

I was honoured to receive a message from Mrs Kismet Marlowe, Roger Delgado's widow, wishing me the best for this project.

Those who made time to share their memories are Katy Manning, John Levene, Victor Pemberton, Claire Nielson, Richard Franklin, Hugh Futcher, Neil Stacy, Timothy Combe, Michael Briant, Terrance Dicks, Pik-Sen Lim, Stephen Thorne, Michael Ferguson, Linda Thorson, Roger Jenkins, Brian Blessed (via AIM LLP), Hildegard Neil (via AIM LLP), Damaris Hayman, Veronica Strong, Jeremy Burnham, and Alvin Rakoff. In many cases their agents and representatives were an essential part of making contact and organising times and I am grateful for their help.

Dexter O'Neill at Fantom Publishing has from the very outset been a source of constant support and inspiration and on hand to answer questions and help about all aspects of this project. Paul Ballard of Fantom gave wise feedback and guidance on the manuscript. I am most grateful to them both for their interest and enthusiasm.

In the process of research I received generous and informative help from: John Kelly; Associate Professor Andrew Hickey of the School of Arts and Communication at the University of Southern Queensland; Tegan Darnell, Kim Moore and Jan Ridley of the University of Southern Queensland

Library; Carolyn Butler White of the University of Southern Queensland; Sally Cholewa and Sophie Volker from the Royal Bank of Scotland Archives; Richard Meunier, Deputy Archivist/Curator, Royal London Hospital Archives & Museum, Barts Health NHS Trust; the Cardinal Vaughan Memorial School including Hannah Staff, Personal Assistant to the Headmaster; Sue Donnelly and Anna Towlson, archivists at the London School of Economics and Political Science; Lisa Kerrigan at the British Film Institute; Shane Brown; Stephen Lacey from the University of South Wales; Martin John Baker; Paul Sutton; Martin Skipworth of the Royal Signals Museum; Ian Hunter from De Montfort University; Marcus Hearn; Jeremy Crang from Edinburgh University; Lottie Alexander from York St John University; Matt Boughton of Hammer Films; Laura Yeoman of York Explore Library Learning Centre; Alan Hayles; Alastair Massie, National Army Museum; Dr Richard Hewett, Salford University; Colin Sparks; Adam Ganz; Dr Matthew Jones and Laraine Porter from De Montfort University Leicester; Sheena Harold, the Teddington Society; Max Sexton; María Paola González Sepúlveda, the University of Melbourne; Beatriz Carbajal, University of Sydney; Tim O'Sullivan, De Montfort University; Gus Barton; James Dearden; Andrea at Mortlake Crematorium; Kate Kuzma; Bruno Kuzma; Hugh Baulcombe, Brunel University London; Richard Temple, Archivist, Senate House Library, University of London; Professor Thiru Aravinthan, University of Southern Queensland.

Throughout this project my family have been an endless source of encouragement and sustenance. Above all else, the idea to write this biography was my sister's. Meredith emailed me one day to point out that 2018 was the centenary of Roger Delgado's birth and, therefore, why don't I write his biography?

Prologue

W ITH A STRANGE WHEEZING, groaning noise, a horsebox appears out of thin air. A man in a dark suit with a devilish beard jumps out. Within moments we learn this stranger is 'usually referred to as the Master'.

This is the first onscreen appearance in *Doctor Who* of the Master and of Roger Delgado, the actor playing him. Delgado was the first, last, and only choice of the producer Barry Letts to bring this character to life. 'There was no casting or anything, no auditioning, it was written for Roger and Roger was always going to play the part,' says Terrance Dicks, the script editor who dreamt up the character.[1] Delgado brought to the role long experience in playing villains on film and television and even longer experience on stage and radio, but not so far any acting in *Doctor Who*. In an early 1970s interview Delgado reminisced that he 'had tried three times to break into *Doctor Who*' before getting the part of the Master.

It was worth the wait. Producer Barry Letts and Dicks provided Delgado with a role created especially for him. They also gave the Master a strong style and he is dapper, dressed in a high-collared suit and black gloves. Beneath the elegant façade Delgado brought onto the screen a vicious, snarling killer with a darkly sarcastic sense of humour and a menacing glare.

His first line, 'I am usually referred to as the Master,' provides my title and gives the viewer much more to think about. Soon after, in a conversation between the Doctor, played by Jon Pertwee, and an unnamed Time Lord, we learn a little more and it seems quite unimpressive. 'That jackanapes, all he ever does is cause trouble,' is the Doctor's opinion upon hearing the Master (his TARDIS disguised as the horsebox) has arrived on Earth. The Doctor and audience hear a different opinion: '[He's] learnt a great deal since you last met him,' cautions the Time Lord, suggesting the Doctor may be underestimating the Master.

In the light of this conversation, and the Doctor's evidently low opinion based on prior knowledge, do the Master's first words start to sound a little defensive, even qualified? Saying he is 'usually' called the Master suggests he may have been known as other things, not least as a jackanapes? Does the line also suggest the self-proclaimed identity may be a new one? Within seconds he has autocorrected and proclaims that his title is 'universally' known. The tension between the Doctor's blithe downplaying of the threat and the Master's assertion of his identity is the beginning of three years of adventures based on the sparring between protagonist and antagonist.

Who is the Master?

Roger Delgado was then in his early fifties and a busy actor in film, television, radio and theatre. This British-born actor of foreign parents had over twenty years' acting in front of the camera under his belt. He had been on the stage even longer and debuted with the Edward Nelson Players in Leicester in 1939. That was after a short-lived career in banking.

His acting career may have been reaching its heights by the early 1970s but Delgado would hardly have thought it had peaked. But these three years playing the Master turned out to be not only the highlight but the end of his career. He first appeared as the Master in January 1971 and in June 1973 he died on location in Turkey for another TV series. His life and career have a beginning and middle but no end. Assuming reasonable health, by 1973 Delgado had several decades left and many more performances, but an accident robbed him of all of that.

A quick look at the page for Delgado on the Internet Movie Database (IMDb) or the screen captures on Aveleyman say a lot about his career. He died aged fifty-five, but even by then he had been enormously productive. IMDb lists over 120 film and television credits (and even then it is not complete), starting from 1948. His radio work is countless.

The same sites show a great deal about the type of actor he became. Look at some screen captures of Delgado and a few themes start to emerge. The greasepaint, the turbans or keffiyehs (an Arab headdress), the roles in 1950s swashbucklers, and the 1960s glossy action series. Even then his range was exceptional. Other actors who joined him in the 'foreigner' niche such as Steve Plytas or Marne Maitland tended to play only a few nationalities. Plytas mostly played Greeks and Turks, from a passenger on the Titanic in the 1958 epic *A Night to Remember* to the plastic surgeon who botched Jack Nicholson's facelift in Tim Burton's *Batman*. Maitland mostly played Orientals. Directors sent for Delgado when they needed a foreigner: French, Spanish, Egyptian, Italian, German, Portuguese, Arab, Indian, Chinese, Czech, Albanian, Algerian, Jewish, and Mexican supporting parts all came his way. Through film and television appearances he appears looking out from underneath not just keffiyehs but top hats, fezzes and kepis (the round flat-topped French policeman's headgear).

What about the man behind the actor and under the headgear? What sort of actor did he aspire to be and where did those ambitions come from? He was born in Whitechapel, a child of Spanish and Belgian migrants but brought up in leafy Bedford Park; he was a scholar at an elite boys' school and at the London School of Economics. He was a bank clerk, a soldier, a repertory player and he did all these things before making his film and television debuts. He had a natural talent but no formal acting training. Like many of his generation, war service disrupted both life and career.

Colleagues, co-stars and friends knew an immaculate man who lived in a house without a speck of dust, whose life and career were equally con-trolled. There was a life story with some mess and heartache underneath this pristine surface. This basic narrative for his life goes something like this: born within the sound of Bow Bells; worked in a bank for eighteen months; educated at the London School of Economics; happily married to Kismet Delgado. All of these have some basis in reality, but that version is a life story with all the rough edges smoothed out and the details simplified.

We are going to see Delgado from different angles. We'll move from a twelve-year-old schoolboy reciting Kipling in front of the Archbishop of Westminster to the mature performer in BBC Television Centre, and we see him get there via a short career in banking and an even shorter time as a student at the LSE, time in the army, repertory theatre, film, radio, and the West End. We also follow him through marriage and divorce, unhappy times in Ceylon, adultery reported in the national press, a happy remarriage, and on his travels to family in Las Palmas, where the profession of 'actor' on the shipping manifests stands out exotically among the housewives and white-collar workers on board with him.

In this life we will follow him from Whitechapel to the comfortable house in Bedford Park that was his childhood home, to the King's Road Chelsea and his second marriage and finally to the lovely little White Cottage in Teddington, from where he departed for Turkey in 1973.

We also follow him around England in regional theatres, and film and television studios, and see an in-demand, highly respected actor who in turn cared passionately and thought deeply about his acting. He was an actor valued and trusted by directors. His controlled professionalism made him a valued member of small companies throughout his career, beginning with the Edward Nelson Players in pre-war Leicester and taking in the BBC Repertory Players and smaller, more informal but still distinct groups of performers centred around producers and directors like Rudolph Cartier, Basil Dearden and Shaun Sutton, and finally in the 'UNIT family' of the Pertwee era.

There is also an amazing cast of characters who rise up from history to be part of his story, from Dr H. Russell Andrews, the eminent obstetrician who brought Roger safely into the world, Dr Vance, the terrifying headmaster of the Cardinal Vaughan School who drummed good diction into the boys, and Sir Charles Haynes Wilson, Delgado's acerbic and decidedly unimpressed tutor at the London School of Economics. There's also the effervescent Misses Betty Nelson and Peggy Diamond, stars of the Nelson Repertory Company, who gave sizzling performances with Roger in Leicester. Edgar Lustgarten, the scholarly but melodramatic criminologist narrated Roger's adventures in British 'B' productions. Then there are the character actors like Marius Goring, Patrick Troughton, John Le Mesurier, Anton Diffring, Wolfe Morris, Hugh Futcher, and Paul Whitsun-Jones, who appeared alongside Delgado year after year in swashbucklers and science fiction. They're all part of the story of his busy life.

In Part One we find him first as a student at the Cardinal Vaughan Memorial School and the London School of Economics, then a bank clerk, then a repertory actor. His film roles develop into parts that are more substantial. He is constantly on radio. He reads the Bible on air, teaches Spanish to Vanessa Redgrave and is a housewives' disc jockey, amongst other oddities. By the late 1960s he is a character actor of substance but one who got there by constant hard work and an enviable reputation for being professional that made directors and managements want to hire a man who was a dream to work with.

In Part Two of this book he is the Master. It's also a story of success with ratings and audiences and the role that brought him immortality. But then a problem: work drops off because everyone thinks he's permanently in *Doctor Who*.

In Part Three Delgado is busy on other projects from Shakespeare to Cervantes and travelling far afield to make guest appearances in television, including one last trip to Turkey.

Let's see what he has to offer.

Part One
Before the Master

D ELGADO'S ACTING CAREER began in repertory theatre, and the rapid pace of repertoire changes, rehearsals, and line learning was essential preparation for his early television work in the 1950s and into the 1960s, where his performances were live with no hope of a retake. From the 1950s it's a madcap rush around the studios in England, anywhere film and television directors needed a foreigner. Early roles were tiny, lasting for mere seconds of screen time. But Delgado was an actor not an extra and was soon making important contributions, even in small parts. Getting to the studios of the 1950s is via the East End of London, a very Catholic education and then a job in a big bank, military service, and marriage.

Chapter One
Beginnings 1918-1937

Tread softly because you tread on my dreams. – W. B. Yeats

B ETWEEN 1918 AND TODAY Whitechapel has changed beyond recognition, in its streetscape and its people. While Delgado was born towards the end of the First World War, it was the Blitz of the Second World War which so drastically changed the appearance of the area. Standing now on the Whitechapel Road after coming out of the tube station, there would still be some views that Mr and Mrs Roger Caesar Delgado could have recognised as they entered the hospital on Whitechapel Road in late February 1918.

The old buildings of the London Hospital still stand. The Whitechapel Bell Foundry is still in its eighteenth-century home.[2] But turning to the west and looking down the Whitechapel Road, the Shard now dominates the skyline. Heading that way we also come to the Wren church of St Mary-le-Bow with its bells and the reason for the oft-repeated statement that Delgado was born within the sound of Bow Bells.

It is tempting to see a curious coincidence between the place of Delgado's birth and the type of menacing roles he was known for, as Whitechapel remains best known as the haunt of the Victorian murderer Jack the Ripper. Some other deliciously sinister associations attach to the district. It was a location for both mass burials for humans and slaughterhouses for animals.[3]

Even the London Hospital, now the Royal London Hospital, has strange associations. It was where the World War One heroine Edith Cavell nursed; but also where the surgeon Frederick Treves kept Joseph Merrick, the 'Elephant Man', a sufferer of neurofibromatosis with severe deformities and who had been exhibited as a freak on the Whitechapel Road.

The East End of 1918 was a place of poverty and charity. But the Delgados saw very little of this. Roger's birth certificate shows he was born in Whitechapel but was just passing through. 'Roger Delgado was born and raised within the sound of Bow Bells in Whitechapel' is the sort of thing normally said about his birth. He was born there, but not raised there and he is far from being an EastEnder.[4] Whitechapel folk were poor, but Roger and Mathilde Delgado were white collar. The family home was not in Whitechapel but in Woodstock Road, Bedford Park, a well-built house in a leafy street.

His birth at London Hospital shows the gulf between the Delgados and the other patients. Just before Mathilde entered the Marie Celeste Ward, the hospital's in-house news-sheet reported on an incredibly elaborate Christmas party for children too poor to have received presents from home. Queen Alexandra, widow of King Edward VII, came to pull crackers with the children. 'The party, we feel sure, was a bright light on the gloomy horizon of the Whitechapel homes. It lifted the children from their sordid surroundings, and transplanted them to a fairy land'.[5]

Our story begins in late February 1918. Mathilde Delgado enters the London Hospital as an inpatient. She will be there until March 20th. What therefore was Mrs Delgado doing there, so far from her comfortable home in Bedford Park? Roger Delgado was an only child who was childless and an immensely private man, so parts of his life are mysterious. Here are some of the mysteries. How even did Mr Delgado get his heavily pregnant wife from Bedford Park to Whitechapel? It's early days for a car, even a taxi, but surely the underground would have been insufferable?

England is at war and so is the hospital. Many of the doctors are away serving, and medical students have been signing up. Not all of them were away on active service. Dr H. Russell Andrews was still there, a famous obstetrician and author of the indispensable technical book *Midwifery for Nurses*, an MD and a Fellow of the Royal College of Surgeons who was active with the Obstetrical Society of London.[6] He had published widely on complex medical cases and now he had another one to deal with, as Mrs Delgado had medical complications from a contracted pelvis and needed surgery.

His expertise may explain why Mrs Delgado came to Whitechapel. Normally the London Hospital treated people from the East End, but Mrs Delgado's medical complications meant her baby would need to be born by caesarean section. In 1918, she endured a complicated, dangerous procedure but made it through safely.[7] All went well but the inpatient registers in the hospital archives show she had to remain at the hospital for some weeks and while there Mrs Delgado registered little Roger's birth.

The birth certificate is a curious document. The registrar made a slip and entered the surname of both parents as 'Delgada'; his subsequent hand-written correction of the 'a' to an 'o' is still there to see. As is often the case with demographic information in this era, the age of Delgado's father, Roger Caesar Delgado Senior, surely cannot be correct. It lists him as aged thirty-one, but he died in 1945 aged sixty-eight. It is more likely that we need to add a decade to his age, which ties him in with the Rogerio Delgado listed in the 1901 census as a Spanish clerk living in a boarding house in St Pancras. By 1911 he was in St Marylebone and in 1915 he married the Belgian Mathilde Robert.

The baby's name on the birth certificate is Roger Caesar Delgado, but sometimes a full name of Roger Caesar Marius Bernard de Delgado Torres Castillo Roberto appears in reference works. His full name is memorably extravagant, but is more concise in official records. He is in the register of the Cardinal Vaughan School as Roger Maria Cesar Delgado and as Roger Caesar Delgado he entered the London School of Economics and enlisted in the Army (and Caesar incidentally was the name of his dog!).

A Spanish speaker would recognise 'Delgado' as the father's name and the last name in the full sequence as the mother's. In this case 'Roberto' is the Spanish version of Mathilde's maiden name, Robert. Long and complex Spanish names can also refer to special saints and religious names, locations or other relatives but Delgado's long name is not quite as Spanish as its initial flourish might suggest. He is Roger Caesar Marius Bernard, rather than Rodrigo Cesar Mario Bernardo.[8] But the 'de Delgado' is firmly Spanish and a nickname for 'son of a thin person', while the 'Torres Castillo' are references to castles and towers.[9]

Delgado was the child of migrants who had made a success of life. All through his life in England Delgado senior was a resident Spaniard and not naturalised but had a good job and a nice home. Roger Delgado senior was a bank clerk. In an age before computers or even typewriters, a clerk needed a good hand. Surviving documents with his writing show his command of English and that he wrote with a beautiful, flowing, copperplate script.

By 1918 Delgado and Mathilde were living comfortably at Woodstock Road. Delgado senior was the breadwinner and his wife, listed in immigration documents as a Spanish citizen and therefore an alien, was a housewife. The house she maintained was and is a large, well-built Victorian home. Woodstock Road's main claim to fame is that William Butler Yeats lived there at number eight as a child.[10] The large homes began appearing on the orchards of the Bedford House estate from the 1870s. The Victorian artist and craftsman William Morris assisted Norman Shaw in the design and decoration of the houses, and according to Yeats' biographer William Murphy the community was 'intended for painters, writers, composers, and people interested in the arts'.[11] In time, handsome, well-built houses appeared.

A community of artistic people sounds perfect for a little boy harbouring ambitions to be an actor, but Delgado senior the bank clerk seems out of place. That said, the few surviving photographs of Delgado Senior show a well-dressed man, almost a dandy, who clearly enjoyed posing for the camera. Boater hats, bow ties and swaggering posture are all in evidence in portrait photographs and more informal snaps, showing that even if Delgado Junior did not follow his father into the bank, he certainly inherited the father's proud mien and ability to look good in fancy clothes.

A Catholic education

As Roger grew up the family stayed put in this agreeable neighbourhood. A serious, dark-eyed little boy looks out from photographs taken during his childhood. Following a tradition that now seems strange but then was normal, the little boy was initially dressed in flowing white dresses. Puppy fat gives him a round little face so different from the angular chin and pointy nose of the adult.

From 1925 to 1929 Roger had his junior education at a school in Bedford Park. Much further west from the Whitechapel Road is Addison Road near Holland Park. Addison Road has been home to the Cardinal Vaughan Memorial School since the outbreak of the First World War. Nowadays it is an established Catholic school with many distinguished alumni and an über-Catholic ethos. For Delgado, it was still quite new, only opened four years before he was born but already a flourishing day school for boys.

A Spanish father, a Belgian mother, and their son were naturally all good Catholics and it is not difficult to understand why Mr and Mrs Delgado chose a Catholic school for their little boy. Years later Delgado played the Cardinal of Rio (one of many Hispanic or Latino characters he would essay) in *The Successor*, an instalment of the *ITV Play of the Week* in 1965 about the election of the Pope. Surviving colour photographs of the production show magnificently dressed sets of the interior of the Vatican and Delgado suavely carries off his sumptuous scarlet robes. As a little schoolboy in Kensington, he saw real-life cardinals looking just as splendid; and throughout his life Delgado remained a man of faith at home with these religious trappings.

Delgado attended from 1929 to 1935 and in later years the school did not forget him. The wartime service of its old boys included many distinguished combatants during the Second World War, especially Flying Officer Donald Edward Garland, who left the school the same year as Delgado, was shot down in 1940 and bestowed posthumously with the Victoria Cross for a daring bombing raid over Belgium.[12] Given the eminence of this honour, Garland's name heads the list of old boys who served in the war. Down in the list is Captain Roger C. Delgado, serving with the Royal Signals.

Delgado the actor and not just Delgado the soldier also remained on the school's radar in later years. A little pamphlet 'A Talk to Parents of New Boys' appeared some time during the headmastership of R. R. Kenefeck, in office from 1952 to 1976. This little document explains the school's religious ethos, its curriculum, its uniform, and what Monsignor Kenefeck expected of the boys and their parents. Then he ends with a page of 'Some successes of past pupils'. A list of civil servants, diplomats, soldiers and pilots, doctors and engineers follows, and then at the very bottom are those old boys 'who have made successful careers in a variety of occupations' including 'in the theatre or with the B.B.C. – Joseph O'Connor, Denis McCarthy and Roger Delgado'.[13]

Oddly, one name left out is Delgado's exact contemporary and fellow pupil, the actor Richard Greene. Greene was also born in 1918 and was a pupil at the Cardinal Vaughan School. Later his career would take him to repertory theatre, Hollywood and a career interruption from wartime service, followed by the immense success of *The Adventures of Robin Hood*, in which Delgado also appeared.

A pleasure and a challenge for a biographer is seeking order and meaning to someone's life, and the presence of two future successful actors at the same school prompts one to wonder where and when their interest in drama came about. Was there something about the Cardinal Vaughan School that fostered the ambitions of the two boys? Certainly the school had outlets for drama and creativity. Alongside the solid academic content of Latin, Greek, French, Geography, Arithmetic and Chemistry, the school had a choir and gave prizes for art and elocution.

On occasion, these activities involved Delgado or Greene and, among the prizes and academic honours given out each Speech Day, both little boys received rewards for creative activity. In 1930, Delgado was in the Upper Preparatory and received a prize for drawing. The child is the father of the man, and as an adult Delgado continued to draw and sketch. Friends and colleagues remember he did so with skill. 'He loved to draw, he was a great cartoonist,' is one of Katy Manning's many memories of her co-star from the 1970s.[14] He collected his art prize at the Speech Day on December 5th 1930 in front of Cardinal Francis Bourne, the Archbishop of Westminster.

Little Roger also gave a recitation of 'The Bee-Boy's Song' by Rudyard Kipling. At the same event Greene recited W. B. Yeats' 'Lake Isle of Innisfree'. Was his recitation on December 5th Delgado's first moment on a stage and his first experience of performance? Small moments like this one are important for understanding where the actor and performer came from. Delgado hardly ever gave interviews. Nevertheless, in his actions he leaves behind the impression of a defiant young man determined not to follow in his father's footsteps, who resigned from a safe bank job and joined the insecure profession of a repertory actor, to doggedly build a career before the war and rebuild it afterwards. Is this where it starts?

The audience for this early performance was distinguished, including the Cardinal and the governors of the school. Kipling's poem is a short but complex piece to recite. The poem is full of exclamation marks and drama:

> Bees! Bees! Hark to your bees!
> 'Hide from your neighbours as much as you please,
> But all that has happened, to us you must tell,
> Or else we will give you no honey to sell!'

The verses have vernacular speech allowing for characterisation:

> Tell 'em coming in an' out,
> Where the Fanners fan,

12

'Cause the Bees are just about,
As curious as a man!

The recitation would have taken careful rehearsal as Kipling's verse presents numerous opportunities to trip up or stumble over tricky constructions that a twelve-year-old will have needed to memorise. Did he practise at home in front of his parents?

Don't you wait where the trees are,
When the lightnings play,
Nor don't you hate where Bees are,
Or else they'll pine away.
Pine away – dwine away –
Anything to leave you!
But if you never grieve your Bees,
Your Bees'll never grieve you.

There was good reason to be frightened of speaking in public at the Cardinal Vaughan School, as the headmaster Dr John G. Vance happened to be a terrifying martinet when it came to elocution and diction (and indeed everything else from handwriting to corporal punishment).

Each year the school ran an elocution competition and Dr Vance would then publish pitilessly detailed criticisms in the school magazine, naming and shaming boys who did not speak properly, picking apart their speech syllable by syllable. In 1934 he was especially unimpressed and let rip. 'Boys suffered from lack of emphasis. When for instance they were reading "Peter and James and John" the proper names did not appear in high relief.' It gets worse. 'Most of the boys suffered from a lack of variety in tone, volume, and pitch.' 'Two boys missed the word "momentous", pronouncing it as something like "murmemtous".' All in all, concluded Dr Vance, 'we are still not within sight of that distinction of speech which I desire as a characteristic of the School.'[15] This was the man listening to little Roger recite the Kipling, and no doubt he was listening critically to every syllable, vowel sound and consonant, and checking for variety in tone.

On another speech day, Greene gave another recitation, this time at the 1934 Speech Day where he recited John Masefield's 'Launching the 534'. Delgado never seems to have given another recitation nor won one of the school's elocution prizes. But 1934, when Delgado was now in the fourth form, shows his academic success and the guest speaker, Bishop Butt, handed Delgado his prize for the best essay on Charles Dickens' character Dick Swiveller (from *The Old Curiosity Shop*, a hefty book for a little boy to have read). It was a big honour as Dickens' granddaughter endowed the prize.

In *The Vaughanian* for that year we learn a little more about this prize. The report on the competition that year was as horrible about writing as Dr Vance was about speaking. 'There was the beginnings of some attempt at criticism, but competitors showed poor choice in their reading of commentaries and slavish imitation or even plagiarism in their use of encyclopedia, dictionary of literature, preface or introduction.' However, in the midst of this mediocrity, 'the best exponents were R. Delgado and P. D. O'Hara. Delgado's essay was remarkable, and maintained a high standard throughout.'[16] As an adult his fascination with literature remained. Delgado lived surrounded by books and made broadcasts on literature.

A Speech Day at the Cardinal Vaughan School was a socially upmarket affair for the masters, the boys and their parents. The event naturally ended with the singing of 'God Save the King', as upper-class English Catholicism has always maintained adherence to both the monarch and the Old Faith. The school was proud of both academic and social success. The school's governors were a who's who of aristocratic Roman Catholics including the Earl of Iddesleigh and Lord Fitzalan. The Duke of Norfolk had been connected with the school's foundation.[17] Old boys always did well in the Classical Tripos for Oxford and Cambridge, in the civil service, and in sport. Like many boys, Delgado departed heading for both university and a good job in the City.

Chapter Two
Mr Banks 1937

Banking is one of the few dignified businesses left in the world. –
Peter Cushing as Fordyce in Hammer's *Cash on Demand*

ANY VAUGHANIANS (OLD BOYS) joined respectable professions, donning bowler hats and pinstripes to work in financial power-houses in the City of London. The beginning of 1937 was a time of major developments for Delgado. He finished with school and took up a job in the City of London at the headquarters of the Westminster Bank. He also began studying commerce at the London School of Economics. He was on track for a secure, respectable career but he had other plans.

The chronology for this part of his life is not at all clear. One of Delgado's obituaries recounted the beginning of Delgado's career in theatre by saying 'one Friday in 1938, after eighteen months in the job he walked out of his City bank and on the following Tuesday began rehearsals with the Nelson Repertory Company at the Theatre Royal Leicester for a production of *You Can't Take it With You*'.[18] This chronology does not work. The Nelson Players did indeed stage *You Can't Take it With You* but it was in 1939. Delgado had been working at the bank, but the staff ledger shows it was not as long as eighteen months. But what is clear is that following matriculation involving three schools, he entered the professional world and university in 1937 before throwing in the towel for both.

For many people their idea of what a great British bank looked like and operated like before World War Two may come from Disney's *Mary Poppins* and the visit Jane and Michael Banks pay to the Dawes, Tomes, Mousley, Grubbs Fidelity Fiduciary Bank in the City of London. If you take away the singing bankers and Dick van Dyke, the film's depiction of the Bank, the pinstripes, and the urgent and high-powered activity in the great Banking Hall is spot on. The sets for *Mary Poppins* filled all the Disney sound stages, one of them being the Bank's enormous interior. A job in a bank was a good one and a great bank an awe-inspiring place to work.

In imagination we can follow Roger Delgado the junior bank clerk from 96 Woodstock Road to the tube stop at Turnham Green on the District Line. The trip would have necessitated going through the interchanges perhaps at Monument and moving to the Northern Line before alighting at Bank. We can only guess at this route but we know his destination was the City of London.

The vast Bank of England dominates the City, both its old bastion walls that withstood the Gordon Rioters, and the 1930s additions on top. Walking up Bartholomew Lane beside the Bank of England, another impressive classical structure comes into view: the Westminster Bank headquarters at 41 Lothbury, designed by Mewes and Davis and put up in the 1920s.

Delgado became a clerk following in his father's footsteps and he joined an established firm of excellent reputation. The Bank was nearly a century old and originated with a stock company formed in 1833.[19] However, the splendid six-storeyed headquarters behind the Bank of England was still new when Delgado joined the Bank's Head Office as a clerk on February 1st 1937; but the handsome classical architecture outside and in creates instant history and solidity.

Inside 41 Lothbury is the vast Banking Hall, still there even though the Westminster Bank itself has moved out. A high ceiling and atrium, glass roof and Ionic columns rise above the black-and-white chequered marble tiles. In the upper storeys in offices with marble fireplaces sat the directors and senior officers of the Bank, including Sir Charles Lidbury, Chief General Manager during Delgado's time and a major figure in mid-century banking and finance.[20]

The old Bank's interior is still overwhelming and really does bring to mind Disney's bankers singing ecstatically of:

Foreclosures!
Bonds, chattels, dividends, shares
Bankruptcies
Debtor sales
Opportunities
All manner of private enterprise
Shipyards
The mercantile
Collieries
Tanneries
Corporations
Amalgamations
Banks!

41 Lothbury and its vast Banking Hall became part of Delgado's world until September 1937. His was a cut above ordinary counter work because his position was in the Foreign Branch Office. Given the multilingual environment in which he grew up with Spanish- and French-speaking parents, and the Foreign Branch Office's dealing with overseas branches in Paris, Bordeaux, Lyons, Marseilles, Nantes and Brussels, the Office and Delgado seem a good match. However, the staff ledgers held in the Bank's Archive do not record that Delgado had a foreign language.[21]

Working at a great bank in the city was a respectable profession that insinuated itself into a worker's lifestyle and recreation. Among the archives of the Westminster Bank for 41 Lothbury are miscellanies such as the chess club papers, the rugby club fixtures, the minutes of the athletics club, hockey club, swimming club and cricket club and the programmes for the golfing society dinners. During an employee's lifetime the Bank was inescapable during work and recreation and even after death. Employment at the Bank meant life insurance; the Bank's impact continued after death in the Widows and Orphans Fund.

Another outlet was drama and the Bank maintained a dramatic society. To understand where Delgado the actor comes from in 1939, it would be satisfying to see a pattern of involvement in opportunities like these. However, the productions for 1937 were in February and December, one too early for Delgado to be part of and the other after he had resigned. Sadly the membership list for the Dramatic Society in 1937 is lost from the archives.[22]

Chapter Three
The university student

Doubtless you would have recalled had you not attended the LSE. –
Bernard Woolley in *Yes, Minister*

A LMOST EVERYONE MAKES the same claim about Roger Delgado: educated at the London School of Economics.[23] The statement is partly but not entirely right, as the education was over almost as soon as it had begun and his tutor thought he had learnt very little in the short time he was there.

The London School of Economics may be more familiar to many from its fictional alumni than its actual students. One of the jibes levelled at Jim Hacker, Minister for Administrative Affairs in *Yes Minister*, was his apparent misfortune at being educated at the LSE, at least according to the Oxbridge civil servants. In the real world, Sir Mick Jagger and numerous foreign heads of state along with many British politicians are alumni, from John F. Kennedy to the Queen of Denmark.

When Delgado applied in the 1930s the School was the 'empire on which the concrete never set', owing to rapid post-war expansion in student numbers and building work at the central London site in Aldwych.[24] It was also starting to offer a commerce degree that some academic economists viewed with snobbish disdain. Lord Beveridge, the director of the School until 1937, said of the degree: 'There are some who fear we may be too technical, and in training for a Commerce degree may lower University ideals. There are others who doubt, because they think that we cannot be practical and technical enough, and that all that is worth learning in Commerce can be learned only in the office and in the world outside.'[25] Delgado came into this gap between the world of the University and the practical outside world.

The Westminster Bank cooperated with the Institute of Banking to let employees gain qualifications but did not otherwise promote higher education.[26] Does that mean Delgado chose of his own accord to study, or was it parental pressure? He applied on January 8th 1937. By February 1st he was working not just for the Westminster Bank but at its city Head Office. In January, he applied to be an evening student and could already list 41 Lothbury as his place of employment.

His student file at the London School of Economics is small and the pages of handwritten and typed documents are in reverse order from April 1937 back to January of that year. Thus it is that, reading the file, the first point reached is his rushed exit from the School having done barely a scrap of work and with no subjects completed. Although small, the file is also a treasure trove of Delgado's professional and personal life up to this point.

But to backtrack, Delgado needed two things to get into the LSE. One was matriculation, the other was references. Biographical statements about him usually say he was educated at the Cardinal Vaughan School and the London School of Economics. Once again that is sort of true; but the reality is messier, in a way the adult Delgado later tidied up and straightened out. His student file adds some of the details.

The Speech Days at the Cardinal Vaughan School show plenty of boys matriculated successfully, meaning they passed public examinations and exited from the high school into university, doing so in the era before A- and O-levels and GCSEs. In 1930s England the choices were Oxford and Cambridge, the University of London and the examinations run by the matriculation board of Durham University. No Old Vaughanians attended Durham University; it was both remote and Anglican.

Boys passed the examinations and gained certificates from the Oxford and Cambridge School Examination Board, including in 1934 Dennis McCarthy, one of the broadcasters mentioned with Delgado in Monsignor Kenefeck's pamphlet for the parents of boys. Delgado did not get to Oxbridge. He instead left the Cardinal Vaughan Memorial School in 1935 to spend three months at the Acton Technical College. By the end of 1935 he had moved on to the Chiswick Polytechnic, for him a local institution on Bath Road, Bedford Park and from which he matriculated in June 1936. Neither the Technical College nor the Polytechnic exists any more, absorbed by what later became Brunel University. But attendance meant Delgado could sit for the London Matriculation and enter one of the institutions of the federated University of London. So he passed matriculation in June 1936, including Latin and Mathematics, and applied to the LSE.[27]

He may not have aimed for Oxford or Cambridge, but Delgado's references for the LSE show a little bit of his parents' life and upmarket social circles among Spanish speakers in London. 'I beg to state that I have known for a number of years Mr and Mrs Delgado, of 96 Woodstock Road, Chiswick, W4, and their son Roger since he was a little boy.' So says the Vice-Consul of the Republic of El Salvador, Signor G. le Bourdonnec, in old-world courtesy. He continues: 'The parents are old friends of ours, and I can testify to their good social standing and high respectability. I have also pleasure in saying that Roger Delgado has been well educated in every sense of the word, and that I consider him to be a deserving and trustworthy young man.' The Vice-Consul lived very nearby in Bedford Park. The file does not recall if the registrar or secretary at the LSE were impressed by this eminent diplomatic reference. It's suspicious, though, how the Vice-Consul skirts around Roger's educational achievements, dwelling instead on his parents and Roger's more general personality traits.

Delgado's other reference is from Robert MacAdam, the principal of the Acton Technical College, who avowed: 'I can speak in high terms of his character and conduct during the whole of his Course, and I am confident that he will prove satisfactory in every way in the pursuance of his further studies at the London School of Economics.' Again there is more about character than academic achievement, and that is a sign of things to come.

By January 8th 1937 Delgado or his parents had paid up £7.12.3 for study as an evening student in the Bachelor of Commerce and with French, although the first three weeks were as a day student. After that, he would have been at 41 Lothbury each work day and needed to finish work each day in the bank and then be out at night to attend lectures.

According to the LSE archives, Roger was undertaking the courses that began the Bachelor of Commerce. Thanks to the LSE schedule for 1936–1937, we can reconstruct what should have been his movements in the first part of the year and they went something like this:

Monday to Friday he was working at the bank.

Monday and Tuesday evenings Course 200: General Regional Geography; the syllabus promised 'special attention will be paid to the study of the great industrial regions of the world and to those regions that produce food and raw materials for them'.

Wednesday evenings Course 40: Elements of Economics with the famous economist Dr Benham.

Fridays 7pm–8pm 151 Accounting (Part 1).[28]

His days were work at 41 Lothbury and most evenings with his lectures. In between time, he also needed to be writing assignments.

And then suddenly it was all over. In a letter with the same old-world courtesy as the Vice-Consul, in April Delgado sent a handwritten note to the School's secretary:

Dear Madam,

Since my first term as an evening student at the School of Economics, I have found it impossible not to miss at least two important lectures a week, owing to certain adverse business arrangements. Rather than allow these to interfere with all my future studies, I think it were best that I discontinue attendance temporarily, and take up my degree course in the faculty of Economics (B.Com) once more at a future date.

Hoping you will notify me of any formalities that may arise in the present situation, I remain yours very sincerely

Roger C. Delgado

The letter is from April 14th, 1937. Prior to this point Delgado had been written about rather than leaving on record his direct thoughts. We find references to him in Speech Days at the Cardinal Vaughan School, descriptions of his good character by referees, and he's in the staff ledger at the Bank. Here is his actual historical voice coming out across the decades. It is also possible to read the letter with Delgado's immaculate diction and beautiful voice in your head. Even when a well-known actor Delgado hardly ever gave interviews and so very few of his direct words are on record.

Most biographers of a subject, no matter how long that subject may have been dead, have a moment which brings home to them that the person they are writing about was an actual human being, not just an historical abstraction or a performer made distant by time and by seeing him in character on the other side of the TV screen. For me when writing this book, that moment came when I opened Delgado's student file from the London School of Economics and saw a letter in his immaculate handwriting and his very human admission that he was not coping with his studies, a moment where the actual person cuts through historic distance.

The importance of the letter as a means of accessing Delgado as a person can overshadow its actual content, including the vague reference to 'adverse business arrangements' and the very half-hearted suggestion he will take up study again at an unspecified 'future date'.

By April 15th his study was over: 'Would you be good enough to cancel from your list of advisees R. C. Delgado,' wrote the Registrar to the tutor Mr C. H. Wilson. The same day the Registrar wrote to Delgado: 'I am very sorry to learn of the difficulties which have interfered with your regular attendance at your course of study. I note that you will withdraw temporarily, and I hope you will be able to resume your course later under better conditions.'

That is not quite that. His student file gives the last word to Mr C. H. Wilson. Of all the voices that come out of the file, from the Registrar, to Principal MacAdam and Vice-Consul le Bourdonnec, Mr Wilson's has the sharpest edge to it: 'Some ability, which is at the moment hidden under a mass of self-esteem. Impulsive, journalistic thinker.' With it is the record Delgado completed two essays and gained not just a B minus but a B minus minus. Ouch. Compared to the Vice-Consul's old-world prolixity or the Registrar's slightly perfunctory courtesy and concern, Wilson tells it like he saw it.

The acerbic Mr Wilson is most probably Charles Haynes Wilson who went on to gain a knighthood and enjoy a stellar career in the British university system as the vice chancellor of Leicester University and then Glasgow University.[29] Delgado meanwhile left the academic system completely and soon would leave the world of banking and commerce entirely. On September 18th that year he had resigned from the Westminster Bank and from the respectable, secure world it represented. What had been stewing in him? His LSE record shows he didn't care for his study. He lasted at the Bank for longer; but the boy reciting Kipling, the artist, the reader, had grown up determined to be an actor.

What on earth did his father think and how did Roger break the news? If Delgado senior were disappointed, he would not have been the first parent to be shocked that his son wanted to go into acting. Alastair Sim's parents were 'appalled' when their son chose acting instead of university.[30] As a banker, Delgado senior could also have done the sums for his child's possible loss of income. As a first-year male clerk, Roger was earning £60 a year, not a huge amount but a respectable wage nonetheless (and better than a female clerk's was), and the work was safe. Acting could actually have paid better. By 1936, Peter Cushing was earning £2 a week in repertory but the work was irregular and far from guaranteed.[31] A small consolation for Mr Delgado senior may have been the increasing professionalism of acting from the 1930s onwards, especially after the formation of the trade union Equity in 1930, but less reassuringly the unemployment rate was enormous and about two thirds of the profession was out of work at any given time. That alone makes Delgado's ceaseless work over the decades all the more incredible, but won't have done much at the time to comfort Mr Delgado senior.[32]

Chapter Four
Doing it twice nightly: Repertory theatre 1938-1940

It's an insecure profession, you know. –
'William Hartnell' in *An Adventure in Space and Time*

THE BRITISH REPERTORY COMPANIES have vanished. The 1952 comedy movie *Curtain Up*, starring Robert Morley, Kay Kendall and Margaret Rutherford and co-written by Michael Pertwee, was a send-up of the provincial companies. The title of the play it is based on was *On Monday Next*, a reminder of the rapid pace of repertoire change and rehearsal and staging in repertory companies.[33]

In the film the company's director, played by Morley, talks disparagingly about the 'cinema house', pronouncing it with an old-fashioned hard 'c'. Even by 1952 *Curtain Up* was a dated comedy, but the small theatre and its demanding schedule was a close version of an earlier reality.

Delgado's earliest professional performances were in that type of environment. Barry Letts knew this world too, saying in his memoirs: 'The world we came from was a world where every town of any size had a repertory company.'[34] That included Leicester and it is here Delgado made his debut, gained professional experience and earned sensationally good reviews. As we'll soon see, this novice, untrained actor was hailed as a 'genius' on stage.

Sometime between the resignation from the Bank and early 1939 Delgado made his way to Leicester. He had made a good choice as the city had a flourishing acting and drama culture including two busy theatres, the Phoenix and the Theatre Royal.

The Theatre Royal in Leicester was a lovely classical building razed in the 1950s to make way for a bank as ugly as only post-war British buildings are ugly. It stood in Horsefair Street, a historic central part of Leicester, and the theatre with its porticoed façade stood near the town hall.[35] Earlier in its history, the actor Henry Irving had performed on its stage, but the theatre closed in 1957.[36] Its destruction in that period is a real-world example of the vanishing theatres and theatre culture dramatised in *Curtain Up*.

The interior of the long-vanished theatre was both beautiful and impressive. Through the foyer and past the box office, a flight of steps with red plush carpet led to the auditorium.[37] Delgado's performances happened beneath the large proscenium arch. Looking out from the forty feet wide by fifty feet deep stage, the performers would see the large auditorium, with two levels of galleries or the circle as well as the seating in the body. The galleries curved elegantly in a horseshoe shape and the theatre accommodated over one thousand people.[38] It was also a beautifully appointed theatre with a pleasant refreshment lounge above the projecting entrance and a collection of stage machinery.

Before its demolition, the Leicester Theatre Royal hosted a number of acting companies, among them the Edward Nelson Players, who were the permanent company from 1938 to 1940. During this time Delgado joined their ranks.[39]

Like other companies, the Edward Nelson group has long since passed into history, but theatre reviews in provincial papers show their journeys around British theatres. In 1935 they were performing in the Palace Theatre in Watford.[40] In March 1938 they're at the St Pancras Town Hall, in May the company is in Peterborough and in time they move on to Leicester: the type of travelling company then typical and now gone.[41] Reviews from 1938 note them performing in their twelfth week of a series of plays and are doing *Miss Smith*.[42] In July 1938 they were still in Peterborough doing *Lover's Leap* twice nightly at the Empire Theatre.[43] The local paper then reported that 'all good things must come to an end' and they began winding up their season in Peterborough with *The Dominant Sex* and then *The Patsy*.[44] By October they had settled at the Theatre Royal in Leicester.

Starting out in rep was typical of Delgado's generation. Sid James had a prolific career in British film and television but started in repertory theatre in Johannesburg.[45] Early in his career, Kenneth More got £5 for doing melodramas in a repertory theatre in Newcastle.[46] Beryl Reid, born in 1919, achieved much acclaim for her comedy and dramatic roles on film and television, from *Tinker, Tailor, Soldier, Spy* and *Smiley's People* to *Cracker*. She was a mistress in *The Belles of St Trinian's*, which also had an early film appearance from Delgado. But she did not attend a drama school and made her professional start in summer seasons, pantomimes and non-stop repertory performances. 'A man called Hyman Zahl seemed to think I was quite a snip at £8 a week, and he gave me tours of theatres which now seem ghastly to contemplate,' was one of her reminiscences. Besides the poor pay, the gruelling schedule and the fact she had to be self-taught in other areas including make-up and lime lighting, Reid also remembered the squalor of actors' digs. When her mother saw one place, her advice was: 'If this is what it's going to be like, I'd just give it up!'[47]

British comic Kenneth Williams, born 1926, also had a long career, although without the critical plaudits Reid received such as her BAFTA and OBE. Like Reid, though, he had no professional training; and, after appearing in revues during his military service, including in the Victoria Theatre in Singapore, he moved on to provincial repertory companies in England. One was the Newquay Repertory Company, and in his diary he recorded his opinion of a 'tat production' in 'which people haven't learned their lines properly'.[48]

His 1940s diary entries remain a vivid record of the rapid pace of rehearsals and often the shoddiness of provincial rep, and help to understand why some of the cast may not have learned their lines. On April 30th 1948 Williams and the rest of the cast were rehearsing *The First Mrs Fraser*. On May 15th 1948 the Newquay Players were performing *The Sacred Flame* but by May 20th they were doing *Night Must Fall*, an Emlyn Williams play. May 27th it was another first night, this time *Love in a Mist* by Kenneth Horne.[49] But during the rush of rehearsals, first nights and matinees, Williams also recorded in his diary: 'Letter from Equity. I am now a provisional member, with 40 weeks' probation before becoming entitled to full membership.'[50] In other words, all his intense activity in repertory had given him sufficient professional experience to become a member of the actor's union.

Memoirs, autobiographies and personal documents like Williams' diary reconstruct the frantically paced, squalid, and poorly paid experiences of repertory players. Instead of somewhere like the Royal Academy of Dramatic Art, the repertory companies were a professional training ground for everything from acting to doing the make-up and lighting. The theatre historian Michael Sanderson distinguishes the repertory companies from the earlier stock companies in that the rep 'changed its players around, avoiding the star system and hierarchy of types'. The reviews of Delgado's performances bear this out. He was characters of all ages and types, young, old, English, foreign.

Newquay may have been tatty; the Leicester Theatre Royal was more upmarket and more prestigious. Delgado performed without professional acting training and he learnt on the job. He was also a *bona fide* professional. By now, Equity had been in operation since the early 1930s. It created a 'closed shop' of members who were professional actors.[51] He was most definitely not an amateur. Throughout his later career, Delgado remained interested in Equity activities and in 1970 added his name to Equity's Living Wage Campaign.[52]

Like his early television appearances, Delgado's theatre performances are mostly lost to us except through reviews. Fortunately the local paper, the *Leicester Mercury*, had an avid drama critic who wrote weekly reviews of the plays that the Edward Nelson performers staged. The reviewer had his clear favourites among the cast, but also produced thorough and detailed comments on who appeared each week and how good their performances were.

The pace for the actors was intense. Not only was there a new play each week, the local billing in the *Leicester Mercury* also shows the cast performed the same play twice a night. The Scottish actress Claire Nielson was another product of the repertory training ground and she vividly remembers the mental pressure of the weekly or fortnightly changes of repertoire. Actors would be 'reading a play that was going to be done, rehearsing a play that was going to be done, and playing a play at night, so you had three roles in your head'.[53]

In April 1939 Delgado is in Leicester, on stage with the Edward Nelson Players. However, the local critic has misread his programme and refers to 'Roger Delago' as one of the actors playing a smaller part in *You Can't Take it With You* and he appeared as another character's son-in-law. The play was of its time. Among the characters are 'a couple of nigger [sic] minstrel comics' and 'a weird Russian'.[54] *The Stage* repeated the naming error. For April 20th the correspondent reports on 'Roger Delago's' participation in *You Can't Take it With You* in what was overall a 'remarkably well acted' play.[55]

Wait a moment, just where has Roger been since leaving 41 Lothbury? If there was not a seamless transition over one weekend from bank clerk to actor, what happened in the meantime between resigning from the West-minster Bank and ending up in Leicester? The likeliest surely is that his part in *You Can't Take it With You*, though a small one, was not something he could simply walk into. To get on stage, did he work his way up, doing menial work for the company such as sweeping the stage, doing the lighting and prompting or eventually understudying? William Hartnell's career with Sir Frank Benson's Shakespeare company began this way, as it has for many actors who have started their careers as a spear-carrier in *Hamlet* (as did Christopher Lee) or played other walk-on roles and doing the chores. Work like that will not have drawn Roger to the attention of the theatre critic and he is lost to sight and lost to historical record until *You Can't Take it With You* gave him a part worthy of comment. There were also those enigmatic references to 'business affairs' in his letter to the LSE, and at this point his military record discloses a little more. In addition to listing his experience as a repertory actor, Army Form B199A in the Ministry of Defence archives notes his pre-war employment as 'confidential secretary to mining rep-resentative in London'. I have not seen this job mentioned anywhere else about Delgado, and it is from this murky period in 1938 to 1939, but the reference fills in a little gap. Which mining representative? It seems the sort of job a well-spoken young man with clerical experience could have done admirably as he looked for opportunities to get on the stage.

By May 2nd 1939 the critic has the spelling right and Roger Delgado was on stage and attracting high praise. The regular 'On the Stage' column for that day sits amidst other bits of exciting local news. There has been vandalism in the Loughborough Gardens and the parish clerk has died. On the stage the Edward Nelson players are performing *Spring Cleaning*. Frederick Lonsdale's play was daring; one of the characters is a prostitute and the plot is about adultery. It was already nearly fifteen years old and, like many plays in the repertoire of provincial companies, it had been on in the West End years before.[56]

The critic loved it: 'one of the finest things they have done' was the verdict. A recurring point in most reviews was lavish praise for Miss Betty Nelson, a young actress in the company. The critic adored her, but other performers stood out: 'The play would be notable for her acting alone, if that were the only cause to rejoice. It is not, for in the more sustained parts, Miss Peggy Diamond, as the wife who is saved from herself; Mr Donald B. Edwards, as the strong silent husband; and Mr Roger Delgado, as the most unlikeable rogue, are all just that little bit more than competent.' There was more, as Delgado has caught the critic's eye: 'Mr Delgado gives a most polished performance. He interprets all the shades of the character of Ernest Steel, philanderer.'[57] At this point he was twenty-one years old, but isn't it satisfying to find the Master of over thirty years later making an early mark as the rogue.

Delgado seems to burst out of a chrysalis as a fully formed and accomplished actor, which again makes us wonder about what he was doing between leaving the bank and appearing in *You Can't Take it With You*; and watching from the wings, understudying and walk-on parts will have been some form of professional preparation.

Later in May 1939 the parts have become smaller. By May 30th the company is doing *Fair and Warmer* by Avery Hopwood: 'Laughter is the order of the day, and they let it rip.' The names are the same. Betty Nelson, Donald Edwards, Peggy Diamond and Frank Woodfield are all on stage and: 'Roger Delgado manages quietly and effectively his less important part.'[58] Reading between the lines was Delgado a scene-stealer, as 'effectively' managing a small part suggests? In his early film and television parts, he would milk a few moments of screen time for all it was worth with exaggerated facial expressions, accents and gestures and was most definitely a scene-stealer.

After such a prominent start as the rogue in *Spring Cleaning* Delgado's next parts are continuing to get smaller. By June the company is performing *If Four Walls Told* which the critic thought was well done but the audiences were not very large. Delgado's performance did not stand out, his mention just being in a list of others at the end of the review: 'Of the others who share in this success are Roger Delgado, Ann Hunter, Isobel Grant, Peggy Diamond…'[59]

Soon the repertoire changes again and next in June the company is doing the comedy *Square Pegs*. The critic's favourite Betty Nelson 'gives a vivacious performance' which is 'as usual'. Delgado is again attracting attention in his own right, this time for his comedy skill in which he and colleague Frank Woodfield 'are outstanding as healthy, exuberant products of the modern age'.[60] Next the pace changed and the company gave audiences a 'tense, dramatic story' which was 'unrelieved by even a line of comedy'. In *The Fake* Delgado again slipped down the cast and we read: 'Roger Delgado, Walter Cutler and Tony Thawton fill the supporting roles well.'[61]

Week by week plays come on and go off and rehearsals for the next play carry on at the same time as the current performances. Like other repertory companies, the Edward Nelson team serve up a mixture of comedy and drama but nothing very new or particularly old. The 'modern' British plays were mostly from at least a decade earlier. Sometimes Delgado had a chance to shine, on other occasions he was competent filling. Some weeks he did not appear at all if there was no role for him.

Next is something special: a lead and, not only that, a lead in a notorious play. John van Druten's *Young Woodley* is set in a public school and is scandalous, for the prefect and the headmaster's wife fall for each other. The Lord Chamberlain could ban any play and banned van Druten's in the 1920s, a move that pushed van Druten to emigrate.[62] The ban had been lifted for over a decade by the time of the performance in Leicester, but the *Mercury*'s review was still alert to the sensitivity of the script.

Delgado was the lead in the titular part of the prefect and the reviewer thought he was sensational: 'Peggy Diamond, as Laura Simmons, the headmaster's wife, and Roger Delgado, as Woodley, the prefect who falls in love with her, make an ideal leading pair.' The chemistry between performers went down well with audiences and the play was a smash. The *Mercury*'s review could attribute why 'the people shouted encore and others applauded enthusiastically' to one factor, the acting between Diamond and Delgado. 'Each has a thorough understanding of a very difficult part and their contributions are no less than acting genius.'[63]

Throughout the next thirty years and more of professional activity, Delgado would go on to get many more reviews, some lousy, most positive, but was there ever one as sensational as this? Remember this display of acting genius was pulled off twice a night at 6:40pm and 8:50pm. Neither is it hyperbole, as the critic consistently judged the performances judiciously and dished out lukewarm reactions with the praise. In the same review another member of the company, Raymond Wallace playing the headmaster, was merely 'competent enough'. Delgado also delivered this performance under the pressure of not just twice-nightly performances but weekly changes in repertoire and gruelling rehearsals.

More than thirty years later, he would be at BBC Television Centre working to almost the same pace and again late into the night, with two episodes of a *Doctor Who* serial recorded each week. The same arduous pace had been part and parcel of making *Doctor Who* for William Hartnell and Patrick Troughton, who each had a new script a week to learn and who both left the programme exhausted. It is not surprising they were shattered by the experience but remarkable that they coped at all. They were products of the repertory theatre treadmill like Delgado. That discipline could become studio discipline and these workhorse actors could survive a killing pace.

The treadmill did not stop Delgado producing especially good performances. It is also worth remembering that, at twenty-one, playing the prefect gave him a role close to his own age. Like the rest of the company members, he was anything and everything. The actresses went from French hostesses to doctors' wives to submissive victims and whores. The men played parts of all ages and types, but in *Young Woodley*, Delgado, an old boy of a private school, was in a part unusually close to himself.

The correspondent for *The Stage* was also impressed. 'An outstanding performance in the title role is given by Roger Delgado.' Normally in these reviews, an actor would get one sentence per review, but clearly his perform-ance as the prefect stood out to an unusual degree. The critic doesn't stop with his comment that Delgado is outstanding but also adds the further detail: 'Delgado holds the audience throughout.'[64] Something very special happened on stage at the Theatre Royal for this play, making it important to remember that Delgado's professional career as an actor was actually only months old.

But treadmill it was, and the acting genius this week could be a supporting player the next. After the lavish praise for *Young Woodley*, the next week he was in the 'remoter part' of a domestic servant in the comedy *Plan for a Hostess*. The reviewer still had a kind line for him as being 'quietly useful'; far from the genius, encores and applause of the week before.[65]

Next month, however, Delgado had the good fortune to play a part that allowed him to share the stage and a love scene with the critic's favourite, Betty Nelson, and where they between them provided the 'high spot' of the play.[66] The local critic had a serious crush on Nelson. Who was she? It is sad that someone who attracted good notices has vanished from history as surely as the repertory companies themselves, but there are a few traces. The *Express and Advertiser* in 1929 reported on local theatre activity and there she is: a small black-and-white photograph shows a stylish young woman posed looking over her shoulder in a dark dress and three strings of pearls.[67] A decade later she was burning up the stage in love scenes with Delgado, but another decade on she's disappeared. There must be many actors and actresses like Betty Nelson, who vanished along with the repertory companies and theatres in the post-war world, but for a time she had an enthusiastic public and a flourishing career.

The weekly changes of repertoire meant each performer could not always have a part and one week the *Mercury*'s critic was pleased with the 'wise selection' of the cast.[68] For an actor who would become a screen villain, the repertory stage gave Delgado a great deal of comedy. He could display 'charm and poise' in *Tony Draws a Horse*, a comedy by Lesley Storm, and his 'enthusiasm' showed in a 'screaming farce'.[69]

The Stage diligently reported the plays out in the regions and noted Delgado in the cast of *Indoor Fireworks*. This reviewer was not so excited about Betty Nelson but thought the play, a 'lighter fare', had a competent cast.[70] The correspondent had thought well of Nelson's performance in *First Episode* in August 1939 but also thought 'Roger Delgado does well as Tony Wodehouse.'[71]

In due course the Edward Nelson team put on *French Without Tears*, a play that sooner or later every company did, and in it the *Mercury*'s critic thought Delgado 'capably deals with a beard and torrents of French'.[72] Both the beard and the French accent are things to note for the future, including for farce in the West End. *The Stage*'s correspondent also thought he made a good Frenchman and appreciated that Delgado 'does good work in a French character'.[73] Watch this space, as future television, film, radio and stage appearances all called upon Delgado to do good work as a Frenchman.

By December 1939 the company is doing Shaw and *The Stage* reports on their production of *Pygmalion*. As is usual, critics think the Edward Nelson members are professional and effective, including Delgado who 'scores' in a smaller role.[74] That is December 7th. The next week Delgado played the Brigade Major in *French Leave* and is 'mixed up in some excruciatingly funny situations'.[75]

But there was something else happening out in the wider world as the reviewer noted that this play, which was about soldiers, was also 'a topical story of wartime humour'. Britain was now at war.[76] Later in December the Edward Nelson team put on another war-themed production and chose *Alf's Button*. Again their local theatre critic appreciated its topicality: 'That great tonic of the last war *Alf's Button* comes back to give merriment at another wartime Christmas.'[77]

By now, the *Mercury*'s critic had been watching Delgado perform for months. The firm favourite remained Betty Nelson, 'always so popular' according to the critic, but the theatre reviews are the barometer of the first months of Delgado's professional acting career. There have been ups and downs of small parts and big parts, small audiences or full applauding houses, but the critic has seen Delgado develop and now at the very end of 1939 realises that Delgado is a big part of the company: 'Roger Delgado has another important role.'[78] Not every role may have been suitable, but the characteristic of a repertory company was that the casts played all types. On December 19th Delgado was in another comedy (with war coming did the company feel that some comic relief was needed?), *Her Temporary Husband*. Still only twenty-one, Delgado was 'a little youthful' for this part as a professional man.[79]

At the very beginning of 1940, Delgado is part of *The Seventh Guest*. The critic for the *Stage* newspaper thought the production was more serious than the wartime comedies recently done by the Edward Nelson team. On this occasion 'the acting honours go to Frank Woodfield' but next in line for praise was Delgado, who 'ably assisted' the leading man.[80]

And then, the acting stops. We must take leave of Delgado as an actor, temporarily. In his time at Leicester his profile and success had grown. He had also been one part of a bigger success. By 1940 the trade publication *Theatre World* reported on the company's success: 'The Edward Nelson Players are well into their second year of residence at the Theatre Royal. It is interesting to note that well over 400,000 people have paid to see these exceptionally fine players.'[81]

Delgado was indeed an exceptionally fine player. From 1940, his career suffered long interruption but he came away from Leicester with parts young and old, foreign and British, rogues, bright young things and lovers, under his belt. He also had discipline. Years later, his colleagues were in awe and even a bit scared of this meticulous, professional, prepared performer. They saw this discipline mostly in film and television studios, but it came from theatre. When working with him in the 1970s, Pik-Sen Lim was in awe of an actor who was word-perfect. But she knew he was of a particular generation when 'you got everything right or you'd be not employed again!'[82] That same iron-clad discipline stays in the actress Claire Nielson's memory when she thinks of the benefits of doing rep. In the 1960s she appeared with Delgado on television, and found that their earlier experience of regular rep made it possible to cope with the ridiculous pressure of live television. 'People were used to theatre, which is the hardest discipline of all. Practically all of the actors had theatre backgrounds.' But actors had to be tough. 'The weaker ones fell by the wayside. It was tough,' she remembers.[83]

The full impact of war came to Leicester a year after the Edward Nelson Players had staged *French Leave* when German bombers blitzed the city on November 19th 1940. Bombs hit factories and homes although the Theatre Royal survived, to await destruction by post-war development. By the time the bombs fell Delgado was gone from the Edward Nelson Players.

Chapter Five
Private, Captain, Husband
1940-1947

The sealed world in which he lives would be broken.
– George Orwell

T HE SOMETIME LEADING MAN and flourishing actor at the Leicester Theatre Royal enlisted in the ranks of the British Army and became number 203338. However, there was still a Leicester connection. Depending on where you look, there are small variations in dates for his enlistment and later commission, which are partly because of the differences between the date of seniority (when he could start to claim rank) and the date of his actual commission. The Leicestershire Regiment records that Private Roger C. Delgado, number 4860699 enlisted on January 15th 1940. From July 20th 1941, he received his commission, the regiment was again the Leicestershire, and in the Army Lists his emergency commission in the Leicestershire has the official date August 30th 1941. Two years later on April 10th 1943 he was in the Royal Signals.

His progression from private to officer is in line with the Army's policy whereby people who enlisted as privates could go to the Officer Cadet Training Unit (OCTU) and thereafter be commissioned from the ranks.[84] Even in wartime, some things never changed including the *London Gazette* genteelly announcing officers' commissions. By September his emergency commission was announced in the Second Supplement of the *Gazette*.[85]

On paper moving from private to officer seems in theory to have been a good idea and many men did so, including Delgado. Many others were reluctant to do so. Because he was commissioned in July 1941, with it becoming official on August 8th, Delgado moved through the OCTU before major financial changes were permitted by the Treasury that allowed men to keep their pay for acting rank while in the OCTU. The war historian Jeremy Crang says that before 1942 those going into the OCTU had to 'forgo any acting rank they held on entry to an OCTU and the extra pay that went with that', Delgado among them.[86] Notwithstanding the possible financial penalty of becoming an officer, Delgado made the transition.

Unlike his acting, Delgado's war service cannot be reconstructed from newspapers. However, his progress up the commissioned ranks is in the Army Lists. Initially a Second Lieutenant, he became a Lieutenant on October 1st 1942. That was his War Substantive Position. He was made up to Temporary Captain in the Royal Signals on March 27th 1944. Serving in the Royal Signals, a communications corps, meant he had a costume of sorts as he wore a cap badge with Mercury, the Greek god, on it. There is also no doubt this tidy young man, who later in life lived in a spick-and-span house and drove an immaculate car, would have adapted well to the spit and polish of army life.

He served in India, along with fully one third of the Royal Signals, and Ceylon (now Sri Lanka) was another important location for the Royal Signals.[87] While his impressions are lost, brother officers and fellow soldiers recorded their experiences of defending the British Empire. Heat, mud, luxury, servants, inoculations, the scale of an enormous country compared to England, are some of the recollections left by British soldiers.[88] Before going to India there will have been inoculations against all types of sub-continental diseases and then training with the other recruits at the camp at Catterick, where Delgado trained from November 1941 to the beginning of 1942.

Like other soldiers, the full expanse of his life before and during his wartime service is laid bare on the form B199A, a 'tremendously complicated document which all officers are required to complete in order to bring their personal records at the War Office up to date', according to the *Spectator*.[89] It fills in some of the gaps about his life before the war that we simply cannot find anywhere else. The young man who joined up in January 1940 was fluent in French and Spanish. When in India, he also made the effort to become proficient in Urdu. He was a well-travelled man, knowing the 'Belgian seaboard and all main cities and the south of France seaboard' from childhood holidays.

Many actors, including Hartnell, Troughton, Pertwee, Shaun Sutton and Richard Greene, had their careers interrupted by wartime service. Some had lucky escapes, including Pertwee and Troughton who both nearly perished. Hartnell was invalided out. Delgado was in the Royal Signals until the end, eligible for the War Medal 1939–1945.

From time to time a web page or comment about Delgado suggests his difficulty in joining up because of mixed and foreign parentage. Was that actually a problem? Roger Caesar Delgado was a British citizen. At school, at the London School of Economics and at the Westminster Bank he enrolled, worked, studied or served as a British citizen, regardless of either a foreign-sounding name or alien parents. On Form B199A his nationality is listed fair and square as British. He was also in the Leicestershire Regiment by January 1940, a reasonably early date for enlistment, and later he received a commission and promotion. However, he never became a major, contrary to an often-repeated claim.

The chances of a delay either in enlisting or in some kind of prejudice against him for being a foreigner may be unlikely. What is clearer is that the momentum in his acting career was cut. His roles at the Theatre Royal had been getting bigger, audiences were enthusiastic and he was part of a tight-knit group with Betty Nelson, Peggy Diamond, Frank Woodfield and others, all of which he had to leave behind. Yet even in war there is some outlet. While with the garrison in Ranchi he was the entertainment officer, the sort of work later immortalised in *It Ain't Half Hot, Mum!*

Form B199A documents the way the army and the war dictated his life from January 1940 up to 1946. Service in the ranks to August 1941; training at Catterick; then, in March 1942, disembarkation in India; stationed at Mhow, a major military hub for the Raj. The next posting was Ceylon in June 1942; back to India; then at last in August 1945 posted back to England. Finally, August 1946 he gets his Class A, meaning his release from the Army.

In 1945 two major events happened. On May 6th his father, Roger Caesar, the bank clerk whose son in the end did not follow in his footsteps, died aged 68 at St Columba's Hospital in Swiss Cottage. The hospital, now closed, was for terminally ill men. In August 1939, perhaps mindful of coming war, Delgado Senior had drawn up his will in his ornate and beautiful handwriting. He was a bank clerk in a world of bank clerks and two clerks witnessed the simple document in which he left Mathilde, his 'relict' in the language of the time, everything. Should she have predeceased him, their son Roger would receive everything. As it happens, Mathilde inherited an estate valued at just over £1,000, which included the family home in Woodstock Road. By May 1945, someone else was coming to live there.

The other major event of 1945 is that a Mrs Olga Delgado arrived on board a ship that docked at Liverpool. The manifest shows she was on board a ship full of housewives and other women, war brides come to take up residence with their husbands. Her intended address was 96 Woodstock Road. Who was Olga? The whole episode is an untold and unhappy part of Delgado's life.

The Family of Anthonisz of Ceylon

The Roger Delgado known to many friends and colleagues was the man happily married to Kismet Delgado and living in White Cottage in Teddington. His first marriage though is one of the most mysterious and unhappy parts of his life. It's not listed on IMDb or generally known and this whole period was one this tidy man neatly packed away out of sight in later years.

Delgado was a newcomer to India and Ceylon, brought there by military service and the deployment along with other members of the Royal Signals to that part of the British Empire. By contrast the Anthonisz family was well-established in Ceylon and deeply embedded in the colonial society. The family name appears throughout colonial records such as the memberships of the local masonic lodges. Their very long genealogy goes back to at least Abraham Anthonisz, born in Amsterdam but who settled in Ceylon in 1736. Over his lifetime he had three wives and seven children, the beginning of a family line of European traders, planters and officials who stayed in Ceylon.

Members of the family also moved into medicine and the military, or both, as army doctors for the British Army that replaced the Dutch East Indies Company as the colonial force in Ceylon. Alfred Anthonisz, born 1844, studied medicine in Scotland and rose to be a colonel in the Royal Army Medical Corps. Alfred's brother Vincent was born in 1865. He did not follow his brother into the army or into medicine, but like his brother and other siblings he made a good marriage. By now the Dutch Reformed faith of family line had given way to the Church of England and family marriages take place in St Paul's Church in Kandy and Christ Church Cathedral.[90]

Vincent was not a doctor but his son, Vincent Henry Ludovici Anthonisz, born in 1894, followed his Uncle Alfred's path to study medicine in Scotland and serve in the Medical Corps. After medical study in Glasgow, he sailed back to Ceylon in 1921.[91] Thereafter he had a distinguished medical career and his social life flourished. Dr Anthonisz received an OBE in 1944 and became the Honorary Surgeon to the British colonial governor.[92] His name still has a place in the history of cricket in Ceylon/Sri Lanka.[93] By his wife, Mary Caroline Treherne de Saram, he had three children and the eldest interests us: Olga Treherne Anthonisz, born on the 19th of September in 1923.[94] This is the Olga who docked at Liverpool, newly married and heading for Bedford Park.

Olga was the product of colonial society in Ceylon thanks to Dr Anthonisz's connections with the governor. A footnote to the family's long and distinguished genealogy is that, in St Anthony's, the Roman Catholic Cathedral in Kandy, Olga Anthonisz married Lieutenant Roger C. Delgado of the Royal Signals Corps. Kandy is in hill country, surrounded by tea plantations. The cathedral is still there, largely unchanged from wartime. Its bright, lofty interior, where paintings of saints look down from above baroque arches, is where Roger and Olga stood and exchanged vows.

The date given in the family genealogy for the cathedral wedding is September 18th 1943, the day before Olga turned twenty. Like so much about dates and ages in Delgado's life at this time, there is room for doubt. The Army Returns for Marriages 1941–1945 lists the Delgado-Anthonisz wedding, but puts the ceremony in Kandy in 1944 and refers to another wedding in 1943. Was one a civil service and one the cathedral service? Their Decree Absolute fourteen years later says the September 1943 wedding was the one in the cathedral. Like for every other soldier, the British Army's impeccable records keep track of Delgado. Presumably, Olga and Delgado met during his posting to Ceylon from June to November 1942. He was back in Ceylon on War Leave from September 5th 1943 to October 4th. Thereafter Olga appears in military records as being one of the officers' wives who was living with her husband.

But here the problems start. Roger did not just get a wife, but a complete package of a close-knit and, as it would turn out, claustrophobic and intrusive family. This phase of Delgado's life and in fact all details of his married life with Olga are obscure, an unhappy period shut away in the past. To go back a few steps, Olga landed at Liverpool on August 9th 1945. She was twenty-one years old. The incoming passenger list for merchant vessel *Winchester Castle* listed her as a housewife, a statement more of what she was going to become instead of the life among the Ceylonese colonial society that she had known.

From time to time during her marriage to Roger she was able to reconnect with her Ceylonese home life. Both her parents were in England in 1948 and Olga went to Ceylon on her own in 1950. In 1952 her father Vincent sailed into England and came to stay at Woodstock Road. He was back in 1954 by which time Olga and Roger had moved out of Woodstock Road to King Street in Richmond. Their move was a significant break with the past. When Roger was born in 1918 Roger senior and Mathilde already lived in Woodstock Road. During his years as an itinerant actor the house had remained Roger's permanent address, and it was where Olga went when she arrived in 1945.

Roger, however, was frequently not there. His post-war life was as a married man, but also a man anxious to rebuild his acting career. Work in the 1940s was patchy and onerous. To keep in work he moved helter-skelter throughout England. York, Maidstone, Coventry, Leamington, Plymouth and elsewhere, anywhere a regional theatre would employ him. The work kept him far from home, far from Olga, and living in digs.

The 1950s would be a decade of outstanding success for him. Thinking back over Delgado's career, the director Michael Briant says: 'If he was good at his trade, which he was, there was no reason to stop working, and indeed that's what happened. He was a good actor, he never stopped working.'[95]

He got there by gruelling work in the 1940s, where he gradually re-established his acting career; and he started where he left off, in regional repertory. In years to come, TV management, producers and directors actively wanted Delgado; he was professional, reliable as well as talented. That was in the future. In the 1940s Delgado assiduously courted opportunities and dropped names and politely but pointedly asked for work. 'Mr MacDonald Hobley, a close personal friend of mine, has suggested that I write to you to ask whether you would be good enough to grant me an interview,' was one letter to the BBC hoping for work.[96] He soon would be performing all over England, leaving Olga and the widow Delgado together at Woodstock Road.

One person who did remember this time in Roger's life was the writer and producer Victor Pemberton.* They worked together professionally in the 1960s, but much earlier they shared a personal link. Pemberton's long-term partner was the actor David Spenser, who worked on stage and in cinema with Delgado in the 1950s and 1960s. David was born in Ceylon as David de Saram, part of the family line from Olga's mother, and Olga and David were cousins. The de Sarams were just as embedded in Ceylonese society as the Anthonisz line.[97] As Roger would discover, that meant the members of these old, established families were watchful, intrusive presences in his life.

Long before their professional association, Victor Pemberton knew Delgado from this personal link. In fact, 'I first met Roger at a dinner party in Colombo' was his memory of a first encounter with a man he would later know professionally in England; but the man he knew in Colombo was deeply unhappy, far removed from the blissfully happy man later known to many other friends and co-stars when married to Kismet. The problem was not just Olga but also the complete package of the family and Ceylon. 'Roger and David were very good friends,' Victor told me, and he recalled them talking at length about Ceylon. It's doubtful Roger had anything positive to say about the place. Roger had married into a family and a society Victor looked back on as 'claustrophobic'. 'The atmosphere in Sri Lanka was claustrophobic, the families are very claustrophobic. You know that you're being watched the whole time.' Everyone didn't just know everyone else, but they were all related to each other. 'They were all intermixed, the whole lot of them,' is how Pemberton summed up this enclosed society.[98]

At least Delgado could keep this dismal, enclosed society at a distance after the war and his return to Britain. His marriage to Olga was, in Pemberton's view, an unhappy one. A problem was where to live. Married life meant spending time in Ceylon, where Victor Pemberton and David de Saram knew the Delgados, but not living there. 'We used to have meals together in Sri Lanka,' recalled Pemberton, although the atmosphere was unhappy. 'I do know Roger was unhappy and I do know that he wanted to live in England rather than Sri Lanka.'[99] That is not surprising. He had served in Ceylon for the war but, following the war, his life, family and his

---

* Victor Pemberton was kind enough to grant me an interview in September 2016. Sadly he passed away on August 13th 2017 as this book was being prepared for publication.

cherished career were all in England. Rebuilding his acting career was going to be a hard slog but it would be outright impossible if Olga wanted to stay in Sri Lanka.

Chapter Six
Post-war: Picking up the pieces 1947-1948

These actors in their middle years know what they're doing and
are good at it. Not rich, not famous, but making a living.
– Ian McKellen

PRE-WAR DELGADO was an active and prominent member of a provincial repertory company. Following demob, he did not return to
the Edward Nelson Players but did return to the provincial stage. He
did so with success and with sizeable parts. Some of his fellow
Edward Nelson alumni also carried on acting careers. For erstwhile
colleague Frank Woodfield there are a handful of television appearances,
and Betty Nelson appeared in a couple of films. A few other memories of the
Edward Nelson team lingered on. As late as 1947 a show in Penzance noted
in its programme that some of the performers were 'ex-Edward Nelson
Players'.[100] Delgado is truly exceptional among the members of that
company in his prolific, successful mainstream career.

Delgado's post-war work follows a different pattern to that before the
war. Prior to enlistment, his professional identity linked with one theatre
and one company in Leicester. To rebuild his interrupted acting career
Delgado travelled the length and breadth of England, from Yorkshire,
around Lancashire, the Midlands, anywhere there was work.

The Stage reports on his whereabouts for July 1947 where he and the rest of the repertory company at the Theatre Royal in York are performing A. A. Milne's *Mr Pim Passes By*. This is an important moment. Delgado had been out of sight to theatre reviewers since 1940. But he was back and his talent was undiminished. Soon he was getting leading parts and good reviews.

The review that reached *The Stage* about the repertory in York thought Delgado and the rest had done a good job with this 'charming play' that was 'being given the correct touch of delicacy'.[101] One way his post-war career did follow that before the war was the same old intense pace, for the next week after *Mr Pim Passes By* the company moved on to a new play.

November 1947 brought him to the Theatre Royal in Nottingham playing the lead in *A Man About the House*, a thriller with some comedy. Delgado was an 'unscrupulous man' involved with a woman who has inherited a large income.[102] The titular 'man about the house' he played was Salvatore, who ran the household of two spinsters. The local critic liked the play and admired the performances, including Delgado as 'the villain of the piece'.[103] We have another perspective on his performance from the *Nottingham Journal*, which liked the way Delgado could be 'so suave and plausible at the outset, and so utter in his final cringing and abasement'.[104]

He moved on and in December 1947 was in Plymouth, still with *A Man About the House* at the Palace Theatre. The local critic appreciated the 'fine acting' on offer from Delgado and the remainder of the cast.[105]

By 1948 he had a major theatrical success that he was taking around the regions. Terence Rattigan's *The Winslow Boy* opened at the Lyric Theatre in 1946 with Frank Cellier, Emlyn Williams and Angela Baddeley. In 1948 Delgado was on tour with the play playing the barrister Sir Robert Morton. Once more at the Nottingham Theatre Royal, he was part of an 'excellent cast' along with Barbara Bruce and Anton Rodgers.[106] In later life, Rodgers found fame and acclaim for television parts in the middle-class comedies *Fresh Fields* and *May to December*. In 1948 he was a boy actor pushed onto the stage by his ambitious mother and had already played Pip in *Great Expectations*.[107] His role as the Winslow Boy, a naval cadet, took him with Delgado around the country but he already knew what a long tour was like. The Empire in Sunderland promised a 'powerful company' and referred back to the Lyric performances: 'Following over a year's sensational run at the Lyric Theatre London.'[108] Then there was a week's performance in Maidstone.[109] Praise for a 'fine study of a barrister who becomes a spearhead of an attack for right' was dished out in the *Rugby Advertiser*, although sadly there were also many empty seats in the theatre there.[110]

Delgado continued almost non-stop around the country in 1948 and into the next year, and for a time found stable work in Coventry. The Midland Theatre Company formed with the support of the Arts Council to provide regional theatre.[111] It started in Coventry in 1946 and it carried on into the 1950s.[112] The company's professional home became the Technical College Theatre but in Delgado's time the productions were on a circuit.[113] Coventry in 1948 was one of the least pleasant places to be. The hideous bombing of 1940 that shattered more than two thirds of the city was still very noticeable and Delgado was working in what was one big bombsite.

Throughout 1948 the Midland Theatre Company staged some Shakespeare including a production of *The Merchant of Venice* where, in a rare encounter with the Bard, Delgado played Shylock with Ninka Dolega, one of Peter Copley's wives, as Portia.[114] We still find him in the Midlands in Coventry in 1949, directed by Bill Fraser in George Bernard Shaw's *The Apple Cart*.[115]

Something stands out, because Delgado is now in the lead. This is a professional first for him and a rarity throughout his career. 'Production is in the hands of Bill Fraser, a veteran at the game and a star performer in his own right in the West End of London. The big cast is headed by Roger Delgado.'[116] He remained in Coventry and with the Midland Theatre Company for Somerset Maugham's *The Sacred Flame* and once more he was in the lead.[117] 'Roger Delgado will be seen as Maurice Tabret,' reported the local paper.[118]

Delgado had many strings to his bow, or what the director Michael Briant calls his 'bag of tricks'. Over his thirty-plus years of acting, he sang, danced, performed as foreigners of every conceivable type and accent, did farce and high drama; but one further talent was as a director. The Midland Company gave him the opportunity and in May 1949 *The Stage* announced that: 'The Midland Theatre Company (Arts Council) are presenting Roger Delgado's production of *The Linden Tree*.'[119] His cast contains a number of names who will stand out to posterity, including Graham Stark and Geoffrey Keen as well as David Dodimead.

Another member of the Midland Theatre Company was Alan Bates, there from 1955 and therefore after Delgado but who years later reminisced about the benefit of being in that particular company rather than somewhere more prestigious like the Royal Shakespeare Company: 'In a way, I was slightly better off, because if you went to Stratford, you walked on, you were the crowd, you might have a line or two, then you would graduate. They would keep you for a very long time before they began to let you emerge.'[120]

In short, a group like the Midland was a good starting point, or in Delgado's case a good restarting point. Apart from Bates, other alumni include the director Michael Langham, who started his career directing Shakespeare and eventually became the head of drama at the Juilliard School.[121] Delgado may have been out in the regions but he was getting bigger parts as he continued to rebuild his career. The Midland gave him another leading role in *The Venetian*. On stage in Leicester Delgado had already played lovers and he gets the opportunity here in a play which 'deals with two of history's great lovers, Bianca Cappello and Francesco de Medici'. Delgado was the great lover Francesco.

The shift to film and television

In the meantime, there had been a further development in Delgado's career as significant as being leading man on stage. Theatre had been good to him. He started there and resumed there after a long break but from now on he would be absent from the stage for a while. Over time, these absences would get longer and eventually be permanent because another medium claimed his time.

The BBC resumed its television service after wartime closure. It needed content to broadcast and for the time being much of its drama output was from contemporary theatre. The Corporation also possessed the technology for outside broadcasts and while many theatres were reluctant to collaborate with television as a competitor for people's attention and a threat to ticket sales, the Intimate Theatre allowed its performances to be broadcast.[122] We find Delgado there in 1948 making his television debut.

Delgado notched up an astonishing number of credits. Someone who was in over 120 film and television productions before dying aged fifty-five, alongside numerous theatre credits and countless radio broadcasts, was obviously a man who said 'yes' to everything. Looking at the big picture of his career, it's also clear he cleverly made important transitions during this career. Further on we'll see some of these. He moved into swashbucklers at the height of their popularity in the 1950s. As they started to fade, he switched again to ITC and ABC adventures. In the early 1970s, he moved to permanent work with *Doctor Who*. These transitions take place throughout his career. After the war, he resumed theatre work but the theatre historian Michael Sanderson points out that although there was a revival in provincial theatre after the war, the same period also saw the rise of television.[123]

Delgado was a theatre actor who moved swiftly to TV. His film debut waited until the 1950s but he was a precocious television performer, precocious because he first appeared on the medium in 1948. Along with a select group of actors including Patrick Troughton, Marius Goring and Peter Cushing and even film star Margaret Lockwood, Delgado was an early and eager performer on a medium that many actors still regarded with disdain when they bothered to think of it at all.[124]

Precious little survives of the first post-war broadcasts. They are the 'ghost' texts to use a term from television historian Jason Jacobs, meaning that scripts and production paperwork exist, also reviews in the daily press and some stills, but not the actual picture or sound recordings.[125] That means there is unfortunately no way to see Delgado's earliest television performances. We know viewers of the BBC Television Service first saw Delgado in action in 1948 and that's a landmark moment in his career.

The BBC's cameras transmitted fourteen productions from the Intimate in the late 1940s, despite numerous technical difficulties with equipment that was dated even by 1948.[126] The busy little theatre hosted in its time actors from Sir Roger Moore to Clive Dunn and its repertory used Delgado a number of times in 1948 in *A Man About the House* and *The Distaff Side*.[127] The Television Service was showing plays from there in January, and on the night of July 8th viewers of what was still the only television service could see the broadcast of James Parish's *Distinguished Gathering*, with Delgado playing Eliot Richard Vines.[128]

It was a good part in a thriller with quite convoluted plotting.[129] Vines is a writer but his new book is going to embarrass a large number of people, who have gathered at a house and are plotting to murder Vines by stabbing him in a darkened room.[130] The play debuted at St Martin's Theatre in 1935 and was revived for this broadcast. Nothing survives of the transmission. Years later when Delgado's obituaries appeared they recalled him primarily as a television performer and the broadcast of this thriller was his first step to that reputation.

To broadcast from the Intimate Theatre (actually a church hall in Palmer's Green) was a major technical achievement for the BBC. A newspaper report of the time described these 'weird objects' at the theatre and the high technology used by the BBC. The 'weird objects' were the cameras, two 1937 Emitrons and a Super Emitron, along with lights, huge cables and the cameramen, all squeezed into an upper gallery. Outside were two large vans, a scanner van and the transmitter van. In the car park a massive aerial, which to the people of north London in 1948 must have looked like an alien object landed in their midst, sent the signal to Alexandra Palace.

Overall, it was a huge effort that continued during the performance. There was a director in the theatre guiding the cameramen, who did more than just point a camera at a stage. Instead the one cameraman was covering 'the long view', one 'the medium view', and the third was for 'close-ups' following guidance from the television director, and Delgado could be seen performing from these different angles. The cameras' output went from Alexandra Palace for 'rediffusion' to the viewing public.

Now it is almost impossible to imagine how marvellous, mind-blowing even, the 1940s television broadcasts were for the few people who saw them; to be able to watch a theatre play live at home was extraordinary. One reviewer was amazed that he could see a live play from the theatre 'with a coffee cup near to hand, a soft carpet beneath my feet and a fire glowing rosily'.[131]

There was one technical hitch during the broadcast of *Distinguished Gathering*, and it is a quaint one. Viewers saw a production with a big cast, but remembering this was about a 'distinguished gathering', a BBC report later said 'owing to the large number of dinner jackets being worn, some of the pictures were not up to the usual standard'.[132]

Delgado's shift to television at these early exciting days of broadcasting shows what his career was now going to be like. He had been on the stage, but from the early 1950s onwards his career was almost totally on screen. He would start to get small roles in film, but he embraced television early: and television rewarded him with big parts, constant work, and fame.

Interlude
Delgado at sea

B Y MOST ACCOUNTS, Delgado hated water. When making the *Doctor
Who* story 'The Sea Devils' in 1972 he found himself in what was
surely an aquaphobe's worst nightmare: in the Solent having to
perform stunts on water while Jon Pertwee showed off his sailing
prowess and Katy Manning good-naturedly teased him by muttering about
'greasy pork chops' when he was feeling especially seasick.[133] On other
occasions he had lucky escapes. While *Sea Fury* and *Ghost Squad* had many
scenes shot at sea, Delgado's were mostly done in studio.

His military service kept him on dry land, but married life with Olga and
his own family connections in the Canary Islands meant that from time to
time he had to put his career on hold and take to the water. At least he did
so in comfort and from the security of a first class cabin.

From time to time in the 1940s and 1950s, his acting was on hold when
he and Olga sailed to Las Palmas. On the shipping manifests, Delgado sticks
out in the list of passengers by virtue of his profession. 'Actor' seems more
exotic than the housewives and clerks on board. One of their trips was in
1949; they sailed from Hull in July of that year and were listed as living at
Woodstock Road. They sailed back into Hull in September 1949.

As the 1940s moved to the 1950s, acting was again temporarily on hold
while Roger and Olga sailed overseas. Olga was on her own in 1950 when she
sailed on the P&O liner *Himalaya* for a return visit to Colombo. In
November, husband and wife travelled to Las Palmas. Once again, the

shipping manifest lists the actor and housewife on board and as always travelling first class. They were still living at Woodstock Road and were back in England by November 1950. By now, the house had been Roger's home since infancy. As a jobbing actor, the old family home was a familiar base as he dashed around England living in digs while acting, leaving Olga at home. As the 1940s turned to the 1950s, the pace relaxed a little. More television and more film meant he could end this remorseless journeying around provincial theatres and work from studios in or near London.

The 1950s were all busy years for Delgado, including more film work and much television, but he kept travelling to see family. By now Mathilde Delgado of 96 Woodstock Road had become Mathilde Martin of 4 General Vives Puerto de la luz in Las Palmas. The widow Delgado had left England on December 2nd 1947 on the ship *Bentacuria*; the immigration records place her among the 'alien passengers' and her country of intended permanent residence as the Canary Islands. She had made a return visit to England in 1948, again coming in among the 'alien passengers'.

After divorce and remarriage his travels continued. Roger and Kismet had been in Las Palmas in 1958, sailing from London on April 3rd. On the way out, they sailed on the *Bruno*, the same ship on the Fred. Olsen line that Roger and Olga had used on their own trip to Las Palmas a decade earlier.

When sailing, Delgado kept good company and on board were Sir Robert and Lady Fraser. Sir Robert made a distinguished contribution to intelligence during the war and his knighthood in 1949 was for his directorship of the Central Office for Information.[134] Now he was in another and equally distinguished position as the Director General of the Independent Television Authority, the ITA. The presence on the same ship of the director of the ITA and Delgado is an intriguing little moment. The ITA was not a broadcaster but the regulator overseeing the various and competing independent broadcasting companies. Delgado was in the frequent employ of these companies. Had Sir Robert watched any of his performances?

Along with Delgado and Fraser and their wives there was a company director, a doctor, a teacher and various housewives, a little middle-class group that makes me think of the social milieu of an Agatha Christie novel. Roger and Kismet returned on May 12th 1958, back to their flat in the King's Road Chelsea. Once more the actor stands out from the accountants and housewives sailing with him.

Mathilde died just over a year later in August 1959. She had remarried to Bernard Martin but in her will she left everything to her son, a modest inheritance of £2,551. Since Roger senior's death she had left Woodstock Road and had travelled backwards and forwards to Las Palmas, where Roger and Kismet visited her. To the end she was also a foreigner whenever she was in Britain. Her death broke the last link to the vanished family life at Woodstock Road.

Chapter Seven
The Cartier Company and BBC Television

I never had a career, only work. – Nigel Kneale

A N ACTOR NEEDED a lot of nerve to do live television. To a repertory player like Delgado the endurance needed for live broadcasts was gruelling but familiar from theatre. Another early television performer was Claire Nielson, also a product of repertory theatre. Live television sticks in her memory as 'the most terrifying thing of all'. However, the exhilarating improvisatory madness of trying to make it all work could offset the terror.

'There were hilarious things that used to happen then,' she told me. 'You'd be acting away and suddenly you'd see someone crawling along the floor beside you putting an essential prop on a table that they'd forgotten to set. And then the director would appear beside the camera and mime slowing down or speeding up with his hands, because all the timings had to be exact.'[135] Who knows what last-minute panics were happening behind the cameras during Delgado's early appearances, but neither the pressure of early television production nor the participation in a live broadcast could hold too many terrors for a disciplined repertory actor.

There was a gap of four years between Delgado's first TV appearance in 1948 and his next in 1952. 1952 sets the scene for the rest of his career. From then on, producers including Martyn Webster and Alvin Rakoff cast Delgado in work including adaptations of Francis Durbridge and in *The Legend of Pepito*, in which Delgado played a Mexican priest for Rakoff alongside Rakoff's wife Jacqueline Hill.[136]

Few producer/directors used Delgado as much as Rudolph Cartier. In contemporary parlance at the BBC, the producer was also the director, hence the many 1950s productions that have the credit of being produced by Cartier. He was casting and directing Delgado by the early 1950s and Delgado's first engagement by Cartier was to play the part of Hatton in the television drama *Portrait of Peter Perowne* in December 1952, Delgado's first appearance in that medium since the broadcast of 1948.[137] There is no recording of the production and little information survives although the science-fiction story was a 'life after death plot'.[138]

As director, Cartier's name is associated with two others, the writer Nigel Kneale and Kneale's creation Professor Bernard Quatermass. Both came into Delgado's life in the 1950s and there is more below about them. Cartier's talents and importance have not just been recognised retrospectively but were seen at the time. A feature about Cartier in *The Times* in December 1958 gives an insightful impression of 1950s television production and Cartier's burning creativity. While it is now possible to watch restored version of the Quatermass serials on DVD, the original experience was the 405-line transmissions on small television screens, a smallness made all the more apparent by the bulk of the TV sets because of the glass electronic valves inside them. Delgado and all other actors were tiny presences inside people's homes and the author of the article in *The Times* was struck by the massive scale of the new BBC Television Centre (which 'seems to have the scale of a mountain already' and is compared to the Colosseum) and 'the little mouse of an artistic end product'.[139]

According to the profile, Cartier was unbothered by the smallness of the end product and saw instead its big impact: 'You can control the viewer's response to a much greater extent than other media permit.'[140] We can remember that when thinking about Delgado's exceptionally dramatic performance in *Quatermass II*. Cartier was also thinking of the future: 'The BBC is producing producers as well as plays. They are feeling their way towards what television drama will one day be.'[141]

The producers work behind the scenes but one way Cartier contributed to the future of television drama was recruiting 'a virtual Rudolph Cartier repertory company'.[142] Among them were actors who would continue to work in BBC drama for the 1960s and 1970s. The importance of this 'Cartier company' to genre film and television is immense. In time Hammer did not just adapt the Cartier and Kneale scripts but took on many of the actors from their pool, including Peter Cushing, Rupert Davies and Patrick Troughton. The impact of Cartier's repertory on the future history of British telefantasy is astounding. Besides Peter Cushing, his players included Cyril Shaps, Paul Whitsun-Jones, André Morrell, Marius Goring, Troughton, and Anton Diffring. Cartier's gift to television was a core of actors comfortable with Lime Grove, Riverside and later the Television Centre and who could deliver the types of performances needed in these small spaces.

Science-fiction roles

Delgado's best-remembered television role for Cartier is Conrad, a journalist, in episode four of *Quatermass II*, sequel to 1953's *The Quatermass Experiment*. The original Quatermass, Reginald Tate, died before a sequel could begin production meaning John Robinson played the Professor for *Quatermass II*, broadcast from October to November 1955. Each episode of the serial had an individual title and Delgado's, 'The Coming', was broadcast at 8pm on November 12th.

By the time of that broadcast, Kneale, Cartier and the whole of the BBC were under unique pressure as the Corporation's broadcasting monopoly ended when ITV began transmission for the first time in 1955.[143] Delgado was only one part of a much larger real-life drama as the BBC braced itself for commercial rivalry, but he was working for the Corporation at a time of great excitement and great anxiety. Playing Conrad in episode four places him for a brief while at the eye of a storm as the BBC for the first time had to worry about audience share. He also dominated episode four, at a moment when the BBC's hierarchy was needing *Quatermass II* to be a success.

According to Andrew Pixley's reconstruction of rather ambiguous BBC paperwork, Delgado, playing Conrad, pre-filmed a scene with John Robinson as Quatermass on October 11th 1955.[144] What is more certain is that Delgado was next at the Mensergh Woodall Boys Club to rehearse the studio sequences for episode four. Then he was in Studio D at Lime Grove for the live broadcast.[145] Playing Conrad involved Delgado in a type of science-fiction production that would recur across his appearances as the Master. Assembling for rehearsal in dismal scout halls, church halls or other rented venues was typical as was recording the episode in one go in a studio in an evening.

By episode four, there are sinister happenings in southern England. Professor Quatermass, still preoccupied with his rocketry, has also investigated a mysteriously abandoned village and an isolated and closely guarded chemical plant. Worse still, strange meteorites falling from the sky infect people, leaving them as zombies.

Delgado appears shortly into episode four playing the Fleet Street journalist Hugh Conrad. The part shows Delgado's full range. In his first scene, there is some comedy business between Conrad and his incompetent office boy who is more interested in preening at his reflection and straightening his tie than running errands. The comedy offsets the later horror when Conrad and Quatermass visit a pub near the plant. Delgado plays Conrad as a smooth, insightful and celebrity journalist who pins down the locals with his sharp questioning. Then Conrad's journalistic curiosity gets the better of him when a meteor crashes through the pub's ceiling.

In the next scenes, Delgado's acting is a powerhouse. What could have been histrionic is chilling. Conrad drives Quatermass away from the pub. In the darkness, the preoccupied and worried Quatermass is oblivious to how inexplicably sinister Conrad's demeanour has become and Cartier's camera gets closer in on Delgado's increasingly inhuman expression.

When Quatermass was looking away, Conrad had touched the meteor and is now becoming a zombie. His final scene is powerful; as the infection takes hold, the personality of Conrad the journalist fights back as he makes one last desperate phone call to the news desk at his paper: 'Sub this to sound right,' he gasps. Kneale's script gives Delgado a vital role to explain plot as the narrative given to the news-desk editor is also for the benefit of the audience. The last thing we see is the telephone receiver falling and rocking backwards and forwards on its cable. Delgado is 'doing some damn fine *explaining-the-plot-over-the-phone-whilst-dying-horribly* acting' as one admirer puts it, gasping in pain, struggling to get the information out before dying.[146]

Although the launch of ITV had created fears at the BBC about loss of audience, *Quatermass II* not only held steady but also increased the ratings. Good advance publicity would have helped and newspapers spread the excitement of Professor Quatermass's return to television. One reported:

'"Quatermass" comes back to television tonight' and 'space suits and gleaming rockets invade the television screen to-night'.[147]

The 7.9 million people watching episode one had risen to 8.3 million who saw episode four and watched Delgado's dramatic death scene.[148] In competition against *Quatermass II*, Associated Rediffusion broadcast *For the Love of Pete*; but audiences stayed with Professor Quatermass. The *Spectator*'s critic compared the tribulations of a charlady in a courtroom on Rediffusion with the ability of *Quatermass* to 'chill the hearts of viewers' and the BBC did have the more exciting programme.[149] A reviewer for the *Yorkshire Post* collected feedback he'd heard from viewers ranging from 'it made me giggle' to 'I dare not look' and concluded overall that 'The Coming' was quite frightening: 'Mr Nigel Kneale, and Mr John Robinson, who plays the harassed professor, have made the world fully aware of the things that go bump in the night and others which slither and crawl.'[150]

Viewing *Quatermass II* nowadays is an object lesson in how well some and how terribly other actors adapted to television. One of the many anecdotes told about William Hartnell (and it is a nice one for a change) was his careful adaptation of performance techniques to television. Remembering that TV actors were not just on the small screen but also in the quite small studios of Lime Grove, Hartnell's instinct was to scale everything down.[151] If pointing in the distance, he kept his arm and hand close into his body as he realised the shot would be close in.

The other factor, besides not pointing your hand too dramatically, is the vexed question of naturalism in performances. *Quatermass II* presents varied levels of performance. John Robinson and Hugh Griffith as well as Delgado already by 1955 had experience in television. By contrast, Monica Grey playing Quatermass' daughter is not so much self-conscious as constipated. Her accent is no different from the well-modulated received pronunciation of the female compère who opened the BBC's first live television broadcast in 1936. It is not just her cut-glass accent, but also her theatrical performance in the small television space that jars with her co-stars' acting style, and her performance has dated horribly.

Grey was not a member of Cartier's 'repertory' and was foisted onto him because of her connections within the BBC.[152] Among the performers he did want in his productions was Delgado and he kept using him. Shortly before *Quatermass II* Delgado was part of Cartier's production of *Point of Departure* in July 1955, along with names to watch for the future including

Arthur Lowe, Laurence Payne, Eric Pohlman and Cyril Shaps. The peculiar little play was an updating of the myth of Orpheus and Eurydice.

In February 1956 Delgado joined the cast of the one-off play *The White Falcon*. Cartier was originally a theatre director and here televises a script written for the stage by Neilson Gattey and Jordan Lawrence.[153] While he had started as a stage director Cartier's vision was often cinematic. Ambitious pre-filmed sequences punctuated *Quatermass II*. With *The White Falcon*, as the British Film Institute's review points out, Cartier retreats from the wider scale of his science fiction and the setting is small-scale.

Paul Rogers plays Henry VIII and Jeannette Sterke (also in *Point of Departure*) is his second wife, Anne Boleyn. What is curious is Delgado's part as Mark Smeaton. There were plenty of opportunities to include Spanish characters in drama set in Tudor England and here Margaretta Scott plays one of them, Catherine of Aragon. But Delgado for once is not a foreigner but an Englishman. Smeaton, a musician, was one of the men accused of adultery with Boleyn and executed by Henry VIII.

As usual, the transmission was live. Surviving descriptions suggest a claustrophobic production without any of the film inserts that Cartier used in other productions to give scale to the broadcasts. However, Delgado's appearance in the fifth scene was on a large set with a gallery and viewers and reviewers at the time were excited with the scene's inclusion of a large number of dancers who performed energetically. Delgado's character has a sexually charged conversation with a lady at the court, and later Jane Seymour implicated him in adultery with Anne Boleyn.[154]

White Falcon was part of the *Sunday Night Theatre* drama strand, and by July 1956 Delgado was again working with Cartier for *The Cold Light*. Marius Goring, who had played the churchman Thomas Cranmer in *The White Falcon*, was also in the cast, as was Vera Fusek. For all concerned it was a major shift from *The White Falcon*. In place of Tudor sexual history, the play used a modern setting and very contemporary themes about modern science.

The play was an important milestone for Marius Goring. He was already a prominent film actor including his part in Powell and Pressburger's *The Red Shoes*. His performance as the nuclear scientist in *The Cold Light* earned him further acting plaudits.[155] While the play was important for Goring, Delgado's part was quite small and he returned to type, playing a foreigner.

The 'Cartier company' was neither static nor exclusive. Working with the same actors was one part of Cartier's modus operandi, but in 1957 he brought the American method actor Eli Wallach onto the screen in *Counsellor at Law* for *Sunday Night Theatre*. The British cast including Delgado, Eileen Way and Cyril Shaps acted alongside Wallach. Although Wallach's major hits including *The Magnificent Seven*, *The Good, the Bad and the Ugly* and *The Godfather III* were ahead of him, *The Observer* was aware that a major American name had graced British television but did not think Wallach's method acting, so different in approach to the classical training of British actors, particularly stood out: 'Eli Wallach, the American disciple of the Method, who flew over to take the name part, was admirably solid, but not noticeably more absorbed in his role than some of our own best actors.'[156]

The Times's television critic was pleased. The review of *Counsellor at Law* recognised that Cartier was doing much more than point a television camera at a stage play. 'In his rapidly moving production Mr Cartier dwelt with mounting urgency on the impending suicide by connecting scenes with forebodingly spasmodic movement and vertiginous shots of skyscrapers.'[157]

Cartier's ability to mix shots from the vision mixer and his use of music and film inserts pushed the broadcast beyond televised theatre. Wallach's performance was impressive and praise of Wallach squeezed out any comment on Delgado's contribution; but he again had work with Cartier and had the experience of working with a major American import.

Cartier's company was performing for an increasingly sophisticated audience with a developing appreciation of television drama as something specific to the medium. When Delgado acted for other producers who lacked Cartier's flair, the results were unfortunate. In 1960 Brandon Acton-Bond directed Delgado in *Conflict at Kalanadi* based on a stage play.[158] The *Spectator*'s reviewer Peter Forster hated what he saw, including the pathetically small and unimaginative realisation of the action. Forster also wrote with considerably informed awareness about what was possible in television and what marked out good direction from inept. He was unimpressed by 'the five soldiers we saw, bunched together to keep in camera'.[159] In other words, the medium drew attention to its shortcomings, something Cartier avoided.

***

Delgado became indispensable to drama directors in strands such as *Sunday Night Theatre*, *Saturday Playhouse*, *Armchair Theatre* and the *Play of the*

Week on ITV. In turn, these drama strands gave him some exposure to critics and audiences. He was part of major successes and along with many familiar faces like Marne Maitland, Rupert Davies, Peter Copley, John Franklyn-Robbins and Cyril Luckham he was in *The Successor*. This *ITV Play of the Week* was an 'Honourable Mention' at the Emmys in 1966.[160] *The Stage* included a picture of Delgado performing a scene with Giorgia Moll in *A Heart and a Diamond* for *Armchair Theatre* in 1960.[161] Directors and producers needed actors of Delgado's calibre. 'It was an era where character actors ruled the day,' says Katy Manning, as the type of work on offer needed strong characters rather than stars.[162]

Thinking back to drama production in that era, Michael Briant said: 'That period was a glorious era for British television drama; we had BBC One classics, BBC Two classics, ITV was also doing classics, we had *Play for Today*, *Play of the Week*, *Play of the Month*, we had series, serials, it was a magical time; and if you were a useful character, there was no reason ever to stop working and you got offered a wonderful, wonderful, variety of work.'[163] European as well as British dramatists had their work adapted which all provided parts for Delgado.

Throughout the 1950s and into the 1960s this 'wonderful work' continued. In 1957 Delgado played a Spaniard, Luján, in Harley Granville Barker's translation of the Spanish play *Doña Clarines* by Serafin Álvarez Quintero and Joaquin Álvarez Quintero. For Granada the next year he was in *The Strong are Lonely* set in Paraguay and broadcast as part of the *Play of the Week*. Or he played foreign parts in works by British writers. On January 27th 1957 *Sunday Night Theatre* broadcast *Myself a Stranger*, billed as a 'play on theme of the colour bar' in *The Times* and featuring Hugh Burden appearing in his own play alongside Bryan Coleman, Barry Foster and Delgado as Hercules de Soysa. The BBC studio recreated Ceylon immediately before the Second World War and it's interesting that Delgado could have compared the sets to the reality. The reviewer for *The Stage* thought the cast, including Roger Delgado, 'were all in tune with the author's intentions' in this play, described in excruciatingly well-meaning language of the 1950s as about the 'coloured point of view'.[164]

If the presence of Eli Wallach may have drawn all the critics' attention for *Counsellor at Law*, on this occasion critics noted Delgado. *The Times*'s television critic didn't especially like the production but thought Delgado and the actress Grizelda Hervey 'were the most mercurial members of a somewhat stolid cast'.[165] To do this work Delgado was also busy moving around England. To appear in *Doña Clarines* he was at the BBC's Midlands studio and to be in *Conflict at Kalanadi* he was in the West of England studios.

During the 1950s and 1960s he made many noteworthy appearances on the small screen, but surely the most terrifyingly memorable of all must be in *One Step Beyond:* 'The Face'. I don't know about anyone else, but his appearance as the ghostly Captain Santoro in this 1961 science-fiction series terrifies the hell out of me. *One Step Beyond* was a paranormal anthology series. The 'face' in question is Delgado's, and in the first scene he appears as a malevolent apparition in a little boy's nightmare. 'The Face' is actually a melancholy little ghost story, told in just twenty-five minutes. The little boy grows up still haunted by the spectral, knife-wielding malevolent figure played by Delgado, before being pressed for service on board a merchant ship and finding his nightmare comes true as the ship's captain is the spectre from his nightmares. In fleeting appearances, Delgado's ghostly figure leers, stabs with a knife and is the very vision of a nightmare.

While Delgado was busy on the very small screen in the 1950s, this decade was also when he made his film debut. That came in 1952. Like with television, once he had started, Delgado never stopped and his film debut led to non-stop activity on the big screen.

Chapter Eight
Film: speaking roles and B films 1952-1955

This is where we came in. – A 1950s cinemagoer

WHAT DID DELGADO offer directors? Mostly, he offered them a foreigner. Throughout his film and television appearances, he portrayed a steady stream of characters who were Egyptian, Arab, Indian, Chinese, Eastern European, Mexican and Spanish. The foreigner would be the backbone of his film career from its beginning in 1952.

Another 'foreign' actor was David Spenser, partner of Victor Pemberton. When I interviewed Pemberton in 2016 he remembered there being a 'nucleus' of actors used for foreign parts. That normally meant a very imprecise understanding of exactly what type of foreigner these people were; more likely, said Pemberton, a director or producer looked at someone like Delgado, Marne Maitland, George Pastell or Spenser, 'this nucleus of actors they used for dare I say it foreign parts', and thought: 'He can play a foreigner!' As Stephen Chibnall and Brian McFarlane say, for Delgado and other 'foreigner' actors, 'it hardly mattered where such actors actually came from'.[166] In any case Delgado came from nowhere more exotic than Bedford Park. All four of these were in *Stranglers of Bombay* in 1959 (of which more later) although only two of them – Spenser, a Sri Lankan, and Maitland, who was Anglo-Indian – were from that part of the world and, in Pemberton's view, 'George [Pastell] was unsuitable to play in *Stranglers of Bombay*; I don't know what his nationality was but it certainly wasn't Indian – and Roger was certainly not an Indian.' He attributed the casting of actors to Hollywood's bad influence over British cinema. 'Hollywood in those days never had the slightest idea how to cast foreigners. If it was a Turkish person they'd cast an Argentinian or something, and if it was an English person they'd cast somebody from America who had the most dreadful accent, or if it was a toff then that person would be playing it with a cockney accent, no idea how to do it. And that drifted a bit into British films and British television.'[167] However inaccurate, the approach did mean constant work for Delgado throughout the 1950s. He wasn't Indian, but that was no reason for him not to play one on screen.

Delgado's ability with accents stood him in good stead as he commenced a series of B films in the early 1950s. His film debut *Murder at Scotland Yard* is also one of the last appearances by another actor famous for villainy, the melodrama star Tod Slaughter (and yes, that was his real name). As one career in film was ending another was beginning, and it would be fascinating to know what Delgado may have learnt from watching this master of Grand Guignol at work on set. Slaughter's film performances are actually a lot more subtle and sophisticated than the production quality of the films or their titles would suggest, and in *Murder at Scotland Yard* he gives a sly, devious performance as the villain. *Murder at Scotland Yard* oozes cheapness, made on the smell of an oily rag at the now defunct Merton Studios on Kingston Road.

Next Delgado made another thriller, *The Broken Horseshoe*, at another cheap little studio, this time Nettlefold Studios. The American actor (but British resident) Robert Beatty plays a surgeon, Mr Fenton, whose patient Charles Constance is murdered. He is implicated in the murder when his cigarette lighter (and, this being a 1950s film, everyone puffs away on cigarettes the whole time) is found next to the corpse. Meanwhile he has fallen for Della Freeman, a glamorous criminal played by the classy actress Elizabeth Sellars.

It's a cheap film and much of the budget must have been spent on the real furs that Sellars wafts around in and which are such a notable part of the production they have their own credit in the opening titles. But it's also a tidy plot and it gives Delgado two good scenes. He plays Felix Galegos, a foreign murderer. He is first seen in a restaurant and makes an immediate impact with his portrayal of sleek, rat-like cunning, all oily black hair and insinuating mannerisms. Mr Fenton enters the restaurant expecting to find Della. He is greeted by an elegantly dressed European man, Galegos, who immediately wrong-foots the surgeon by acting as though they know each other, leaving Fenton confused and trying to recall where they have met before.

Galegos is lying and deliberately setting out to confuse. He is part of a criminal gang doping professional racehorses. He has murdered Constance but now needs to get back a railway ticket in the surgeon's possession that has a message written on it in invisible ink. He drugs the surgeon's Dubonnet and makes a getaway with the railway ticket.

On paper, there is not much to the part of Galegos; but already, in only his second film performance, Delgado is achieving much with small touches. As he talks to the surgeon he spins his small glass with his aperitif in it round and round in his hand. Fenton tries to leave, but Delgado lays a hand lightly on his wrist, a small touch but it stops the doctor in his tracks.

In his next scene, we see Delgado's character standing over the body of a woman he's just murdered. Again the small, sharp movements add to the performance. With a short, brutal tug he rips out a phone line to stop Fenton calling the police, holds the surgeon at gunpoint, and darts out of a doorway, locking the surgeon in with a dead body. However, at the end it's an anti-climax when the police arrest Galegos off-screen.

***

A lot of Delgado's credits are for roles in fantasy, horror or science fiction, but popular comedy also occasionally appears. Early film roles find him in this territory. He has a minor part in the 1953 comedy *The Captain's Paradise* as 'Kalikan Policeman'. The film was a financial success but Delgado's moment is brief and he only really a footnote in it, as it is a footnote in his career.[168] It starred Alec Guinness and Delgado's old director from repertory in 1940s, Bill Fraser.

Another foreign comedy part comes in 1954's *The Belles of St Trinian's*, released to good box office in September that year.[169] His part is a blink-or-you'll-miss-it moment, but Delgado is performing and not merely part of the background. His role is 'Sultan's Aide', referring to the Sultan of Makyad, a Middle Eastern millionaire and horse trainer and owner who sends his daughter to the girls' school St Trinian's. Eric Pohlman, often in films with Delgado, plays the Sultan.

At the beginning of the film, the Sultan's aide delivers the Sultan's daughter Fatima, played by the British actress Lorna Henderson, to the railway station to travel to St Trinian's. As the aide, Delgado looks resplendent in morning dress, spats and a top hat and carrying a furled umbrella. Delgado has one line, asking a stationmaster 'St Trinian's?' but the fruity, high-pitched voice that comes out sounds like it has been dubbed. For the moments he's on screen, Delgado hams up gestures and facial expressions, including his look of horror when the stationmaster is dragged away because the naughty schoolgirls have looped a rope around his feet and tied it to a porter's luggage trolley.

Delgado stayed in B films for much of the 1950s. He was in a number of B shorts collectively called the *Scotland Yard* series, the sort of popular, rapidly made fillers where the actors were paid per day and there could be up to fourteen camera set-ups at one time to ensure speedy production. These half-hour B productions are nifty little thrillers, often made by people who were stepping up to bigger and better things. Ken Hughes directed one of Delgado's shorts, later to move to prestige projects like 1970's *Cromwell*. Their stark black-and-white photography owes a lot to Hitchcock, and overall they're directed with flair despite tiny budgets and running times.

Edgar Lustgarten introduced these shorts. He was a famed writer who was rather like a criminological Alistair Cooke, but introducing gruesome murders rather than *Masterpiece Theatre*. Filmed in a grand, book-lined study, sipping sherry and sitting in a wing chair, Lustgarten gave a scholarly class to the gory details (houses all over the Home Counties are littered with the bodies of the shot, gassed, strangled and poisoned) and to overblown dialogue like 'A passenger who didn't know that his destination was death!' The B shorts also showcased the up-to-the-minute crime-solving technology at the Yard, from the chemical analysis of poisons to the telegraphic transmission of the suspects' photographs to Interpol, and watching them now there is a quaint propagandistic tone to these little films about 'the great police organisation'. But the plots are tight, the actors are amazing, and often the shorts feature the lean and wily Inspector Duggan, played by Russell Napier. Duggan goes to any length to solve crime. In one he smuggles out incriminating evidence, burnt pages from a fireplace grate, in the crown of his homburg hat.

The television writer Susan Sydney-Smith calls the shorts 'unremittingly middle-class', but that misses the point that Inspector Napier would also travel anywhere in the world he needed to when following a clue, which is where Delgado came in, playing in succession a French, a Portuguese and an Italian police inspector.[170]

In his first, *The Missing Man*, Delgado is a very Gallic inspector at the Sûreté, assisting the Yard trying to find a vicar's missing son. At this point his film acting is still in its infancy and he doesn't waste a moment on screen, shrugging with over-the-top Gallic insouciance, pointing emphatically with a cigar, and delivering lines in an accent perfect for *'Allo! 'Allo!* (or perhaps *The Pink Panther*): 'I have zee information for you. Zis man Neil, we have not found him but he has been in Paris. *Oui, mais certainment!'*

Being in B films meant Delgado appeared at a particular point in a cinema audience's evening's entertainment.[171] An evening at the cinemas meant watching the A and B features, the commercials, newsreels and travelogues on a continuous loop – hence the expression 'This is where we came in,' said as cinema patrons caught up with the loop.

We can imagine cinemagoers seeing Delgado in his B films in the midst of other parts of the evening's programming. His appearances could be amongst commercials advertising the miracles of nuclear technology, maybe a newsreel item about Princess Margaret, or adverts for local businesses. The cinema patrons watching him will have entered a cinema through a door opened by a commissionaire, possibly seen the cinema manager hobnobbing in the foyer and could buy their cigarettes from the usherette (naturally patrons in the cinema smoked as much as the actors on the screen). In the midst of all this, the B films were obviously cheap and cheerful but could provide part of a good evening's entertainment. They were short and did not outstay their welcome like an overblown epic could.

1957, a year where he was busy in both film and television, included an uncredited part in *Violent Stranger* (or *Man in the Shadow*), a *noir* about a man accused of a crime he did not commit. In 1958 he made *Mark of the Phoenix*, playing a good guy, a government scientist.[172] The movie is a Butcher's production, a byword for films that are cheap even by B movie standards. But as the young lead, a jewel thief, Sheldon Laurence gives a lively performance; and Anton Diffring and Delgado add some class to a

62-minute B film acted on cheap, badly dressed sets – in other words, doing what Delgado did for much of the decade.

Interlude
Breakups and new starts

A MONG DELGADO'S MANY 1950s screen credits was a part in *The Alien Sky* on January 26th 1956. There is no recording surviving of this BBC Television Service broadcast; but, in another way, it did have a lasting impact. Apart from Delgado, there are some familiar faces in the cast, including Marne Maitland. The broadcast was adapted from Paul Scott's novel. Scott wrote a lot about India and, like his *Jewel in the Crown*, the story of *Alien Sky* was set on the subcontinent; Delgado and Maitland were cast from the usual talent pool of 'foreigner' actors. Also in the cast playing Kamala was a young model and actress, Kismet Dinah Shahani.

Kismet was born in 1929 and was British, but like Delgado she had the exotic looks to perform as a foreigner in 1950s British shows. At this point her acting career was still young and her only other credit was as one of the beauty contestants (a young Joan Collins was another, and more tragically so was Ruth Ellis, a few years later hanged for murder) in 1951's *Lady Godiva Rides Again*.

In 1952, under the headline 'Kismet is the Name', she appeared in the *Portsmouth Evening News* wearing a daringly low-cut white frock. Readers were told that this 'daughter of a Sikh' had been 'selected as model of the month' by a local arts group.[173] The front page is a little snapshot of dreary post-war Britain. The same page carries reports of the Presbyterian ladies meeting for religious devotions and the local council's demand for more zebra crossings; the glamorous photo of Kismet must have been quite the most exciting thing to have happened in Portsmouth for a long time.

From early days in Colombo through post-war years as Delgado trudged around provincial rep looking for work, his marriage to Olga had strained and eventually broken down completely. Possibly the only person who knew Delgado before and after was Victor Pemberton, who saw their unhappiness and was unsurprised they divorced.

And so 1957 was a year like many others, with one major difference. There was lots of work on television, lots on the radio, small parts in film, but then an appearance in March in the divorce courts. While all actors need exposure, this was one piece of publicity that Delgado could have done without. An unhappy marriage cracked and broke, but this is the 1950s and there is no such thing as no-fault divorce. It's instead an era of private detectives and where getting a Decree Absolute depended on airing dirty linen.

For a man as dignified and private as he was, we can only guess at his mortification at appearing in the press not for his acting but for his adultery. 'Roger Delgado' was the simple headline in the *Telegraph* March 26th 1957 and the matter-of-fact report stated: 'Mr Roger Caesar Delgado, radio and television actor, offered no defence in the Divorce Court yesterday when his wife, Mrs Olga Treherne Delgado, King Street, Richmond, was granted a decree nisi because of his adultery with Miss Kismet Shahani. The wife was awarded costs.'[174] A few days before, *Radio Times* had noted his broadcast in *Children's Hour* playing a Belgian merchant in *The Adventures of Samuel Poppleton*, but here was something sadly different.

Delgado married Kismet Shahani in 1957 after the Decree Absolute came through on May 9th that year. It was a registry-office ceremony rather than a Catholic cathedral like the first. Under no circumstances in the 1950s could a divorced Catholic remarry in a church.

Olga was single for longer but, in the end, both Roger and Olga moved on to happy marriages. After her divorce from Roger, Olga gained a profession and became a secretary and then the associate editor of the *Museums Journal*.[175] During her marriage to Roger, however, she is never described as anything except 'housewife'.

For a while Olga kept the surname Delgado and was living under it in Knightsbridge by the late 1950s. In 1962 she married the eminent scholar Gordon Rattray Taylor and was his second wife. Taylor's writings enjoyed large esteem in his lifetime including *Sex in History*. As a precursor to writers such as Stephen Hawking and Richard Dawkins, Taylor wrote books on serious scientific works that found a popular readership. Another outlet was the BBC such as the script for *Your Mysterious Brain* shown in August 1962 and directed by Innes Lloyd.[176]

Olga's marriage to Gordon lasted until his death in 1982 and his last book, *The Great Evolution Mystery*, appeared posthumously. Olga wrote a preface for it and her passion to see the book published is tribute to her years of happy marriage to Gordon Rattray Taylor. The book was a labour of love for Taylor and its editing and completion was a labour of love for Olga. Her secretarial skills subsequently brought the manuscript to completion by revising, typing and editing and sourcing illustrations.

She wrote the preface herself and referred to Gordon working on the book but 'battling all the time against an illness which grew steadily more serious and debilitating'.[177] Her preface is a rare and precious instance of a comment by her that survives on record, although her signature is on her Sea Arrival Card when she returned from New York in November 1960.

As for Roger and Kismet, their union was a triumph that brought them both joy for seventeen years. Friends and visitors saw a delightfully happy couple. In her only interview on the subject, Kismet reminisced about a union where they hardly ever quarrelled, where she travelled by his side (except for the fateful journey to Turkey in 1973) as he made his way on and up in his acting career and they moved together into the lovely little White Cottage in Teddington (number Teddington Lock 1540).

Delgado was a tidy, dapper and carefully controlled man and, after his divorce, that part of his life was carefully packed away and the lid put on it. Friends and colleagues in the 1960s and 1970s, meaning those still around to speak about him now, know his life with Kismet; but he left his life of the mid-1950s and earlier neatly but emphatically in the past.

Chapter Nine
On the air 1947 onwards

To inform, educate, entertain. – Lord Reith on the BBC

FTER THE WAR, Delgado doggedly rebuilt his stage career and began
his film and television careers, but as an actor he was busiest of all
on the wireless.

If anything, his radio career was more varied and more distinguished than
his film and television work. Co-stars included luminaries like John Gielgud,
Edith Evans and Michael Redgrave and he extended his performance range
into areas absent from his film, television or stage work, with acting in works
from Oscar Wilde to Chekhov. It's also where we find this private man sharing
in public one of his private life's strongest feelings: his religious faith.

As an actor, Delgado had many assets: his eyes, his presence, his superb
posture, but one of his best assets was his rich, resonant voice. From 1947 up
to his death, Delgado broadcast constantly. He mixed discs for housewives.
He read the Bible and great literature and acted in radio plays.

Delgado's broadcasting took a number of forms. A lot of it was as a cast
member in full-cast drama broadcasts. He started on the Home Service in
1947 with *Flags on the Matterhorn*, which also included in the cast the future
'Q' from the James Bond films, Desmond Llewelyn. At this point he was
touring extensively around the regions and working with the Midland
Theatre Company, and he is next on the Home Service in *The Ivory Tower*.

His producer was Val Gielgud, who like Shaun Sutton, Basil Dearden and Rudolph Cartier would find work for Delgado on a regular basis.

By this time BBC Radio was moving on. It is well known that Lord Reith, the first Director General of the BBC, insisted the announcers wear dinner jackets; and, as Victor Pemberton remembered, the actors in drama also wore evening dress when performing in Saturday-night radio drama, the men in dinner jackets and the women in evening gowns.[178] That 'eventually faded', but the BBC remained a powerhouse of radio drama.[179] Although the television service resumed after the war, the number of licence holders was small and building a successful career in radio was a good idea.

David Spenser, a de Saram from Ceylon but resident in Britain from a young age, also began acting in the later 1940s when he played William Brown for the BBC. He later said of radio acting in this period: 'Difficult though it may seem today, radio actors and actresses were considered to be "stars". Their voices were as recognisable as faces in *Coronation Street* today. There was no television.'[180]

Acting in radio called for particular acting skills that Delgado had in spades. Radio actors, unassisted as they are by props, costumes or settings, have to create a reality, according to Victor Pemberton, and they need the imagination to do so. Acting in this medium means 'reality and imagination go hand in hand'. Sometimes that imagination gets a helping hand. For example, if the play had a scene of characters at a conference, then the producers would sit the actors around a table.[181] Nonetheless, most of the time it was a group of actors huddled around a microphone and, that being the case, Pemberton believed: 'It's very important you use your imagination as to where you are.'[182]

The pace and diversity were even greater than Delgado's repertory theatre days in Leicester. From the early 1950s, his voice was constantly on BBC radio productions, and *The Stage* (which also reported on radio acting as well as the new medium of television) regularly noted his participation in plays on the Third Programme. The diversity of his broadcasts is extraordinary. His radio work did sometimes parallel his television and film work. He swashbuckled on the small screen and on the wireless. One of Christopher Lee's memories was of a time 'I had to caper about the studio with Roger Delgado, using actual foils in a duel'.[183]

If he eventually was known primarily for his villains on film and television, there is no such consistency in his radio acting. In 1950 alone his performances in drama covered instalments of *Dick Barton Special Agent* to *Six to Ten* written by Hugh Burden, whose television play *Myself a Stranger* had a part for Delgado later that decade. The range of the plays was immense. In February 1950 Delgado was in Balzac's *The Red Inn* and John Galsworthy's *The Country House*. In May it was Virginia Woolf's *The Legacy*. There were plenty of parts needing a Spanish accent including *Bridge of Estaban*, a comedy set during the Spanish Peninsular War. Along the way there were adaptations of Mark Twain, Molière, Sir Walter Scott and A. A. Milne. His co-stars included Marius Goring, Catherine Lacey, Patrick Troughton and Francis de Wolff, colleagues who would be part of Delgado's professional circle for years to come.

Much of this radio work has faded without trace; however, Delgado was part of a legendary broadcast of *The Importance of Being Earnest* in 1951, in which Delgado played Merriman the butler in acts two and three. Here his voice is at its fruitiest, in line with the performances of his co-stars, who had all been playing these parts for decades. A languid John Gielgud played Worthing and Edith Evans the formidable Lady Bracknell, whose declaration 'A handbag!' sums up the entire play. Evans repeated the role in Anthony Asquith's 1952 film version and for many years the type of posh, enunciative acting captured in this broadcast, including Delgado's, dominated all later performances of the play on stage.[184] Angela Baddeley and Gielgud had played their parts in a 1939 stage production, which had also featured Evans as Bracknell.[185] Lady Bracknell may have been Evans' signature role, but this type of comedy was a rarity in Delgado's career.

There was some other comedy in his broadcasts on the Home Service including *Men from the Ministry* with Dickie Murdoch in 1967. Meanwhile in drama he acted alongside Flora Robson in *Mary Tudor* on the Home Service. His superb voice was also used for narration and in 1951 *The Stage* reported: 'Roger Delgado will also be heard as the narrator in *No Heaven for Me* by Lady Cynthia Asquith.'[186]

Acting on the radio gave Delgado the opportunity to perform with distinguished actors, more than his co-stars in B films and television. Performing on the BBC placed Delgado among a host of performers, some well-known and some who become well known. *The Stage* for August 1951 reported that there was to be a broadcast of *Murder at the Ostrich*. Delgado was in the cast and so was Patrick Troughton.[187] Troughton and Delgado worked together the same year on *Watch the Wall, My Darling!* along with

Valentine Dyall and Richard Hurndall, and in *Under the Red Robe* on the Light Programme, which starred Peter Bathurst.[188]

Although his radio experience was enormous, critics did not always feel the volume and scale of his performances suited the microphone. In 1952 he performed with Michael Redgrave in a production of *Ivanov* by Chekhov on the Home Service. But the critic for the *Manchester Guardian* listened and thought 'one high pitched scene' was 'not attuned to the capacity of the microphone, though on the stage it would have been fun to see these two mutually irritating and irritated fellows bawling at each other.' This listener was clearly very unimpressed, ending up by saying 'the chief women's parts were rather better played than those of the men', adding the final nail to the coffin of a flawed broadcast.[189]

Radio directors, as much as their film, theatre and television counterparts, needed the man of many voices. Delgado's accents were at their service, sometimes in plays that sound seriously weird by now. In 1952 he was an Arab houseboy in *Only Got Egg* on the Home Service, in what *The Stage* reported was a 'farce on life in the Middle East'.[190] In 1953 he played the Spaniard Captain Montserrat in a powerful broadcast of *Montserrat*, which the BBC's announcer kicked off with 'a warning to sensitive people'. One critic thought the play was '100 minutes of almost unbearable horror' about the 1812 uprising against Spain. The quality was also apparent as it was 'a moving experience of the power of language'.[191] Here is Delgado at his very strongest, with his magnificent voice (courtesy of Canon Vance at the Cardinal Vaughan School?) matched with equally strong words.

His Italian-accented Signor Orlando, a statesman at the Paris Peace Conference in 1919, also gained critical praise. These broadcasts relied on strong ensemble playing, which in this case the critic for the *Glasgow Herald* thought was achieved admirably. Delgado's 'eloquent' performance, in a debate with characters played by Howard Marion Crawford (who would later be on set with Delgado in *The Avengers*) and MacDonald Parke, 'left the strongest listening impression of the immense and perhaps ultimately hopeless task which lonely statesmen undertake'.[192]

Delgado grew up in a multilingual household but as an actor he hardly had the opportunity to show his own knowledge of languages beyond the occasional use of '*olé*' or '*signor*' and a little burst of French in the *Sherlock Holmes* story 'The Disappearance of Lady Frances Carfax'. The exception is

73

some broadcasts called *Starting Spanish* he did in 1957, which was already a super busy year for him on film and television.

Nowadays Vanessa Redgrave is a major star; in 1957 she and the actor Basil Jones were slumming it playing Dorothy and Basil Street. Starting on 30ᵗʰ September the *Radio Times* announced: 'Basil and Dorothy learn how to ask for rooms in Spain and how to avoid some of the more obvious mistakes of pronunciation. The lesson begins slowly in George's study in Hampstead and ends at full speed in a Spanish pension.' The lessons went on for weeks in different scenarios; Basil and Dorothy found themselves in a tramcar, a post office, a shoe shop and a tavern, with Delgado somewhat surreally popping up to impart lessons like 'Basil and Dorothy Street learn that they cannot get along without understanding the double negative.'

In July 1959 Vanessa Redgrave once again found herself acting out ludicrously contrived scenarios so Delgado could teach key points of Spanish grammar like 'Basil and Dorothy Street learn about radical changing verbs.' How did listeners cope with the excitement!

While the content may sound mind-numbingly boring, it's not surprising to find Delgado in these pedagogical roles. Roger Delgado looked and was intellectual. His co-stars and directors remember an actor who 'intellectualised' or thought deeply about his parts. His house was full of books and with his own neat dress, dark-rimmed spectacles and cultivated voice, he was perfect for the type of cultural broadcasting that is so quintessentially BBC, including his religious broadcasting.

If some of his Spanish-language broadcasts on Spanish grammar sound heavy going, his radio work is a reminder of an age when broadcasting included serious plays lasting for up to one hundred minutes, strong educational content, and deep and complex religious content. For example, from April 1961 Delgado was a reader on the BBC Television Service for *Meeting Point*, during which sermons by Karl Barth, John Donne, Fray Luis de Leon and C. S. Lewis were given. Of these, only the last may be familiar now but all were major religious thinkers from the seventeenth to the twentieth centuries. In 1963, viewers watching the BBC Television Service late at night had Delgado reading from the Gospel of Saint Luke, normally at eleven o'clock.

Along the same lines, Delgado participated in a broadcast from the Church of All Hallows on London Wall in April 1964 for *Seeing and*

Believing, a series of readings from seventeenth-century spiritual writers. Delgado's rich voice was ideal for both the florid language of the seventeenth century and the acoustic of an old church. This broadcasting remained important to him and he carried on making religious broadcasts well into the 1960s. *The Stage* reported in 1966 that 'Roger Delgado, Gwen Watford, Gary Watson, and John Alldis are among the artists paying a return visit to the BBC-1 series *Seeing and Believing* for its 200th edition on Sunday.'[193]

At home and in his life Delgado liked things spick and span. He dressed neatly, kept his house immaculate and all around him was an overwhelming impression of neatness. His scripts had no scribbles on them, his car was washed and polished, his clothes neat. But a tidy mind and a tidy life did not come at the expense of a powerfully creative imagination. Acting in radio meant an actor had to be even more creative than on television. If the actor could not see the setting in their mind's eye, the audience would not either.

Someone who knew this well was Victor Pemberton, prolific writer for radio and whose partner David Spenser worked often with Delgado, including the films *Stranglers of Bombay* and *In Search of the Castaways* and on stage in *The Power and the Glory*. Pemberton had a chance to see this serious but creative actor when Delgado played the leading role of Professor Gomez in *The Slide* in February 1966. This BBC science-fiction radio series is of interest to *Doctor Who* fans as it's often hailed as a precursor to Pemberton's 'Fury from the Deep', a season five *Doctor Who* story with Patrick Troughton. Pemberton thought differently, telling me firmly that they are 'two totally different stories'. Be that as it may, it's a miracle the series survives at all and the only copy of it turned up in Pemberton's garage in Spain smothered in dust.[194] Pemberton had made it himself in 1966 by pointing a microphone at his wireless. That is a reminder of how precious many of the surviving television and radio broadcasts are, surviving only through random chance.

To play Gomez, a Chilean seismologist, Pemberton asked especially for Delgado. They knew each other already because of the common Ceylonese connection in their private lives but that had been earlier, when Delgado was unhappily married to Olga and caught up with oppressive Ceylonese society. By 1966, he was remarried to Kismet and much in demand, including as South American characters. For Pemberton he played a Chilean but over time Delgado had acted characters from all over South America including Uruguayans and Argentinians.

Pemberton's script was set in and around a New Town, a setting he chose deliberately as in 1966 'they'd just built a town called Harlow, so new towns were in fashion'. Vivid dialogue also describes huge seismic cracks under the English Channel. The sentient mud and the unfolding horrors made for scary drama. 'It scared a lot of people,' remembered Pemberton with relish. To sell all of this the serial needed strong actors but also, in Pemberton's view, it needed intelligent actors. What is one of those? 'An intelligent actor is someone who does his homework,' someone who doesn't turn up on the day and just read the part but who comes having read the script and thought about the character and then 'will do everything in his power to bring the character to life'.

Pemberton got exactly that with Delgado. While Delgado was by no means a method actor, he was a creative, imaginative one whose characters lived in his own mind and Professor Gomez took on an imaginative life all of his own. Pemberton learnt something of this when he talked to Roger about Gomez and asked him some questions about the character. 'Where do you think he was born, Roger?' asked Pemberton; and, as it turned out, Roger had the answers ready in his mind. Delgado knew that Professor Gomez had been born just outside of Santiago and gone to university there.

It's not an accident or luck that Delgado worked so much in radio. It is because he worked so hard and so creatively. As film and television producers also knew, radio producers knew they were getting an intelligent, professional actor, not one who would turn up and read lines or whose attitude was just 'Oh, I'm doing that on Tuesday.' Delgado cared.

Chapter Ten
The Hammer contributions
1953-1967

We don't always get the kind of work we want, but we always have a choice of whether to do it with good grace or not. – Christopher Lee

THE UNGODLY HOUSE OF HAMMER is as far removed from the Bible and sermons as possible. But Delgado was many things. In private he was religious and in public he was happy to show that with his respectful, sonorous readings of biblical texts. But, as Katy Manning remembers, he was 'funny, irreverent'.[195] Being religious did not stop him playing the wicked Magister and acting out a Black Mass in *Doctor Who* and it certainly didn't stop him working for the House of Hammer.

In the 1950s and 1960s Delgado joined a host of character actors who were finding employment in the horror films made cheaply, often in colour, and profitably although not with any critical success, by Hammer Film Productions. The production facilities at Bray, a studio converted from a stately home in Berkshire, were intimate in scale but its managing director Sir James Carreras had big ambitions and solid acumen and there were big profits from Carreras' distribution deals with major US studios including Columbia and the healthy ticket sales in British circuits.

But there were other strings to Hammer's bow besides its gothic horrors and Delgado was part of atypical Hammer productions. A second tier of thrillers, wartime dramas and science-fiction films sit alongside the gothic horrors, often with actors other than Cushing and Lee. This variety gave Delgado employment.

Delgado's route into employment at Bray was actually through the B *noir* thrillers. One was *Blood Orange* in 1953, in which he played a murderer. The quick pace of production and the range of parts Hammer gave him meant his repertory background stood him in good stead. These are emphatically 'B' pictures, often directed by Terence Fisher. At least the people concerned went on to better things. Terence Fisher directed *Blood Orange* and would re-use Delgado in *Stranglers of Bombay* in 1959, by which time Hammer and Fisher had both become horror specialists.

From February 1954 Delgado was on set at Bray making *Third Party Risk*, released in March 1955 and known in the USA as *Deadly Game*. His role was a Spanish police chief. The film is of a type with the thrillers that James Carreras was then making at Bray and distributing in the USA via Lippert. It does however stand out from the pack because Carreras allowed the unit to travel to Spain for some location shooting. Doing so was and remained a novelty for Hammer. For years to come locations including Egypt, Cornwall, Tibet, India, Blood Island in South East Asia, Transylvania and the Alps were realised in the studios and on the backlot at Bray and later at Pinewood and Black Park. But for once, the location used was the actual setting.

Delgado's part was not enormous but was important as his role as police chief involved him in the film's climax and the thwarting of a plot involving a scientific formula, a roll of microfilm and exciting incidents including a fire and a murder.[196] The part also gave Delgado a role alongside reasonably big-name actors including the American Lloyd Bridges and Maureen Swanson, the so-called 'pocket-sized Venus' who soon after quit acting and married an aristocrat, becoming the Countess of Dudley and turning her back on her time as a 'starlet'.[197] There are no acting honours from this film for Delgado or anyone else and he was one member of an 'insipid cast of characters' in *Third Party Risk*.[198]

Delgado's next employment at Bray was a different matter. By 1959, several things had happened for Hammer, Fisher and Delgado. Hammer had broken out into both British cinema circuits and American cinemas with outstanding successes for their adaptations of the Frankenstein and

Dracula stories in 1957 and 1958. A recognisable and publicly bankable teaming of Peter Cushing, Christopher Lee and Terence Fisher, as well as less publicly prominent but essential work from Phil Leakey, Bernard Robinson and James Bernard for make-up, design and music respectively was now in full swing. *The Mummy*, *The Hound of the Baskervilles* and more Frankenstein all followed in 1959.

Thus Delgado was back at Bray in 1959, and this time the studio was recreating nineteenth-century India in its backlot for *The Stranglers of Bombay*. Terence Fisher was directing and had his usual team including Robinson and Bernard, as well as Arthur Grant as cinematographer with Anthony Nelson-Keys writing the script and Anthony Hinds producing. Any attentive cinemagoers among the many who were now queuing to see Hammer films would have seen these names in the credits of almost all the recent successes, especially the gothic horrors. Other familiar names were missing, as there was no Peter Cushing and no Christopher Lee.

Hammer had several strings to its bow and had a second tier of films and actors. *Stranglers of Bombay* is such an example and in the lead were Guy Rolfe and Andrew Cruickshank, two quality character actors. Neither were as bankable as Cushing and Lee, but Hammer was prepared to use leading men other than its two most recognisable stars.

A cinemagoer would not have needed to be attentive to notice one other major difference to Hammer's recent films, as *Stranglers of Bombay* is in black and white, not the garish Eastman Color used for the adventures of Baron Frankenstein and Count Dracula. To make up for the absence of colour, Hammer promoted the film with a tawdry flair that makes William Castle look timid. Although not in colour, the film's posters promised a movie shot in 'Strangloscope', an otherwise meaningless term that just served to point to the astonishing violence in the movie.

Leaving nothing to subtlety, the lobby posters also promised 'Murder cult strikes terror in exotic India' and 'See the goddess of murder command her thuggees to Kill! Kill! Kill!' Rather more opaque and figurative was the promise to cinemagoers to 'See India's throat choked in their strangling silks'.[199] The film lives up to the hype and is violent, even more so because the horrors are in stark monochrome. Critics were horrified and even Terence Fisher was shocked by just how brutal it was once the final cut was assembled. *The Times* thought it 'juvenile' but admitted: 'The film may be acquitted of revelling in the cruelties it describes, but it nevertheless describes them in some detail.'[200] The 'Thuggees' in the film, more properly the 'thagi', were a cult of religious assassins, which the British East India Company sought to eradicate.[201]

Delgado's part in *Stranglers of Bombay* did not give him much dialogue but gave him a great deal of screen time. Some of his film roles gave both limited dialogue and limited screen time, of which he would make the most. For this Hammer film, Delgado is on screen from the first scene among the worshippers of Kali, the goddess presiding over the cult of the thuggees. Their leader is played by the Cypriot George Pastell, another actor useful to Hammer (and *Doctor Who*) as a sinister foreigner and Delgado is his second in command, Bundar. The part gives him some good moments as he presides over brandings, blindings, and murders. As always Delgado stands out even on a set filled with actors and extras. While playing a sweaty killer, he even brings dignity to the role. Many British actors in the 1950s could look distinctly uncomfortable showing off bare puny chests, but Delgado's excellent posture, good build and bearing gets him through with his dignity intact.

Stranglers of Bombay is, says Terence Fisher's biographer Wheeler Dixon, a film where the director was at his 'most Sadian'.[202] The black-and-white photography helps to disguise that the Hammer backlot is standing in for India and the costume and make-up convincingly shows the heat of the colonial environment. Characters are drenched in sweat, down to details such as patches of moisture under the armpits of Andrew Cruickshank, playing the Colonel. The black and white also mutes some of the horror as the Eastman Color processing Fisher used in his other Hammer horrors highlighted the red of blood and wounds. Even so, the numerous scenes of torture and one remarkable sequence when the thugs slaughter a camp full of people have kept their impact.

One of the most horrifying moments comes early. Two brothers of the cult have strayed from the right path and in punishment the thugs gouge out their eyes. Naturally the British Board of Film Censorship would not let the actual blinding be seen, but we see the aftermath and the sight of the two men with gore dribbling from empty eye sockets down their faces is still disturbing. The thugs' ally Patel Shari, played by Marne Maitland, another actor who was adept at playing sinister foreigners for Hammer, looks away in horror. In silent mockery Delgado's character offers him a cloth to cover his eyes and is rewarded with a slap in the face.

Behind the scenes Delgado enjoyed himself. He was already friends with David Spenser, who had been on stage with him a few years earlier but who also knew him from earlier days in Ceylon during his unhappy marriage to Olga. Victor Pemberton recalled that Roger and David 'had a lot of fun together' on the set, although Spenser also firmly declined Fisher's request to perform some ridiculously dangerous stunts himself.[203] Others at Bray including Marne Maitland and Terence Fisher were friendly and familiar faces.

Delgado worked for Hammer but made horror films for other companies in this period. He has a small part in the 1959 horror *First Man into Space* but, through hand gestures and accent, he makes the three-minute cameo stand out. Like so many of his parts, Delgado made the most of any opportunity to be on screen. In *First Man into Space* he also has the advantage of being on screen with bland actors giving bland performances against bland sets while his performance was the complete opposite.

The plot of *First Man* retreads *The Quatermass Experiment*. A strange alien entity comes back to earth from a rocket launch. The entity spreads and consumes human hosts. Towards the end of the film the character Prescott is called to his commanding officer's room where he has to explain a rocket launch that came back to earth dangerously near the President of Mexico. He explains what happened to the exuberant and wide-eyed Mexican Consul, played by Delgado.

Delgado is not on screen for long but makes the most of every second. Brushing off reassurances he replies, 'What is ten miles Signor, when you do not know where the missile is?' before going on to describe in vivid terms how the rocket fell down to earth at a bullring. 'A great silence descended in the crowd. Five thousand people, ten thousand eyes; suddenly there is a... a roar from space.'

Delgado is on screen to provide a few moments on comedy relief. Miles Malleson did the same in Hammer; here Delgado makes noises imitating the sound of the crashing rocket, presents an exorbitant bill (for 20,000 pesos) to replace a prize bull that nearly squashed the President of Mexico, and he gets the last word. He leaves the office with a patronising parting shot. 'I hope that next time you lose a missile you shoot it in some other direction.'

There was more horror when Hammer found use for Delgado the next year when filming *The Terror of the Tongs*, again at Bray, from April 1960.[204] By now Delgado had provided Hammer with a murderer, a modern-day

Spanish policeman and a Raj-era Indian killer. Now in 'yellow face' make-up he was a Chinese villain.

Joining him under the make-up to play Chinese criminals were Marne Maitland and Charles Lloyd Pack, both Hammer regulars. Another regular was Christopher Lee. In his two previous Hammer films, Delgado had missed appearing with either Cushing or Lee. Now he was a Tong henchman of Chung King, Lee's character and the Tong leader who spends the film plotting and ordering killings.

The production of *Terror of the Tongs* was a happy one according to the director Anthony Bushell, although the reviews were mediocre. Hammer was not offering Delgado anything especially notable, although he does have good screen time with Lee. Delgado plays Lee's henchman, working in the Tong headquarters hidden behind a seedy café. His part is to look sometimes menacing and sometimes aloof, exchanging inscrutable looks with Lee and asking, 'Why is it these occidentals indulge in their vices the same way they run their lives?'

At the very end, when the police overrun the Tong headquarters, Lee's character evades capture by having Delgado stab him in the back. Lee gives a convincing performance as Delgado plunges in a stiletto blade. The moment connects Delgado with one of the best known anecdotes about Lee, who refused to take direction from Peter Jackson on the set of *The Lord of the Rings* on how to act the experience of being stabbed in the back, telling him, 'Have you any idea what kind of noise happens when somebody's stabbed in the back? Because I do.'[205] Way back in *Terror of the Tongs* Lee was applying the same knowledge, dying breathlessly in line with his expert knowledge of what it's really like to die from a stab wound and a punctured lung.

Delgado's final employment at Bray Studios gave him his biggest role in a Hammer, in a film with many detractors. So far Delgado had given Hammer a Spaniard, an Indian, a Chinese, and finally he was an Egyptian in *The Mummy's Shroud*. Delgado was also in one of the best casts ever assembled for a Hammer film. Again, he is in a second tier, or a Hammer without Lee or Cushing (actually the film was the B feature accompanying another Peter Cushing Frankenstein film).[206] However, André Morrell, Elizabeth Sellars and Catherine Lacey are distinguished contributors and Delgado's part for once is sizeable. By now, after *Storm over the Nile*, *The Sandwich Man*, *Khartoum* and many television roles, he was an expert in playing Arabs.

He is a sinister presence throughout the film. Early on he makes a dramatic first appearance in a dark underground tomb when he leaps out of darkness and shouts a warning to a party of archaeologists led by Sir Basil Walden (André Morrell, formerly Delgado's neighbour in Chelsea). Characters throughout the film refer back to the 'madman' in the tombs and his warning as one by one the archaeologists start to die.

The film has a very boring start; a long flashback to a *coup d'état* in ancient Egypt with a voice-over explaining events, before the action shifts to the 1920s when the tomb of a boy Pharaoh and his guardian are uncovered by Sir Basil's team.

After this slow start, John Gilling's direction improves as the film gets going. Throughout the film, Gilling finds interesting ways to show the characters. The set is dressed with the grilles and screens of a Middle Eastern bazaar and rather than showing the mummy fully, Gilling has inventive ways to bring it onto the screen. It looms up behind Sir Basil, who sees its reflection in a crystal ball. Another character just sees its reflection in development fluid in a photographic studio. A blurry, intimidating outline is seen from the point of view of a shortsighted character. Most shocking is when it leaps out of an alley and murders the rich financier backing the excavation.

The murders, orchestrated by Delgado's character, are also genuinely nasty. The mummy's hands crush Sir Basil's head. The mummy kills another archaeologist in the photographic studio by dousing him in acid and setting him on fire. The financier's assistant is brutally bundled into a mosquito net and hurled from a window.

Delgado is in his element. He's at the eye of a storm, unleashing mayhem and murders. Delgado's character is orchestrating this violence in concert with Haiti, a deranged but accurate fortune-teller played by Catherine Lacey. Other directors have testified to Delgado's ability to add suggestions for his performances, in ways that even underwritten and stereotyped parts become interesting. Here he is playing what one reviewer has called a 'politically incorrect filthy Arab'; that may be so, but Delgado sells us the part with little touches. He is at the centre of a powerful sequence the first time the mummy reanimates and murders Sir Basil. In anticipation of the killing, he flicks out his tongue momentarily. Watching through a beaded curtain, his hand comes up and lightly takes hold of the strands, his soft touch the reverse of the powerful, crushing hands of the mummy. Best of all is his mad laugh at the climax, deranged cackling being something he used in moderation but here to good effect.

In this, his fifth appearance at Bray, he came as the studio was closing and Hammer moving out to other premises, mostly Pinewood. But Bray's backlot was in service one last time to appear as Egypt in the 1920s.[207] Most of the cast were Europeans playing Europeans but Catherine Lacey and Delgado both darkened their skin and teeth to play Egyptians. Lacey, who had been a phony nun for Alfred Hitchcock in *The Lady Vanishes*, was the only thing the film critic John Russell Taylor liked about a film he found 'static and stodgy' and where: 'Only Catherine Lacey as a toothless Cairo soothsayer has the sense to ham things up enough to make them momentarily diverting.'[208]

Ultimately, Delgado's work for Hammer is a tight impression of what he could offer and what directors asked of him. His parts were all foreigners, getting more exotic and more violent as his appearances developed. Hammer horror films were profitable and impactful but they were not mainstream. All but one of Delgado's was released with an X certificate from the British Board of Film Censors, meaning audiences were restricted and the films notably *recherché*. Other films placed him firmly in the mainstream.

Chapter Eleven
Big films, small parts
1955-1968

I can't remember a time when I didn't want to be an actor. –
Charlton Heston

D ELGADO'S FILM WORK assumed a distinctive pattern. In B films (and
to be honest, some are more like C films) he has sizeable parts; in
larger and in more prestigious films his roles were smaller. What
therefore of Delgado's mainstream career, including films with big audiences,
big stars and mainstream appeal?

For much of the 1950s Delgado languished in small parts in small B films
from Poverty Row filmmakers like Butchers and the Hammer *noirs*. In 1955
there is a change of pace when he plays the 'native spy' in *Storm over the
Nile*, a big prestigious picture in which Delgado was a small cog. James
Robertson Justice (who was in just about every British film made in the mid-
1950s), Laurence Harvey and Anthony Steel co-starred in what was almost a
shot-by-shot remake of *The Four Feathers* from 1939.[209] James Robertson
Justice ensured there would be boisterous fun on the set and even brought
his massive pet eagle to the studio. Justice was one of the biggest stars of the
era, and it was the stars who attended the premiere with the Duke of
Edinburgh, whereas Delgado was down among the bit players.[210]

It's a film full of stiff upper lips. Lieutenant Faversham worries his upper lip isn't stiff enough to fight the Sudanese at the Battle of Omdurman (fans of *Dad's Army* will recall Corporal Jones was there) and resigns from the army. His army friends think he's a coward and so does gruff General Burroughs, who comes out with lines like 'Shot to pieces at the head of his men, as a soldier should be,' and 'Fine old service family. Father killed at Inkerman, grandfather blown up with Nelson, uncle scalped by the Indians. Splendid record.'

Delgado's scene reunites him with Ferdy Mayne, yet another of the nucleus of actors who could do 'foreign'. Mayne had been murdered by Delgado in *The Broken Horseshoe* a couple of years earlier but now both of them were in colour and in an A film. By the time Delgado appears, the ex-lieutenant Faversham has travelled to Egypt and hatched a complex plan to prove he is not a coward. He disguises himself as a Sangali, a tribe branded on their foreheads and whose tongues have been cut out.[211] He tries out his disguise on the native spy, who is duly fooled. While Delgado's role is not a big one, it still has importance. Faversham, with dark make-up, a branded forehead and his head lolling to one side, convinces the native spy. 'Sangali, huh,' says Delgado, while toying with a nasty-looking curved dagger.

The *Evening Express* chattily reported: 'Anthony Steel, who rarely has a hair out of place, and always looks as though he has just stepped out of the shower, will surprise us all in *Storm over the Nile*... he will be disguised as a native... a very scruffy one at that, complete with beard, whiskers, bedraggled clothes and scar on forehead.'[212] The film is a curiosity. Steel is a white man playing a white man who disguises himself as a native, whereas in the same film and same scene Delgado plays an actual native. It gives the film a level of unreality, as does the fact that Michael Hordern, James Robertson Justice and Geoffrey Keen play men much older than their actual ages at the time and perform with their hair very obviously full of talcum powder.

The next year something similar: a small part in a prestige film. Delgado played Captain Varela in *Battle of the River Plate* (or *Pursuit of the Graf Spee*), another big, prestigious movie. Also among the cast in the Powell and Pressburger epic were Douglas Wilmer, Patrick Macnee, John Le Mesurier and Christopher Lee, co-stars of Delgado's into the next decade (and Lee was also in *Storm over the Nile*). Of his own role in *Battle of the River Plate*, in which he played a Spanish-speaking café owner, Lee said: 'It was a small role in a big film, a situation common for me during the decade.'[213] The exact words could have issued from the mouth of Delgado, whose biggish parts in B films were balanced by small parts in A films. He was also fortunate in his casting. Assuming the audience had stayed alert until the last minutes of this two-hour epic, Delgado has a high-profile cameo at the very end as Captain Varela. He booms at a merchant vessel through a microphone, boards it, and takes the English sailor Captain Dove (Bernard Lee) to capture the Nazi sailor Captain Langsdorff (Peter Finch).

Then in 1957 he was the 'Stranger' in *Stowaway Girl*. He was still getting far more work in television than he was in cinema but he is used to brilliant effect in *Stowaway Girl* as a greasy, menacing figure stalking a young girl through the streets. So often in his career, Delgado played characters with flair, elegance and grace in dinner jackets, period courtly costumes or well-tailored suits. But in addition to the grubby stranger in *Stowaway Girl*, the next year he was Salgado in *Sea Fury*. Both films rather bizarrely indicate there was a short-lived demand in 1957 for grim movies about old sea dogs having inappropriate relationships with young girls. *Sea Fury* is also close in style and tone to *Hell Drivers* of the year before, a tough, unsentimental and shocking film made by the blacklisted American director Cy Endfield. The veteran actor Victor McLaglen arrived in Britain with great fanfare in January 1958 to play the part of an old sea captain who falls in love with a young Spanish girl.

In *Sea Fury* it's shocking that the elderly seaman Captain Bellew would even consider a relationship with a young woman, but even more shocking that her father, played by Delgado, pimps her out to the old man. Delgado, cast against what was increasingly his type, plays a foreigner but not a theatrical villain. Here the villainy comes from his shabby desperation to make some cash by offering his daughter to the old man. 'She very young, she dance well, she sing well,' he wheedles to the captain, while at the same time pulling the girl's coat off her shoulders and exposing her bare shoulders.

The part is not large but is a fascinating detour from the sort of work Delgado was now doing. As we'll see soon, by this time he was swash-buckling his way through role after role on television (sometimes with Robert Shaw, who plays a sailor in *Sea Fury*); but here his shabby drunken father, who emotionally manipulates the old Captain and sexually exploits his only daughter, is a performance that still has the power to shock.

The Singer Not the Song is a rarity: a film that gave Delgado a good-sized part in a big film with big stars. He shares screen time with both Dirk

Bogarde and John Mills, although behind the scenes the film was unhappy. Bogarde did not want Mills in the picture and was on his worst behaviour while on set, having promised 'I will make life unbearable for everyone concerned.'[214]

It's not hard to predict what Delgado, the professional's professional, would have made of this petulance, or of the strange beast that is the finished film. At least he comes away with dignity intact from a much-derided film but one which does have a cult following for its weird excesses and queer subtexts. A character performer, given a reasonably prominent part but far from being the star, Delgado turned up to the filming in Malaga in Spain, got paid and walked away.[215] Kismet came with him on location. He is also insulated from some of the silliest moments in the film, not least Roy Ward Baker's extraordinary final shot: a close-up on Bogarde's crotch, encased in tight leather, as his character and John Mills' priest die holding hands. It's one the moments of 'telegraphic queerness' that make it both a bad film and a cult film.[216]

The Singer Not the Song opened in Britain in 1961 and in New York the next year, to derision. Spain stood in for Mexico and the half-Spanish Delgado stood in for a Mexican. His part is Pedro de Cortinez, father of the town beauty Locha. De Cortinez is paying off the gangster played by Bogarde and in turn lives unmolested in his magnificent house. In most of his scenes Delgado is surrounded by the grandeur of the hacienda and explains that he lives quietly by means of bribery. Delgado is also on screen at a dramatic high point when his daughter is to marry an American. Outside the church Bogarde's character arrives oozing dangerous, seductive villainy and the bride abandons her father, her groom and her wedding ceremony by going off in the car with Bogarde, leaving Delgado's character to eat his dust.[217]

Delgado carries his part off well, including his well-tailored suits and gaucho hat. He knows how to bring a foreigner, especially a Latino one, to life. His hand gestures are on display as he flaps his hands, waves them in distress and slams them onto a desk while exclaiming, 'My daughter is kidnapped and the police can do nothing about it.' Other parts of his performance are controlled and immaculate. Before we see Delgado for the first time, his daughter tells the priest: 'When you go in, he'll mark his place in his book with a finger, and then if you go on talking he'll sigh, and put the book marker in and close the book.' Indeed, once inside, Delgado uses fussy little gestures to carefully mark his page and put the book aside.

Delgado assumed a foreign accent to share the screen with Dirk Bogarde again in *Hot Enough for June* in 1964. He was Josef, a menacing waiter in a Czech hotel. Initially Josef seems benign if a little pompous. *Hot Enough for June* mixed comedy with drama and Delgado mixes his menace with some delicious comedy. 'Will you require anything else, a glass of beer perhaps?' he asks politely if a little randomly as the inept British spy played by Bogarde checks into the hotel. Bogarde clearly doesn't want to talk but Josef keeps going. 'I hope that you will do good business, we need businessmen back here,' before lamenting, 'It's a different class of people sir, it's not like the old days.' Bogarde pulls out some money to give a tip. 'Tipping is a product of the capitalist system; it no longer has a place in our way of life,' Josef says in a suddenly bored voice, as though reciting a lesson he doesn't care about; but his hand snatches the money. It's a beautifully judged comic performance and shows Delgado doing what he did best in most of his work before the Master: imbuing even small parts with life and personality and making the most of limited screen time.

Later in the film Josef has become more menacing and is clearly in cahoots with the head of the secret police, played by a thuggish Leo McKern. The British-made film used a corps of reliable actors to provide the British and Eastern European spies. *Variety* thought the casting was effective: 'Among the actors who fit engagingly into the scene are Roger Delgado, Richard Vernon, Alan Tilvern, Eric Pohlmann, George Pravada and Richard Pasco.'[218]

We can detour for a moment, as Delgado's part is one of a small, strange subset of his roles that could be classified as 'dodgy hotel managers' (or more accurately the floor waiter in *Hot Enough for June*), who are sinister or just eccentric characters that make Basil Fawlty look good by comparison. On television in *Danger Man* he played a conniving hotel manager who knows where the Nazis buried their gold and who tries to stop Drake finding out. There is a chase through the hotel and a climactic fight. The episode was early in the series before John Drake's character was British rather than American and was another of Lew Grade's ITC adventures. Delgado played another hotel manager in *The Saint* in 1962. This manager was more benign and was unwittingly caught up in Simon Templar's little plot to punish a spoilt heiress.

As the hotel manager Monsieur Moser, Delgado was part of one of Sherlock Holmes' cases in 'The Disappearance of Lady Frances Carfax', when an English noblewoman vanishes from his Swiss hotel in an episode directed by Shaun Sutton and broadcast on the BBC in May 1965. Douglas Wilmer played Holmes. Delgado performs the worldly-wise hotelier with his much-practised French accent, hand gestures as ostentatious as his voice and facial expressions. He winkingly suggests to Dr Watson that the disappearing lady may have run off with a missionary and in a small part as ever makes his impact, getting across swagger, haughtiness, servility and shock in turn as he learns more about the case.

These small television parts were interspersed among more film roles. *The Singer Not the Song* required Delgado to be a Mexican and *Hot Enough for June* to be Czech, and his other 1960s film appearances continued to use him as foreigners. Another occasion where Delgado turned up and got paid is *Road to Hong Kong*, made the year after *The Singer Not the Song*. Once again Delgado is a foreigner, playing 'Jhinnah' and wearing a fez. The film is an interesting one because comedy is not a major part of Delgado's career, but directors could use him in comedy parts.

The film is horrifyingly bad, although it puts Delgado among a seriously impressive cast with Bob Hope and Bing Crosby obviously, but also every-one from Peter Sellers and Robert Morley to Dorothy Lamour and David Niven, although Zsa Zsa Gabor's cameo was deleted (which could only have been a blessing to her career).[219] The film itself was an unfunny shambles that harmed Bob Hope's career.[220] Delgado's part was small and insignificant enough to walk away with his reputation unscathed although this film must compete with *Sands of the Desert* as the absolute dregs of his career.

A more successful film in 1962 with critics and audiences was *In Search of the Castaways*, based on a Jules Verne story and starring Hayley Mills in one of a series of six pictures she made for Disney. Audiences were promised 'A Thousand Thrills, And Hayley Mills!' in the story of two children, their scientist friend and a rich aristocrat sailing along the 37th parallel to find a missing sea captain.

One of their adventures en route brings them to a South American village, where they excitedly learn the villagers are holding three castaways prisoner. To their disappointment, the three prisoners are Patagonian sailors, not the missing father. A door opens and three ragged, desperate men run out and fall at the feet of the English party babbling madly. Among them is Delgado, looking atypically scruffy for an actor normally seen looking suave in more upmarket surroundings and costumes. The role is small but colourful and is a reunion with David Spenser, his co-star from *Stranglers of Bombay*, playing a South American guide.

1962's *Village of Daughters* is a whimsical little black-and-white comedy. It even starts with a breathy voiceover saying 'Once upon a time,' establishing a fairy-tale tone to the proceedings. A big comedy cast includes Eric Sykes and John Le Mesurier, and Eric Pohlman appears, having been in films already with Delgado. George Pastell, a villain with Delgado in *Stranglers of Bombay*, plays a pickpocket.

The plot can written on the back of a postage stamp. A Sicilian village has run out of young men and there are lots of lusty young women who need husbands. Into this situation comes Herbert Harris (Sykes), a naïve and inept young English salesman who is a victim of mistaken identity as the villagers believe he is Antonio Durigo, a local boy who has made it good in London.

Events build to a climax when Harris is about to marry the mayor's daughter and they exit the mayor's house to get in a carriage that will take them to the church. Edwin Richfield plays the carriage's driver. Out of the carriage step three Mafioso brothers: Giovanni Predati, Alfredo Predati, and Francisco Predati, the last played by Delgado. All are waving nasty-looking shotguns and, because they believe Harris is really Antonio, they've come to shoot him and finish off a vendetta.

It's a small, mute part but does show his range. Having a small role with no dialogue does not mean Delgado is just an extra. His character and name are in the end credits and he is definitely performing. As his brother asks a bewildered Harris, 'You've forgotten what happened in 1815?' (the origin of the blood feud), Delgado looks puzzled and then stern as Harris denies being the man they want to kill. He gets to prod Sykes in the back with his shotgun. He also joins in the big comedy chase seen at the end when the mayor, all the village women and the Mafia chase Antonio around the village.

In other ways it shows his range. A couple of years later Delgado played another Mafioso with a shotgun in *Court Martial*, the television series about the Judges Advocate General. But that time the tone was serious not comedic and the performance of a similar part is totally different. In *Village of Daughters* he's a comedy bad guy. In *Court Martial* he is utterly chilling. There his gun is for killing old women, not for waving around for comic effect.

As usual by now Delgado is playing a foreigner, and the entire cast of the film barring Sykes were playing Italians. While it was very normal in that time to have British actors putting on accents and doing foreign parts, it does not mean the effect was always successful. The review of *Village of Daughters* in *Illustrated London News* remarked on 'a company of mainly English players grotesquely pretend to be Italian villagers'.[221]

Although he was now in the public eye as a villain, directors still offered him comedy parts. Michael Bentine and Robert Hartford-Davis collaborated on the 1966 comedy *The Sandwich Man*. On paper, it is a film with a lot going for it. Bentine was enormously popular on television and the cast was incredible. The central plot device of Bentine's character wandering around London with sandwich-board placards over his shoulders allowed him to meet a galaxy of stars. Across the film Terry-Thomas, John Le Mesurier, Fred Emney, Dora Bryan, Diana Dors, Stanley Holloway, Suzy Kendall and Burt Kwouk appeared. Delgado played Abdul the Carpet Seller, a part that gave him several scenes with Bentine. To play the part he wore a fez and a robe and dark make-up, and in one badly realised special effect he rises from the ground on a flying carpet.

The film flopped. Another actor under dark make-up was Hugh Futcher. He has a clear impression of why the film failed despite its good cast and big names. '*The Sandwich Man* was an idea of Michael Bentine's; and with the greatest respect to the memory of Michael Bentine, I thought Michael Bentine's big mistake was the fact that he insisted that he play the Sandwich Man.' The issue was the star: 'Michael Bentine was a very skilled comic; I don't think Michael Bentine was a particularly good actor, and what I think would have helped the film enormously is if the part had gone to Ron Moody, because Ron Moody had all the qualities to play the Sandwich Man.'[222]

Even if sometimes films were flops, that was the fault of stars and directors, not character actors, and even being in massive disasters did no harm to Delgado's career. Futcher is in no doubt about why directors and management cast Delgado so frequently, and that's his professionalism. There's a reason so many of his friends and former colleagues think of his professionalism first and foremost when talking about him. By no means all actors were as professional as Delgado but then not all actors were in work so much. Delgado could be trusted, and Futcher saw in action a man with a busy career because 'management, particularly TV bosses, knew that he delivered the goods and he could always be trusted to be a professional and give a good performance'.[223]

But another reason is that audiences liked him. By the mid-1960s he had been on the big screen and the small screen for close to fifteen years. There had been big roles and small roles but with his distinctive looks and voice he stood out even in tiny parts. Audiences, so Hugh Futcher told me, like familiarity; they like seeing the same faces in the same way they like catching up with old friends. That theory certainly explains the financial success of the *Carry On* franchise when audiences paid to see the same actors in the same scenarios from *Carry on Sergeant* in 1958 to *Carry on Emmanuelle* in 1978.

When they worked together Futcher was younger than Delgado and as 'a young actor having an ambition' he thought: 'I used to say the joy would be when you appear on the screen there is a chuckle in the audience watching the film, because they know it's like a friend suddenly appearing on the screen.' Likewise when audiences saw Delgado, thinks Futcher, 'You always believed, when Roger appeared, in whatever guise he was playing; people identified with the fact, and maybe they didn't even know his name, and I say that with the greatest respect to him, but it really became that thing: he was a familiar face.'[224] And so he was. His appearance was unmistakable even if accent, nationality and costume changed from film to film. Even if someone did not know his name, they would recognise him as that actor who played foreigners.

Even in another incredibly busy decade there were some things he missed. It's striking he was never in a James Bond film. These had big international casts but British character actors like Richard Vernon, Cyril Shaps and James Cossins filled out the smaller parts. Given his prominent work in the ITC and ABC adventure series, the fact there was no part for him in a Bond is curious, although he did have parts in spoofs of the franchise like *Masquerade*.

But otherwise Delgado by the mid-1960s was everywhere and working without stop. That meant he became a very familiar face in certain places like the Elstree Studios in Hertfordshire. Delgado was often there, as were people like Hugh Futcher who remembers: 'There was a period particularly with people working at Elstree Studios, people either liked us or we were just in favour at that time, because you seemed to meet the same faces all the time.'[225]

Elstree was almost a second home to Delgado. It's where he made *The Saint* and *The Avengers*, but also many other programmes that kept him busy in his career like *Overseas Press Club – Exclusive!*, in which he appeared in September 1957 in the episode 'Two Against the Kremlin'. Elstree was one of several second homes and the speed at which he moved from job to job meant he was equally a familiar face at Lime Grove, Teddington, Pinewood and at the start of his career at the studios that churned out the B movies like Nettlefold and Merton.

The mid-1960s continued to see a flurry of film activity for Delgado. Many of his films in the 1950s had been cheap B movies made in the smaller studios like Merton, Nettlefold and Beaconsfield. His 1960s works were more substantial; bigger budgets, longer running times and major stars, and bigger parts for Delgado. In quick succession from 1963 he made *The Mind Benders* (another one with Dirk Bogarde), *The Running Man* and *Masquerade*. In this last, *Variety* noted his performance alongside bigger names: 'Jerold Wells, Roger Delgado and John Le Mesurier all contribute to varying degree.'[226] It's a step up from earlier film work because Delgado had dialogue, reasonable screen time, and a reviewer knew he existed.

One of Delgado's most regular television employers was Rudolph Cartier, but directors in film also valued and re-hired Delgado. One of them was Basil Dearden, director of *The Mind Benders* and *Masquerade*. After his own untimely death in a motor-car accident, critics obituarised Dearden as not 'in the big league of directors whose every work is marked with a distinctive personality'.[227] The comment might be a reflection of the diversity of his films, starting with Ealing comedy and ending with *The Man Who Haunted Himself*. He made 'problem pictures' focused on key social justice concerns including homosexuality, brought onto the screen in *Victim*, and racism, which was the focus of *Sapphire*.[228]

Dearden cast Delgado as Dr Jean Bonvoulois in *The Mind Benders* in 1963, originally announced as starting production in 1962 but like other Dearden films delayed in production.[229] Delgado appears briefly when a Security Service agent played by John Clements (a blast from the past from the days when Delgado worked for the Intimate Theatre) watches a film of a strange scientific experiment. A French physicist, Dr Bonvoulois has spent four months locked away in a remote cabin to test his endurance for isolation. When he emerges, he is a wild haired and wild-eyed madman, issuing creepy warnings in broken English about being visited by angels. His madness is part of the 'suspense and gruesome space-age qualities' that *Variety* liked about this odd little film.[230]

There's no doubt Delgado liked playing Arabs and found great amusement in the parts. Several Dearden films gave him the opportunity to put on the greasepaint and headdress. 'I'm the nastiest Arab of the lot in the film *Khartoum*,' he once commented, 'a thoroughly treacherous, sinister and conniving character. Then there was the Audrey Hepburn film *Masquerade*, in which I had another villainous Arab part.'[231]

The Mind Benders was the start of an association with Dearden that would span several films and television programmes. The film historian Gus Burton thinks that Dearden's background at Ealing made him familiar with the approach of making films with an informal repertory. But he also thinks Delgado had a particular recommendation: as he puts it, directors would have thought, 'We need a Latin, send for Delgado!'[232]

Someone who was behind the scenes and saw Delgado interacting with Dearden was the director's son James. His memories of how the two got on well make sense of two things. One is why Dearden kept using Delgado, and the other is why Delgado would be happy to accept very small roles. As James remembers the relationship between them, Delgado 'certainly seemed on good terms with my father, who could be difficult to say the least with actors he felt were not giving him what he wanted, and clearly liked having him around on set'. Once more there is a behind-the-scenes glimpse of the arch-professional, an asset to a company and a director's dream. That's how Basil Dearden felt. What about Roger? James thinks: 'Even if the part was not that large, the actor in question would probably agree to come and do the role in appreciation of the continuing relationship and the shared respect that existed between them.'[233]

To say the least, Delgado was a member of a horribly insecure profession. Most other actors were in the same boat, but the insecurity of his chosen career seems strangely at odds with his controlled, settled private life. Basically, he seems to have been an actor who lived like a banker. I do wonder if, with the good quality clothes and wine and the gorgeous little house in Teddington, he had champagne tastes on a beer income. However, little glimpses like the snapshot James Dearden remembers of his quite difficult father liking Delgado and wanting him around on his film sets fill in some blanks of how his life worked. Delgado did his utmost to be an asset and employable.

Delgado is one of several actors wearing dark make-up and a turban in the epic *Khartoum*, about the events leading up to the death of General Gordon of Khartoum in 1888 (the events that happened ten years before the main action in *Storm over the Nile*). His part is a tiny one in a large and troubled production. The project was announced as a colour United Artists film long before any filming began. Work on the film was delayed and the original director Lewis Gilbert (later to direct James Bond films) had put the project on hold to make *Alfie* with Michael Caine.[234] Eventually Dearden and his usual collaborator Michael Relph joined the project although neither man was happy during production. After release, the film suffered in comparison with *Lawrence of Arabia* from four years earlier.[235] As always, Delgado had the knack of making the most out of small material. He had little dialogue (and that which he had was dubbed by Robert Rietty) but was part of a lengthy scene where he sat next to Marne Maitland glowering at Charlton Heston.

Also under the greasepaint was the leading classical actor Laurence Olivier. His presence in the film brought home the difference between a star and a character actor like Delgado. Each day Olivier would be 'purring to Pinewood in his Rolls', compared to people like Delgado who caught the train.[236] Reactions to Olivier's performance reinforce how carefully Delgado judged his own performances in foreign and exotic parts. He could walk a fine line that kept the seriousness of his performance intact despite outlandish make-up and costumes.

Not so Sir Laurence. *The Times*'s critic thought: 'We are given a formidable display of eye-rolling and lip-licking, a weird Peter Sellers-oriental accent, and a valiant but unsuccessful attempt to disguise Sir Laurence's all-too-English features with false hair and green lipstick.'[237] The actual Mahdi was a striking-looking man with 'a birthmark on his right cheek and a slight V-shaped gap between his two main front teeth'.[238] As played by Olivier, he looks like a freak. Delgado as ever could give a director a credible, dignified foreigner, something better-known and better-paid actors could not always pull off.

Dearden gave Delgado another small role in 1968 in the lush *Assassination Bureau Ltd* which starred Oliver Reed, Diana Rigg (fresh out of *The Avengers*) and Telly Savalas. The film was under way in May 1968 at Pinewood.[239]

Where we find Delgado in *Assassination Bureau* is alongside actors such as Kevin Stoney, Olaf Pooley, Vernon Dobtcheff, John Abineri and others, familiar to *Doctor Who* fans from their appearances in 1960s and 1970s stories (Dobtcheff and Stoney were in season six Troughton stories, Abineri and Pooley were both major villains in season seven), actors who gained substantial parts on television but much smaller roles on film.

Delgado's part as 'Bureau Member' is almost a mute one although at the very end he catches sight of Oliver Reed on board a Zeppelin and shouts out his name. We first see him on the enormous and complicated set that is the Bureau's headquarters. A gathering of immaculately dressed European noblemen is joined by Oliver Reed and at a signal a servant starts winding a winch. A large bookcase parts in the middle and we see a huge circular room, surrounded by murals on the walls. The members file in and take their places at a table to stately incidental music. Dearden shoots from a high angle, capturing the grandeur of the setting.

We learn the Assassination Bureau (of which Delgado's character is a member) has existed as a shadowy organisation for a long time and its members have carried out notable assassinations over the years. The members are played by Warren Mitchell, Curt Jurgens and Kenneth Griffith amongst others, plus Savalas and Reed. Rigg's character, in an effort to stamp out the Bureau, has commissioned the assassination of its leader, played by Reed. He challenges the other Bureau members: can they kill him before he kills them?

Although he has almost no dialogue, Delgado is well used and visible in a sprawling film that has a massive cast. In the major scene in the head-quarters of the Bureau he makes the most of his screen time, banging on the table in approval when other members speak, reacting in amazement when Count Dragomirov announces the commission to have himself assassinated and comforting Kenneth Griffith's character when the Count throws a gavel at him and strikes him on the head. He manages to communicate a lot without any lines.

Behind the scenes working as a 'lowly assistant' was James Dearden, Basil's son. While in the final film Delgado's role is small and quiet, James still remembers 'Roger's name was on the call sheet a great deal, even though his part was fairly small, but as one of the bureau members he was in all the scenes involving the assembled board members.'[240] A small part could still mean much work and decent fees if it was a big movie.

Assassination Bureau received good reviews on release in March 1969. 'Elegant, quite witty, engaging,' thought Richard Roud, the critic for the *Guardian*.[241] 'An amiable, diverting comedy thriller,' was the verdict in *Illustrated London News*.[242] It also had a good box office.

By contrast one of the biggest films and biggest flops of 1968 was *Star!*, showcasing the singing and dancing talents of Julie Andrews, Bruce Forsyth,

Daniel Massey, Beryl Reid and many others, but not a hit with audiences and marred by Andrews' abrasive performance. In a sprawling film lasting nearly three hours, Delgado is on screen for about thirty seconds.

Star! is the life story of Gertrude Lawrence, the music hall star and actress. At about half way through the film, she and Noël Coward are acting out scenes from his new play *Private Lives* in front of the Lord Chamberlain, who is concerned about its decency.[243] Lawrence and Coward are throwing themselves into a scene of the lover's tiff, doing so in a room just off the Horse Guards Parade and a growing number of spectators are gathering at the window, unaware they are seeing a demonstration in front of the Lord Chamberlain and thinking they are seeing some torrid love-making.

Across the parade ground strolls the immaculately attired French Ambassador, wearing a morning coat and top hat, flanked by a French soldier in his flat kepi and an aide in a top hat. They see the commotion inside the room as Coward and Lawrence claw lustily at each other's clothes. 'Les Anglais: never underrate them,' says the Ambassador to his country-men, watching on with sardonic enjoyment.

Delgado's brief appearance brings back memories of his small role in *The Belles of St Trinian's* as another superbly dressed foreigner. The contrast, though, says a lot. In the intervening years Delgado's film acting has matured. In contrast to the eye-popping ham on the platform in *St Trinian's*, where Delgado was determined to make the most of every second on screen, in *Star!* his acting is far more subtle. Seeing Lawrence and Coward cavorting on the sofa through the window, his face registers brief surprise, moving to a quizzical, supercilious look; and, as he speaks, he gently flaps his suede gloves under his face. He makes the most of his time on screen and makes his mark in a film with a gigantic cast, which is what he had been doing on film throughout the 1960s.

Chapter Twelve
West End interludes
1956-1967

An intractable trouser dropping frenzy.
– Ben Venables describing farce

D ELGADO'S LIFE AS an actor began in theatre and continued there
after the War, but his theatre career never flourished and eventually
fizzled out. While he never stopped performing on film, television
and radio and could always squeeze in another character part, the stage was
not his natural home. He is far from alone. Troughton famously disliked
theatre, or what he called 'shouting in the evening'. Theatre work disappears
almost completely from the lives and careers of other contemporaries
Christopher Lee and Peter Cushing. For Delgado there were a few West End
appearances, which were a mixture of drama, music and comedy, but these
are rare.

Although theatre was not his priority, there were some sizeable West End
productions in Delgado's career and a cluster of them from the mid-1950s to
the mid-1960s. For an actor obituarised and thought of as a villain, his West
End parts are a real medley from the sinister police chief in *The Power and
the Glory* to high farce and musical theatre. He doggedly rebuilt his career
after the war, starting in regional theatres. Delgado's stage work in the 1950s

and 1960s received lukewarm reviews, and for good reason his energies were mostly being directed to film and television.

Like his film and television work, though, his stage appearances show a jobbing actor taking on anything and he moved from *avant garde* (and poorly received) European theatre to religious plays. There were also long gaps. The review of *The Rising Sun*, in which Delgado appeared in 1953 with the International Theatre, moved from the lukewarm to the lousy. Delgado was in 'this travesty of a play' full of 'cliché and platitude'.[244]

In 1954, Delgado participated in *The Prince of Peace*, a 'modern Nativity play' that was 'presented in aid of the National Society of Cancer Relief'. It was a worthy cause but I suspect the audience was bored rigid. Getting onto the stage of the Phoenix with Paul Scofield two years later was a major step up from Christ Church hall in Turnham Green for *Prince of Peace*.[245] In 1955 *The Stage* announced: 'A reading of Pirandello's *Grafted* (*L'Innesto*) is to be presented by Play Forum,' and among the cast was Delgado, along with Cyril Shaps, one of Cartier's repertory company.[246]

Then something bigger and better happened – his West End debut. In 1956 Delgado joined Peter Brook and Paul Scofield part way through their season with H. M. Tennent productions.[247] Both Scofield and Brook enjoyed spectacular success with their tour of *Hamlet* to the USSR. *Hamlet* was at the Phoenix Theatre in January 1956 and came off on March 24th and *The Power and the Glory* opened on April 5th. It had already had a first performance at the Theatre Royal Brighton on March 26th 1956 and ran there for a week.[248] The little programme produced for the week's run in Brighton is a time capsule of theatregoing in the era, including the request to audiences that 'Smoking is permitted in the Auditorium, but no pipes or cigars please.'

Denis Cannan adapted Graham Greene's novel. Advance notice promised a play about a priest eluding authorities in Mexico. Scofield was the whisky priest and Delgado the chief of police, an antagonist.[249] At the Phoenix, it ran to sixty-eight performances or a season of six weeks but did not lead to a Broadway debut for Delgado.[250] He was not in the cast that opened the play in New York.[251]

The part in the London run did give Delgado some profile. A large photo of Delgado in character as the chief of police interrogating Scofield's priest accompanied *The Times*'s review. Delgado is bearded and has a cigarette hanging loosely from his lips while he leans menacingly over Scofield.[252] His part of the chief of police was a powerful one and meant he was on stage almost from the beginning. His character is the second in speaking order. When the curtain rises, the scene is a dentist's surgery where a dentist played by Brian Wilde is peering into the mouth of Delgado, who is looking up in significant concern. The dentist as it turns out is not to be trusted, as his surgery is a front for the smuggling of Roman Catholic priests; and the dentist enjoys the police chief's worry: 'One good pull and it's over. It's the principle of the revolution, isn't it?' he says in cruelly insincere sympathy to the police chief.

Later in the play Delgado is in a scene marked out by critics as a dramatic high point. As explained by the reviewer in *Theatre World* the priest 'risks everything to procure the wine he must have to celebrate secret masses in the outlying villages'. However, in Act II the priest 'watches the precious wine he has bought illegally for his masses "knocked back" by unscrupulous men'. One of these unscrupulous men was Delgado. Photographs of the production show him with a cigarette in the corner of his mouth, bathed in sweat and staggering around as he gulps down the wine. *Theatre World* also pointed to the importance of Delgado's role as one of 'two representatives of the secular power, the one a corrupt tyrant (played by Roger Delgado), the other an idealist of the best intentions (Harry H. Corbett)'.[253]

We see Delgado keeping seriously impressive theatrical company. Apart from appearing with Scofield and receiving direction from Brook, Graham Greene himself attended the dress rehearsal. For Brook and Scofield the rehearsals were intensive and worrying because the play just wasn't coming together. Scofield was under the pressure of performing *Hamlet* by night and rehearsing *The Power and the Glory* in daylight hours.[254] One strange anecdote tells of Scofield's inability to get into character throughout the rehearsal period. At a dress rehearsal in front of Graham Greene, the part finally came good after Scofield had a haircut, losing the long hair he had grown to play Hamlet and finally feeling comfortable as the whisky priest with an ugly buzz cut.[255]

To pause and compare the careers of Delgado and Scofield shows the type of actor Delgado had become and that he would remain. They did know each other and had done a broadcast of *The Portrait of a Lady* on the Home Service in 1952. Otherwise, they are a study in contrasts. Throughout a long career, Scofield made twenty films and two of these are classics, *A Man for All Seasons* and *The Crucible*. His career was primarily in the classical theatre with the National Theatre and the Royal Shakespeare Company. Delgado began in the theatre, but his career was almost entirely with film, television and radio with the stage coming in a distant fourth and Shakespeare hardly at all. There were plenty of hits and misses but it was to the broadcast mediums that he nailed his colours.

Even though it's the prestigious West End, *The Power and the Glory* used Delgado in the same way Roy Ward Baker would in *The Singer Not the Song* a couple of years later: a man of Spanish descent playing a Mexican. He was in distinguished company with Brook, Scofield and Greene, but Delgado was just a visitor to their world. Brook long collaborated with Tennent's productions, not surprisingly as Tennent's, under the control of Binkie Beaumont, was the 'General Motors of British show business'.[256] Brook and Scofield were also collaborators; they worked together before and continued their association long after.[257] After doing *Hamlet* together, they joined forces on an enormously successful *King Lear*.[258]

The Power and the Glory had a large cast and received mixed reviews, but the praise for the acting focused mainly on Scofield who was a familiar performer to all the major theatre critics. *The Times* found it 'quietly absorbing' but singled out Harry H. Corbett as the deputy chief of police for praise of his 'light, easy touch'.[259] The review in *The Stage* pointed out that with a very large cast, it was possible for the individual actors to get lost in the crowd: 'The company is large, but most of its members have individually little to do,' said 'R.E.L'. However, the same reviewer did think that 'Roger Delgado, as the corrupt Police Chief' was one of the cast members who 'make an impact with well-managed character sketches'.[260]

Much reaction was negative, in the bitchy, biting-tone theatre reviews at the time. For the critic Peter Hall the entire Brook-Scofield season was an example of how in the theatre 'things go terribly wrong'. In particular, writing of *The Power and the Glory*, there was 'a great performance by Scofield in a poor play'.[261] *Theatre World* thought the play 'fails to present a dramatic whole' and did not mention Delgado at all. However, it may have been the better outcome to be ignored by reviewers in a play struggling to get good reviews.[262]

He had been in the West End not just on stage with Scofield, but in the theatres down Shaftesbury Avenue where there were many other leading lights. Hugh Griffith was having success in *The Waltz of the Toreadors* at the Criterion, Robert Morley was in *A Likely Tale* at the Globe Theatre, and Peter Cushing was in *The Silver Whistle* at the Duchess.

This West End appearance did not lead in any important new directions for Delgado. The play closed in 1956, and in 1957 he was rarely off the television screen. He had made one stage appearance but that year was enormously busy for Delgado on television. He clocked up seven television appearances in *Nom-de-Plume*, *The Scarlet Pimpernel*, *The Advancing Shadow* and *The Alien Sky* (with Kismet); in addition were *The White Falcon* and *The Cold Light* for Cartier. Most of these are footnotes as the programmes are lost. Cast lists show Delgado was firmly in his foreigner niche including 'Andre' in *The Scarlet Pimpernel* and 'Mahmoud' in *The Alien Sky*. He was also in the major film *The Battle of the River Plate* playing a Uruguayan sailor. Playing the Mexican chief of police on stage was an extension of that type of role.

The next year did not take him into further West End work but sustained his television work as a foreigner, including appearances in eleven separate television programmes. He appeared in multiple episodes of *The Buccaneers* as Spanish characters and all episodes of the miniseries *Huntingtower* in 1957 alongside familiar faces like Paul Whitsun-Jones and Frazer Hines. But television work ranged across everything from a comedy French role in *Billy Bunter of Greyfriars School* to Lt. Lachaise in *Assignment Foreign Legion*.

In the 1960s he returned to the stage from time to time, taking a break not just from film and television but from villainy. Some of Delgado's theatre work is now chiefly interesting as a reminder that his range extended to singing. He had used this talent in between West End roles in performances of *One Girl a Day* at the Coventry Theatre in March 1959 and at the Palace Theatre in Manchester in April.[263] The light musical was of a piece with the sort of entertainment the Palace Theatre offered; later that year Norman Wisdom starred there in pantomime.[264]

The local reviewer for the *Manchester Guardian* found *One Girl a Day* a musical that was old-fashioned and 'full of all the clichés of English musical comedy that one would have thought Sandy Wilson's satire had killed stone dead'.[265] However, a dated and clichéd production was also one which gave Delgado a strong opportunity to stand out, as 'what little bite the piece has comes from Lucille Gaye, as a diamond-bright American matron, and the one topical song, sung by Roger Delgado'.[266] In line with the type of roles he was playing in film and television, whether comic or straight, Delgado was playing a foreigner, in this case the Arab Ali Bey.[267] Cast photos show him surrounded by a harem of glamorous young women in diaphanous clothing.

Delgado's theatre career is of a piece with his work in film, television and radio: there is astonishing variety. In 1961 he was in *Little Old King Cole*, playing the substantial part of the Duke Rollo. Charlie Drake starred and Delgado and the diminutive comedian were together again in the film *Sands of the Desert*. Delgado's role in the pantomime reminds us of the comedy parts which recur during his career. A sudden illness meant he had to bow out of playing a hotel manager in an episode of *Hancock's Half Hour* on television, but he did do comedy with Harry Worth and Reg Varney.

Whenever he did comedy from the 1960s onwards critics' reactions showed that by now Delgado was firmly established in the public mind as a villain making occasional detours into comedy. The television critic Bill Edmund saw Delgado in an episode of *The Valiant Varneys* and thought 'it was grand fun seeing that arch villain Roger Delgado – who has menaced us in so many serious dramas – enjoying himself in a knockabout rôle'.[268] Comedy parts extended his villainy. He was a menacing Eastern European in Harry Worth's show in 1968, not far removed from his part in *The Protectors* from four years earlier. He even wore the same sort of karakul fur hat. For the episode of Worth's show 'James Bond – Where Are You?' he was second in the credits and singled out as a 'featured' performer. What a sign that his star had risen, to make not just a guest but a special guest appearance. A comedy appearance by Delgado by then was something special. He was not just a familiar face but was well entrenched in the acting scene with a name linked to a strong professional identity.

The surviving tape of the episode is not in brilliant condition, but it's possible to enjoy Delgado's comedy cavorting as he finds Worth in his Eastern European embassy, thinks he's a spy, then realises he is not, then tries to wriggle out of the confusion (having mistakenly notified his superiors he's captured a spy) and gets Worth to stage an escape by knocking him out, with Worth eventually smashing an occasional table over Delgado's head.

But we digress. Delgado used his comic timing in 1961 in *Little Old King Cole* at the London Palladium from December 30th with the show running until March the next year. The production was pure show business, 'the large show with the little hero' as the *Spectator*'s reviewer said.[269] A big cast of actors, nineteen musical numbers, dancing girls, dancing boys, the Bill Shepherd Singers, Kirby's Flying Ballet, the Aida Foster Children and the Palladium Orchestra all joined forces. The finale was so lavish it even had a separate designer. The show was immense and went on and on for months.

This pantomime was the biggest success of Delgado's stage career, albeit very much a shared success and if we measure success in box office and the sheer scale of the production. It was Leslie A. Macdonnell's production and by March 1962 he placed a full page ad in *The Stage* with the cocky boast that the show was the 'longest running pantomime in the history of the London Palladium' and had 'the greatest gross revenue for the corresponding of any previous London Palladium pantomime'.[270]

Although the production gave Delgado the chance to do comedy, his role was still villainous. A big report in *The Stage* while rehearsals were in progress said: 'The traditional fight between good and evil is waged, this time between Ariel, played by the dark-haired 17-year-old Sandra Michaels, and the wicked Duke Rollo, portrayed by Roger Delgado, an actor whose whole career has been spent in the playing of the hissable character.'[271] Delgado couldn't control what people wrote about him, but comments like that did very little harm. They just showed the reality: he was a typecast villain and there was no shortage of that kind of work. Patrick Troughton famously had a horror of being typecast and leapt from project to project to stave off typecasting until his own untimely death in 1987. Other actors, including Peter Cushing and Christopher Lee, co-stars of both Troughton and Delgado, embraced typecasting, or at least pragmatically accepted that it paid the bills.

For Delgado the panto was a big success in raising his profile. A wonderful photo of him in his costume and make-up as the Duke Rollo appeared in *The Stage*. Under a cap and long dark wig, a beardless Delgado looks out with a sneer on his face and a big fur collar around his shoulders. Underneath there is more comment on this villainous actor being in panto: '43-year-old Roger Delgado is a villain once more… Roger, who began his career in 1938 playing a villain has since appeared in films, TV and radio roles, 75 per cent of which have been villains.'[272]

At this point in his career Delgado's profile was scaling new heights. He was a special type of actor, the 'hissable' specialist in playing villains, but producers and directors continued to cast him in all types of parts out of regard for his professionalism and ability. He could play comedy villains or straight villains. Huge numbers saw *Little Old King Cole* and his stock with British children around 1961 to 1962 must have been very high. As *The Stage* pointed out, while appearing in the pantomime ITC was showing his appearances in the swashbuckler *Sir Francis Drake*. By now Delgado was not just a villain specialist, but a foreign villain specialist. *Sir Francis Drake* was yet another time playing a character called Mendoza and would not be the last!

His time in *Little Old King Cole* also reminds us of the professionalism of the man under the roles as his approach to work was totally unlike that of the panto's star. The star was Charlie Drake, the diminutive but physical comedian. By the end of his life, Drake had gambled his way through millions of pounds and his private life was a shambles.[273] Nothing could be further from his panto co-star Delgado, with a home life and affairs kept in immaculate order.

Then, Delgado's immaculate private life was very different from so many of his contemporaries. At home at White Cottage he lived in strict order with no dust, dirt or chaos. He invited a select few to charming dinner parties with fine wine. Meanwhile some other British actors had different home lives. Consider Hattie Jacques. 'Her big home in Earl's Court was crammed with out of work actors, window-dressers, homosexuals wanted by the police, and the alcoholic and incapable Joan Sims.' Her *Carry On* co-star Sid James once arrived home to find an axe embedded in his living room floor, a present from an irate husband whose wife was having an affair with James. The *Carry On* stars may be extreme cases of personal dysfunction, but they do put Delgado's peaceful, tidy home life into perspective.

There was a gap of two years in stage work after the pantomime and then Delgado appeared in *Enrico* at the Piccadilly Theatre from July 1963. It was one of three Italian musicals produced by Pietro Garinei and Sandro Giovannini from 1959 to 1963.[274] The show lasted for 86 performances but was not a particular success. Delgado was part of the problem. 'Its huge success in Italy was not repeated in London, where a chiefly British cast and Rascel in his original role, didn't go down well.'[275] *Enrico* is basically plotless with a loose linking story for a musical about modern Italian history. Renato Rascel arrived in London in May 1963 to begin rehearsals. If there seems to have been a long gap between his arrival and the opening, it's because the musical was meant to open on June 13th, after transferring from Liverpool.[276] There was another delay and the musical should have opened on June 28th but the show's scale and complexity meant that, behind the scenes, there were delays in the arrival of 'several mechanical staging devices'.[277]

According to most critics, it was not worth the wait. Once again Delgado had mixed reviews for a stage appearance. *The Stage* was kindest in a vaguely patronising way with comments like the music was 'tuneful but unmemorable'.[278] *The Times*'s theatre critic had spiteful fun with 'this Italian musical', which 'limped bravely into the Piccadilly Theatre last night'. 'Mediocrity', 'facile', 'inconsistency' and 'dull witted' are some of the acidic descriptors. The musical stretched all its performers into a variety of characters and types. Renato Rascel himself appeared for some of the musical in make-up to look exceedingly old. Delgado appeared throughout from the prologue onwards. He was a priest in the Christening scene, the dancing instructor in the Coming of Age scene, a socialist in First Love, Cavaliere Rapisaldi, in the last part appearing in two separate scenes and appearing older in the second one. Backstage photographs show the range of the make-up and costume changes from scene to scene.

Delgado comes in for criticism: 'The show misuses a number of good performers, such as Bryan Blackburn and Roger Delgado, who are required to work outside their proper range.'[279] It would have been interesting to know more. By 1963 what did the reviewer think was Delgado's proper range? Should he have stuck to being a villain? The comment is however of a type with negative comments on the use of British actors in the Italian musical.

Next time he was on stage the reviews were positive. He moved from musical theatre to farce in *The Diplomatic Baggage* at Wyndham's Theatre in 1964. There was the usual regional preview in Brighton from September 14th and the production then transferred to the West End, where it opened on September 29th.[280] Brian Rix, a brilliant farceur who once said he'd lost his trousers over twelve thousand times on stage, cast Delgado as Monsieur Martell, a Frenchman and diplomat.[281] Ads promoting the play promised 'laughter signed, sealed and delivered'.

The 'baggage' of the title is a young blonde Frenchwoman who looks like Martell's wife but actually isn't.[282] Delgado's part was a big one in an ensemble piece, which also included John Barron, Elspet Gray (Mrs Rix) and Charles Heslop. Critics and audiences both liked it and no doubt it would have been an enjoyable evening's entertainment. Amongst other pleasures, there was a saucy French chambermaid and a solid farce plot or what the reviewer in *Plays and Players* called 'all the standard farce apparatus'.[283] It was at Wyndham's but was of a type with the Whitehall farces.

In the play, there is a dinner party of four people, but the two women are not the wives of the men at the table. Then their real wives arrive and the two girls have to be smuggled out of the room, hiding underneath trolleys.

Derek Royle played the waiter having to push the people around under the trolleys, prefiguring I feel his part as the corpse in *Fawlty Towers* dragged from room to room. In farce manner, more and more characters arrive on stage and eventually the two wives and the two young women come face to face. 'In the course of the evening the stage gradually fills up with whores, executives and ladies of good standing, none of whom is aware of the presence of the others until the final curtain,' is how critic Jeremy Rundall summarised it.[284]

Delgado played a suave Frenchman. Photographs of the production show him stylishly dressed and enjoying the company of the young blonde played by Suzanne Vasey, who spent part of the play sitting on his lap. The reviewer in *Theatre World* enjoyed the 'uproarious comedy' and noted Delgado's contribution to the goings on: 'Roger Delgado as Monsieur Martell and John Barron as Harrison Tweedie, the government official complete with mouth syringe and medicaments, were individually excellent and collectively brilliant.'[285] The farce was light relief from the more serious works playing in the theatres down Shaftesbury Avenue: the Welsh actress Rachel Roberts was playing the whore Maggie May at the Adelphi, and *Scent of Flowers* with Ian McKellen was a play about suicide.

Even though Delgado was on stage, his appearance actually reinforced that he was by now primarily a television and film actor. The blurb about him points out that by 1964 he was rarely now on stage: 'He is delighted to be back in the theatre, after a long period in films and on television, especially to play in farce.'

His appearance also showed that in the public eye he was by now more than a jobbing actor, but a character actor with a clearly defined identity and a face and name people recognised. We glean this point from the programme, which says: 'Roger Delgado is a professional villain, who has found that crime does pay. That is to say he specialises in playing villainous parts. He was that wicked character who murdered Torrance in *Maigret*, and he has perpetrated other terrible crimes, strangling with scarves and knifing with ceremonial choppers, all for the sake of entertainment.'

The biographical blurb harks back to a number of recent film roles, the strangling being in *Stranglers of Bombay* and the ceremonial chopping in *Terror of the Tongs*, as well as his part in *Maigret* the year before. Undoubtedly the appearance in the farce was by now a detour from the main line of work that he was clearly associated with in the public eye. Well before he played the Master, anyone seeing him on screen could expect to see him do something wicked and villainous. Thinking of the many villains, Katy Manning defines his career: 'His major roles as an actor were those kind of castings.'[286]

The next time Delgado was on stage on Shaftesbury Avenue was again as a foreigner, this time playing Senor Sanchez in *Cactus Flower* at the Lyric Theatre. The comedy opened on March 6th 1967. The programme for the show contains a biography that is a source for some of the most familiar stories told about Delgado and often repeated since. Referring to his job as a bank clerk, the programme says: 'After eighteen months he walked out and fourteen days later he walked on to a stage in Leicester.' In a type of Chinese whispers, one of Delgado's obituaries kept the same basic story but shortened the time period to just the following week.[287] The programme also noted he was a go-to actor for playing foreigners: 'Of his many films the most recent are *Sandwich Man*, *Khartoum* and *The Mummy's Shroud*, in all of which incidentally, he plays Arabs.'

The play was an exuberant production and Delgado danced on stage. As in *Diplomatic Baggage* Delgado played a well-groomed foreigner and he appeared elegantly dressed in a dinner jacket. The whole production was in fact well designed and the sets notably expensive.

Its reception was more lukewarm than for *Diplomatic Baggage*. Hugh Leonard, the reviewer for *Plays and Players*, thought: 'As a comedy it is by no means unfunny: the situations are nicely arranged and many of the ripostes are neat.'[288] Nonetheless the same reviewer thought the play so formulaic that it was as though it had been written by a computer. In the pompous language often found in theatre reviews of the time, his patronising judgment was that the play was written for audiences 'to whom form, style and innovation are all equally anathematical'.[289] *The Stage* was kinder about the play although it still thought the comedy was familiar stuff and predictable. But the direction was 'swift and snappy'.[290]

These West End appearances were a mixed bag of styles and success levels. *The Power and the Glory* received mixed reviews, but gave no glory at all to Delgado whom Scofield overshadowed in reviewers' comments. People hated *Enrico* but *Diplomatic Baggage* was a pleasant farce and *Cactus Flower* was predictable. Was Delgado's natural home the television and not the stage?

Chapter Thirteen
Swashbuckling 1954-1962

I'm the Master here now. – Don Esteban in *The Buccaneers*

FOR MOST OF his career Delgado appeared with a neatly trimmed and pointed beard. His appearance resembles the courtly gentlemen, aristocrats and kings in paintings by Van Dyck or Velázquez, especially so when Delgado appeared in period costume. Has there ever been an actor so completely in the right place at the right time, with just what programme makers were after to be villains in their swashbucklers? For TV roles across the 1950s and 1960s, directors and producers constantly wanted him. Professionally his interests were looked after by Fraser and Dunlop, an agency with among others Beryl Reid and Diane Cilento on their books, and his career was flourishing.[291]

The BBC and the independent companies churned out swashbucklers and always needed foreign villains. 'There were always parts around for good villains,' is how Terrance Dicks explains Delgado's success.[292] Delgado was a perfect swashbuckler. Stories about Robin Hood, adventures set in the Middle Ages and during the reign of Elizabeth I, or adaptations of Alexandre Dumas, all required Arabs, Frenchmen, and Spaniards, often as villains. With his Velázquez looks, Delgado could fill these parts. His appearances in swashbucklers in the 1950s are preludes to the Spanish Ambassador Mendoza in *Sir Francis Drake*.

Sadly some of Delgado's earliest swashbuckling is lost from television archives: ghost productions that have left behind paperwork, some photographs and stills but no sound or image. To judge from surviving evidence, Delgado looked magnificent in *The Three Musketeers*. He appeared as Athos in all six episodes of the 1954 series made by the BBC, with Laurence Payne, Paul Whitsun-Jones and Paul Hansard filling out the other roles. Charming publicity photographs show the Musketeers in their flamboyant costumes striding around the streets of London.

The reviews were kind to it. *The Times* offers some intriguing hints of a quite sophisticated television production and refers to film sequences and a 'rich and fast-moving spectacle' played out across numerous sets, including the courtyard of Monsieur Treville's house and at the Red Hart Inn.[293] There was also a good fight scene and the final verdict was of an 'entertaining episode'.

One report from the press shows a behind-the-scenes moment during rehearsals at Lime Grove and has cast members Delgado, Whitsun-Jones and Hansard posing in costumes with the young actress Clare Austin. While the episodes are lost, it was evidently an attractive production. Delgado is in a doublet, large lace collar and sweeping hat.[294] Whitsun-Jones looks like the Laughing Cavalier. Another surviving still shows a lively sword fight in action with Porthos, Aramis, Athos and D'Artagnan ranged against Richelieu's men.[295]

The whole 1950s were remarkably busy for Delgado in television. For the BBC he also contributed to a lost version of Robert Louis Stevenson's *St Ives* along with William Russell, who before becoming Ian Chesterton in *Doctor Who* was also an active swashbuckler on British television.[296] For ITC he appeared in cheap, production-line programmes, but remained an actor prepared to thoroughly rehearse and who gave his parts more depth and consideration than they really deserved.

By the mid-1950s Delgado had the BBC, ABC, Associated Rediffusion, Granada and ITC to work for and the companies like Sapphire making programmes that Lew Grade distributed. In succession, he moved through *The Three Musketeers*, *St Ives*, an appearance in *The Scarlet Pimpernel* and *Sword of Freedom*. Not all of these programmes survive but it is possible to see a great deal of Delgado's work in the immensely busy 1950s. His episode of *The Borderers* is gone. However, his part in an episode of *The Scarlet Pimpernel* has been retained. It reunited him with Marius Goring, another actor used extensively by Rudolph Cartier on much more serious works like *The Cold Light*.

BBC programmes like *The Cold Light* are a reminder of a period when Sunday-evening entertainment on the national broadcaster could be grim dramas made in the studio and lasting for over an hour and a half; or else viewers could get half an hour's jaunty adventure. Delgado usually played suave and stylish roles, including immaculate costuming and tailoring, so his part in *The Scarlet Pimpernel* is a rare glimpse of a scruffier role, in this case playing an ally of the Pimpernel.

Thinking back to actors in television drama in the 1950s and 1960s, the director Michael Briant reminisced how 'Part of an actor's bag of tricks is sword fighting, horse riding, those were the two things you really had to have under your belt as an actor to make a decent living.'[297] Delgado's swashbuckling bears him out. There is plenty of sword fighting throughout the 1950s but in *The Scarlet Pimpernel* he also takes a tumble off a horse. We last see his character with his chest bandaged and gasping in amazement when he gets to see the Pimpernel face to face.

Many of these swashbucklers were the brainchild of Hannah Weinstein, the formidable American executive and producer. Prior to blacklisting, she had an amazing career in broadcasting and journalism in the United States. In 1944, she had visited the White House as a member of the Committee of the Arts and Sciences to meet Franklin Roosevelt. By the 1950s, she was among many left-wing broadcasters and writers working in Britain and had taken over Walton Studios to make her Sapphire Films swashbucklers.

Weinstein's company and the studio were friendly and familiar territory for Delgado, and Walton was where he came to make *The Adventures of Robin Hood* among other swashbucklers. It was an enjoyable place to work and even the normally acidic Kenneth Williams found the studio 'all very pleasant and convivial' when he was there for a guest appearance in *Sword of Freedom*.[298]

Sapphire did not just make swashbucklers, and one of their international successes was *The Four Just Men* in 1959, distributed by ITC and set in the present day. Jack Hawkins, Dan Dailey, Vittorio de Sica and Richard Conte played the four men. They rarely appeared together but the episodes alternated between them, meaning the settings were international and some filming took place overseas. Film directors including Don Chaffey and Basil Dearden were behind the cameras. Dearden directed Delgado in 'Rogue's Harvest', a 1960 episode with Vittorio de Sica's crime fighter in the lead.

While Sapphire sometimes put Delgado in contemporary settings, more often the company used him in their period adventures. He contributed a villainous part to 'Angelica's Past', an episode of *Sword of Freedom* broadcast in August 1958. Edmund Purdom, at this time at a halfway point in his career between some limited success in lavish costume dramas and a later career in trashy Italian films, plays the artist Marco del Monte, a republican living in Medicean Florence. Francesca Annis is Angelica, his lover but also a former thief.

The pattern of the adventures follows other Sapphire productions. A crisis, some ensuing adventure, and a happy resolution after a sword fight leave the audience ready for next week's adventure and it all happens in the space of half an hour. In this case, the crisis is the reappearance in Florence of Virelli the Cord, played by Delgado at his most sleekly and murderously charming. Virelli is a thief whose nickname comes from the cord with weights tied on it that he can quickly throw around someone's neck and strangle them, or flick over their wrist and tie them up. He has come to reunite with the former thief Angelica and for a time it looks like the awful Virelli will succeed in breaking up the happy relationship between Marco and his reformed thief girlfriend.

Happily Virelli is outwitted and the episode ends with a dramatic fight between Virelli and Marco. Both Delgado and Purdom throw themselves energetically into a fight scene filmed quickly on a cramped set. The fight is also a showcase for one of Delgado's many skills as an actor: his dexterity. In a menacing fashion, he squares off with Marco and quickly tosses a dagger backwards and forwards from hand to hand while grinning slyly. Not all actors could coordinate props and acting so well. One of the worst was Kenneth Williams, whose inability to coordinate what he was saying with what he was doing was a source of frustration on the sets of the *Carry On* films when producer Peter Rogers and director Gerald Thomas wanted to get scenes shot as quickly as possible.[299] Not so Delgado, who showed remarkable dexterity with the dagger and the cord, which, quick as a flash, he could throw and ensnare someone.

His business with the dagger and the violence of the fight scene show us by now what producers could expect from casting Delgado. They got a reliable actor who was on set on time with his lines learnt but who also added extra to each of his parts. The fight scene could have happened without the dagger tossing but it adds a wonderful touch of menace.

Between 1957 and 1958 his swashbuckling took him through parts in *Huntingtower*, *The Adventures of Robin Hood*, *William Tell*, *Queen's Champion* and *The Buccaneers*, sometimes for the BBC and sometimes for the Incorporated Television Company. Actors could return to these serials in different roles. Paul Eddington played several parts in *The Adventures of Robin Hood*, and in *The Buccaneers* Delgado was first Captain Mendoza and then in two episodes Don Ferdinand Esteban. In both cases he was a villain.

The Buccaneers is another one of the serials made on film by Hannah Weinstein and in this case follows the crew of the *Sultana* in the early eighteenth century. Captain Tempest (Robert Shaw) is a pirate who is on the side of the British, and the rollicking theme song invites us to 'go a-roving'.

As Captain Mendoza in 'Dangerous Cargo', Delgado comes into conflict with two British ships while wearing a magnificent jabot with his hair in a ponytail. His wickedness is wonderful, including throwing around bags of gold as bribes and tying up women. He is back in 'Conquistador' but now playing Don Esteban. Although the scripts are basic and the sets cramped, there are some flourishes. At the opening of the episode, the camera pans across the familiar deck of the *Sultana* and we think we see Captain Tempest, but it's not: it is Esteban disguised as Tempest, and he turns around to face the camera accompanied by a blast of dramatic incidental music.

Some of his dialogue as Esteban has a familiar ring to it. 'You are confused; good, that is exactly what I set out to do: create confusion,' he says, a line the Master could have delivered. He gives his dialogue in a clipped Spanish accent with a few foreign flourishes. Telling of his capture of the *Sultana*, he says, 'And *olé*, it was all over in two minutes.'

Delgado's most substantial contribution is in episode 25, 'Conquest of New Providence', broadcast first in March 1957 and also shown in the USA like many of the ITC series made on film. The episode is Delgado's second outing as the villainous Don Esteban. Previously Esteban has taken over the *Sultana*. Now he has captured all of New Providence and imprisoned the British, news reported to the crew of the *Sultana* by the boatswain Sam Bassett (Neil Hallett).

As in other ITC series, Delgado has good screen time and a good character. As Don Esteban he struts around in rich clothes, interrogates people, bribes others and presides over a hanging while seated on a throne, keeping people in suspense until giving the signal by dropping his kerchief. In time the crew of the *Sultana* arrive and lead a revolt on New Providence and the Spanish are defeated. The sword fight between Delgado and Robert Shaw, playing Tempest, is an early glimpse of the vicious snarl we will see later.

Richard Greene had an acting career that for a short time ran almost parallel with Delgado's. After the Cardinal Vaughan School, Greene joined a provincial repertory company in the 1930s. However, from there their professional pathways separated. Greene scored major success in Hollywood, including working with Basil Rathbone and Shirley Temple. He returned to the United Kingdom for military service, but after the war moved to television and in 1955 began his run in *The Adventures of Robin Hood*.[300] It is difficult to type or read those words without hearing the show's distinctive theme song about Robin Hood 'riding through the glen'. The adventures it accompanied were a major success on British and American television.

Delgado makes his contribution late into the series' run and appears in 'The Minstrel', broadcast in April 1958. He plays, surprise surprise, a Spaniard, in this case the Ambassador from the Kingdom of Aragon. Delgado appears halfway through the episode, drawn up to the castle gates in Nottingham on a litter borne by bearers and sitting next to Prince John (played by Brian Haines). The story as usual features the battle of wills and wits between John and the Sheriff of Nottingham and Robin Hood and his Merry Men. In this instance, their weapon is a minstrel in the district improvising offensive songs about the Sheriff and John.

As usual, the episode's plot moves along briskly. The Minstrel is locked up because John and the Sheriff don't want to be embarrassed by the rude songs when the Ambassador visits. Friar Tuck infiltrates the prison, memorises the catchy songs and soon has taught them to merry drinkers in a pub. The Sheriff issues an edict banning singing; and then the Ambassador arrives.

Delgado looks magnificent and saturnine. His costume is a long robe and high hat, and he bows his way courteously through formal greetings. 'Your popularity is very impressive,' he tells John. Compared to the neurotic Prince John and the Sheriff, Delgado plays the Ambassador suavely.

Unwittingly, the Ambassador becomes a means to humiliate the Prince as the elaborate fiction of Prince John's popularity comes crashing down. Leaning back casually on a high chair, the Ambassador asks, 'You must tell me all about this Robin Hood.' The Prince and the Sheriff tense up: 'We haven't seen him for a long time, ever since the people started clamouring for our gracious prince to assume the throne,' replies the Sheriff uneasily. 'I heard he was the greatest bowman in England, witty, clever,' replies the Ambassador to the continuing discomfort of the pair.

A banquet then follows and Friar Tuck cunningly brings in a small group to children to sing for the Prince. The Sheriff refuses the offer and the Friar drops a reference to the ban on singing. 'Death penalty for singing, but why is that?' exclaims the Ambassador in surprise. The Sheriff has no choice but to let the children sing, but out of their mouths comes a song proclaiming loyalty to Richard the Lionheart. John is furious; the Sheriff realises that 'Only one person could be behind this: Robin Hood,' and the fiction collapses that Robin Hood is dead and Prince John popular with the English people.

In ten minutes of screen time, Delgado makes the most of the part. He gives the role of the Ambassador courtly grace but also a sense of humour and a worldly wisdom. Having come to England to see for himself if John is telling the truth that the people want John to replace his brother Richard, the Ambassador instead embarrasses the Prince and the Sheriff and further witnesses their humiliation in the singing orchestrated by Robin and the Friar.

The Ambassador also gets the last word of the episode. Left alone with Maid Marian on a balcony as the Minstrel escapes from Nottingham, Maid Marian tells him, 'There's only one Robin Hood.' 'And only one king of England, it seems,' the Ambassador replies with shrewd awareness of the political situation in England, and they walk back into the castle.

Over a decade later Delgado would impress his *The Avengers* co-star Linda Thorson with his willingness and indeed determination to properly rehearse even small parts and small scenes, compared to other actors who came on set, did their scene, and left again. 'The thing that Roger liked to do was rehearse.'[301] His meticulous and finely judged performance in *The Adventures of Robin Hood* gives the same impression of an actor treating material, even a ten-minute part in a children's programme made on a production line, with due seriousness and preparation.

The Adventures of Robin Hood was set when Richard the Lionheart was away fighting the Crusades. In 1962 Delgado appeared in 'The Norman King', an episode of *Richard the Lionheart* set in medieval Sicily. This time he is a Saracen. Viewers and Delgado are both on very familiar ground. It is an ITC series, made on film for children, with over thirty episodes being churned out on what television historian Tise Vahimagi calls the treadmill of the productions made by Edward J. Danziger and Harry Lee Danziger.[302]

Nothing in terms of tone, production or style sets *Richard the Lionheart* apart from the umpteen other film series including *The Buccaneers*. 1962 also marks the dying days of such productions.

'The Norman King' is not focused on the scheming of Prince John against Richard; this time Tancred in Sicily and the King of France are conspiring to kidnap Richard. The plot, such as it is, is to lure Richard away during a masquerade ball. Their Trojan horse to do so is Laki, a Saracen and son of Mahmoud, Saladin's admiral. Delgado plays Laki, clean-shaven for once but looking out from underneath one of the many keffiyehs he would put on for ITC. For a 1960s children's serial Delgado is suitably exotic and frightening, brandishing his sword and shouting in Arabic. The episode has secret passages and swordplay. Like the Aragonese ambassador in *The Adventures of Robin Hood* Delgado gets some depth, helped by some vivid dialogue including the threat to 'crush you between his armies like a walnut'.

For the early 1960s it's also remarkable that the character is given the moral high ground compared to the squabbling and plotting Christian kings and knights, and he says with a smirk: 'See how Christian kings smell treachery.' He also gets to go out with a laugh. Laki, who is the same height and size as the king of France, was to have infiltrated the masquerade ball and lure Richard away. To aid the disguise he is given the French king's ring with the royal seal. But Laki turns the tables on the scheming French king, helps Richard and walks out happily with the royal ring saying, 'If anyone stops me I shall say I am the King of France!'

As a jobbing actor, Delgado's only other regular work in his whole career besides the Master was Don Mendoza, Spanish ambassador to the court of Queen Elizabeth I in *Sir Francis Drake*. ITC showed the serial across the end of 1961 and 1962 although Delgado was cast by April 1961.[303] Prior to broadcast it had been hyped as the 'most expensive TV film series ever made!', not quite true although it did use a full-scale replica of the *Golden Hind* that sailed around Plymouth.[304] ABC also threw a blowzy launch party at the HMS *Drake* barracks at Davenport, although it didn't go to plan and the young sailors invited 'jeered and hissed throughout'.[305]

Is Mendoza the quintessential Delgado role? Terrance Dicks thinks so: 'The wicked Spanish ambassador, probably dressed in black velvet,' is how he sums up Delgado prior to *Doctor Who*.[306] Michael Briant also saw the natural fit between Delgado and the Spanish roles he so often played: 'Inevitably with a name like Delgado you're going to be regarded as something of a foreigner.' Taking that association further, Briant thinks back over Delgado's career and judges: 'He had Spanish heritage. And there was a pride about him, now I think about it: there was a dignity and pride about Roger, he had that Spanish mien.'[307]

Delgado is not in every episode of ITC's *Sir Francis Drake* but he is a highly impactful participant as the principal antagonist against the heroic Drake, played by Terence Morgan, and the stately Queen Elizabeth, played by Jean Kent. All of the principal cast were very much at home in Tudor England and period settings. Kent had been a major Gainsborough star and spent the 1940s in ornate period dramas, and by now Delgado had been in practically every ITC adventure series.

Delgado is on hand to scheme and plot but always to be defeated. As Mendoza, Delgado again gives more depth to a part than the scripts always called for. His courtly graces cover his scheming and plotting, meaning his villainy is all the more dramatic for being disguised. 'I am desolated at this intrusion,' is one of his flowery, gracious lines when entering a Countess's castle, but the grace soon gives way to some hard-headed scheming. What was Delgado aiming to achieve with this part? While the role on paper is a wicked foreigner, his approach to enacting villainy is, thinks Michael Briant, to show through his acting that 'he's got another point of view, and he is trying to perpetuate what he thinks is right'. Briant, pondering if Delgado, as the Master, was acting out an evil role or not, considered: 'I don't think Roger went around going "How do I perform this as evil," he went around going "I want my point of view to prevail; I am prepared to tell any lie, do anything, in order to make my point of view prevail."'[308]

The point is also true for Mendoza, where Delgado could have chewed the scenery with Spanish villainy but instead gave audiences a charming, courtly ambassador who was determined to prevail at all cost. Naturally that never happened but, in the midst of defeat, Delgado also gave audiences a shrewd, alert character. In the episode 'The English Dragon', Drake and Lord Oakeshott, played by David McCallum, escape from a cell via a secret tunnel. 'No one could have got in,' exclaims the Constable of Calais in bewilderment. 'But someone got out,' is Mendoza's perceptive response.

The formulaic adventures gave Delgado exposure overseas, as NBC took up the filmed series for broadcast as a filler after *Car 54, Where Are You?*[309] Not everyone was a fan. *Variety* thought the programme was 'mindless'. *The Stage*'s reviewer was grudging: 'The series will probably be a commercial

Roger aged four
(Image © Kismet Marlowe)

A childhood studio portrait
posing with a Kepi cap
(Image © Kismet Marlowe)

An early theatre appearance
as La Hire in *Saint Joan*
(Image courtesy of John Kelly)

On stage in Manchester in 1959:
One Girl A Day as Ali Bey with
his harem
(Image courtesy of John Kelly)

Delgado as Don Ferdinand and Robert Shaw (right) as Captain Tempest in 'Conquistador', a 1957 episode of *The Buccaneers* (Image © ITV/REX/Shutterstock)

Delgado as Virelli the Cord and Adrienne Corri as Angelica in 'Angelica's Past', an episode of *Sword of Freedom* and one of fifteen television appearances Delgado made in 1957 (Image © ITV/REX/Shutterstock)

More swashbuckling with Paul Whitsun-Jones and Paul Hansard as the Three Musketeers
for the BBC in 1954
(Image © ANL/REX/Shutterstock)

As Major Sayid with Martin Wyldeck as the Emir in *Ghost Squad*: 'Quarantine at Kavar'. Playing Arabs was the backbone of Delgado's career. (Image © ITV/REX/Shutterstock)

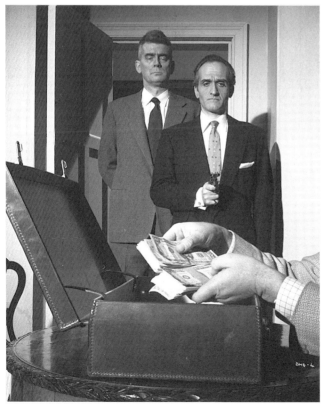

Delgado playing Von Golling, the Nazi hotelier in *Danger Man*: 'Under The Lake' (1961) (Image © ITV/REX/Shutterstock)

Inside and out, Delgado's White Cottage in Teddington was kept immaculate
(Images © Kismet Marlowe)

In 'The Liberators', an episode of wartime drama *Court Martial*, Delgado played Mafia thug Salvatore Fratuzzi (Image © ITV/REX/Shutterstock)

On familiar ground in a glossy ITC adventure series, this time playing the casino manager Tapiro with Mary Merrall as Aunt Clara in *Randall and Hopkirk (Deceased)*: 'The Ghost Who Saved the Bank at Monte Carlo' (Image © ITV/REX/Shutterstock)

One of Delgado's biggest film roles was the Soothsayer in Charlton Heston's hand-picked cast in *Antony and Cleopatra* (1972)
(Image courtesy of John Kelly)

Playing the villainous Victorian gambler Silva with George Murcell as Inspector Vandeleur in *The Rivals of Sherlock Holmes*: 'Madame Sara' (1971)
(Image © FremantleMedia Ltd/ REX/Shutterstock

Before the Master, Delgado's quintessential role was the wicked Spanish Ambassador Mendoza in *Sir Francis Drake* (1961-1962)
(Image © ITV/REX/Shutterstock)

With Jean Kent in *Sir Francis Drake*: 'Drake on Trial' (Image © ITV/REX/Shutterstock)

Playing the Cardinal of Rio in *ITV Play of the Week*: 'The Successor' (1965). Delgado was at home playing Latinos and Catholics. (Image © ITV/REX/Shutterstock)

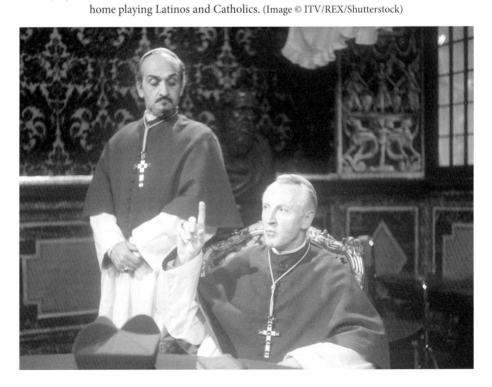

At the Casa Pepe restaurant in Soho with Kismet (Image © Kismet Marlowe)

On holiday in 1961 (Image © Kismet Marlowe)

The Doctor shadowed by
the Master and Azal in
Doctor Who: 'The Dæmons'
(Artwork © Alister Pearson
with thanks to David Lavelle)

Delgado's final role on British
television was playing the freedom
fighter Pedro in *The Zoo Gang*: 'The
Lion Hunt', broadcast posthumously
(Image © ITV/REX/Shutterstock)

success but it offers nothing new as television entertainment.' Chapman suggests the serial is 'the least remembered of the ITP/ITC swashbucklers, despite good productions, good action sequences and an overall quality look'.[310] That's very true and the sets in particular are solid and well-designed compared to the shoddiness of *Richard the Lionheart*.

Some ten years later, a tiny joke in the *Doctor Who* story 'Colony in Space' paid tribute to Delgado's role as Mendoza. 'The man they arrested turned out to be the Spanish ambassador,' comments the Doctor when told UNIT has had a possible sighting of the Master. As is well known, the line is a reference to Mendoza, but actually one of Delgado's routes to *Doctor Who* came via another swashbuckler where he acted with Barry Letts, the man who would without hesitation cast Delgado as the Master.

People who knew both Delgado and Letts sensed an affinity between them. 'Barry was a very thoughtful man as well; he was of the same school as Roger Delgado,' thinks Briant.[311] At the same time as Delgado joined *Doctor Who* the RADA-trained actor Richard Franklin joined the cast, playing Captain Yates. Thinking back, Franklin also considers having been an actor made Letts a good, empathetic producer: 'Barry was a very good producer but a very good director as well and of course he had been an actor, which I think is always a great help; he knew what the problems were, and therefore I think would have appreciated working with somebody like Roger.'[312]

There were also a number of professional links between Letts and Delgado even before they swashbuckled together. One was the Theatre Royal in Leicester, where Letts worked (after Delgado's time) as an assistant stage manager. Besides the theatre, a further link was the producer and director Shaun Sutton. Sutton cast Delgado in a variety of parts including as a Nazi in 'Over the Line', an episode of the 1960 wartime drama *The Long Way Home* which also starred Letts (he also used Delgado as a Nazi in *The Silver Sword*, another series with Letts, although he and Delgado were in different episodes). Sutton had earlier brought Delgado and Letts together in *The Three Princes*, first produced in 1954 and repeated (as in restaged, and with Kismet in it) in 1959.[313] *The Three Princes* broadcast in 1959 brought together Letts, Delgado and John Woodnutt, all later reunited on the set of 'Frontier in Space'. *Queen's Champion* of 1958 had already brought them together, also with Patrick Troughton appearing and with Shaun Sutton producing. For once, Delgado played a good guy, while also remaining true to type in playing a Spaniard. Viewers and critics recognised just how good these actors were at their swashbuckling and the panache they brought to their work. The *Telegraph*'s Maurice Wiggins liked the 'sterling romantic battlers, such as Mr. Paul Whitsun-Jones, Mr. Roger Delgado, Mr. Barry Letts and Mr. Patrick Troughton'.[314]

He had been in period costume again with Troughton but for once not playing a Spaniard in *The Splendid Spur* for the BBC. The 1960 serial adapted Arthur Quiller-Couch's story as a robust children's adventure, and critics received it well. Guy Taylor wrote a positive review saying, 'Head of BBC-TV's Children's Programmes, Owen Reed, must have been spurred on by the success of previous costume dramas to attempt another one.' Among the excitements were 'spies at every cross-road, traitors at every inn'.[315]

By now Delgado had been doing period swashbuckling for nearly a decade. His beard, his face, even his complexion had made him perfect for the parts. His parade of foreign villains for these adventure series shows Delgado in the right place at the right time. In Briant's view the sort of work Delgado accepted was pragmatic: 'He's not stupid, and of course having the little beard and moustache I think, certainly having the beard, gave him a more Spanish, swarthy look. Inevitably if you're making a TV production or you're making a feature film in the UK studios, you're going for your important characters to employ a quality actor like Roger who looks the part, and indeed he can swashle his buck and wear a nice costume and make a leg.'[316]

Nothing shows better that Delgado was *the* go-to actor for wicked Spanish characters than the fact he plays two different roles in *Sir Francis Drake*. In six episodes he is Mendoza. But in one, 'The Governor's Revenge', he plays Governor Ancuna. Viewing the episodes for the first time the casting is confusing. Delgado as always shows he has thought hard about this part and the script and he shows us differences between the parts of Mendoza and Ancuna. Mendoza is more darkly Spanish while Ancuna has more surface charm and gives a lighter performance. Nonetheless, as 'The Governor's Revenge' begins, it does jar somewhat to have Delgado on set, performing in a Spanish accent but playing a different part, and I wonder how much it confused the watching children. But it does show his value on the ITC production line as a regular, reliable foreigner.

Sir Francis Drake is Delgado's biggest part outside the Master, but it was also the end of an era. According to Chapman, ITC 'would change direction, turning its back on the costume adventure series in favour of contemporary detective and secret agent series'.[317]

Delgado effortlessly transitioned and remained a stalwart of ITC in particular. His swashbuckling included *Sword of Freedom* for ITC and Lord Grade, the same mogul who produced slick, glossy thrillers from the early 1960s. If the 1950s had been his era of swashbuckling for ITC and the BBC, the 1960s would be the era of Delgado's appearances in the adventure series made by ABC and ITC.

Interlude
The home front

T HE 1960S WAS A SIGNIFICANT decade for Roger. He had married Kismet Shahani in 1957. Married but with no children, in 1962 he requested the solicitor Anthony Sumption draw up a will and be its executor and trustee. The paperwork was finished by January 20th 1962 and witnessed by an actress and a property management assistant.

In 1962 Sumption was at Mark Lane in the City of London. The will lay undisturbed until 1973 when Sumption, now at Lowndes Square, executed his sad duty. The signature Delgado added to the document in 1962 is a little more flamboyant and a little less neat than the signatures on his application for entry to the London School of Economics in 1937.

The will itself was a straightforward and tidy document, exactly what you would expect of Delgado, leaving no loose threads in its straightforward provision for Kismet. It was the will of someone with no siblings and no children who lived tidily. He was a natty dresser and an organised man, for example selecting carefully each morning the television programmes he was going to view that evening at home.[318] The will is part and parcel of a man who planned everything.

In the midst of film and television work, Delgado's domestic circumstances changed again and took on the pattern they would follow until his death. By 1962 Woodstock Road was long gone and the Delgados were living in the King's Road, Chelsea. It was a fashionable area and near neighbours included André Morrell, Peter Ustinov, and the film director Sir Carol Reed, who cast Delgado as a Spanish doctor in *The Running Man*.

In 1964 he and Kismet moved to Park Lane, Teddington. White Cottage was and is a charming little double-fronted house near the corner of Park Lane and North Lane. It has a good-sized garden and Kismet recalled the house was 'practically filled with books'.[319]

Delgado's good taste showed in his living arrangements. All the places he called home, Woodstock Road, King's Road, King's Street and Park Lane, are still standing and in good condition. They show he rented or bought good-quality premises, usually quite old and charming and in nice parts of London. Inside, his good taste continued. He liked good wine and was a delightful dinner host. He liked good things and, for the early 1970s, he was quite cutting-edge in owning a colour television.

There is an amazing consistency about him that comes through from the memories of his colleagues in terms of how he lived, how he acted, and how he organised his life. He was 'professional', 'meticulous', 'controlled', all words used by former colleagues to describe him.

At home in White Cottage as at work, Delgado was a neat, meticulous man. Richard Franklin once visited White Cottage in Teddington and over forty years later his memory is fresh of someone 'very punctilious'. 'I suppose some people might even call him too precise at times,' mused Franklin, and he told me: 'I went to their house once in Teddington, it was a little house, but again absolutely reflected his character, meticulous, absolutely neat, not a speck of dust anywhere.'[320]

Outside White Cottage was Delgado's car, as neat as his clothes and his house. 'He had a little Mini, a tiny car, but it was absolutely immaculate,' remembers Franklin.[321] Teddington was a congenial place to live. It was near the TV studios and locals there still remember seeing the villain from *Doctor Who* at the nearby railway station.[322]

His good taste showed in other ways. Out of character and out of costume he normally dressed smartly, even intellectually. He wore spectacles with thick, dark frames. It may not be surprising that his co-star in 'The Mind of Evil', Pik-Sen Lim, when thinking back to rehearsing with him, thought: 'In my mind's eye, from what I recall, there was him in costume; I don't even remember, what did he wear when he came to the rehearsals?' In her mind's eye the immaculately dressed Master and the immaculately dressed Mr Delgado come together.[323]

After moving to Teddington, his life took on settled patterns for both work and play. To relax, he enjoyed driving holidays.[324] In terms of work, he continued to do occasional theatre, some films and a great deal of television. Throughout the 1960s the independent companies employed him and his vocal talents to play a whole host of wicked foreigners in glossy, colourful series that would get his face onto American television.

Chapter Fourteen
Independent adventures
1961-1972

You play well, Signor. – Estoban in *The Persuaders!*

Yussuf, Estoban, Kreer, Rodriguez, the Vizier: the names of characters among the foreign roles Delgado contributed to the glossy adventure series made by the competing independent companies like ITC, ABC and ATV. The swashbucklers kept Delgado in the past, whereas the independent adventures placed him in glitzy contemporary settings.

Among the writers are names familiar from *Doctor Who* credits like Malcolm Hulke, Terrance Dicks, Bill Strutton and John Lucarotti. Many of these series had up-tempo jazzy themes by Ron Grainer. While some had the budget for overseas filming, many evoked glamorous overseas locations in the studios at Teddington, Pinewood or Elstree and on the high street in Borehamwood. The adventure series, many of them initiated by Lord Lew Grade, were a more glamorous proposition for their casts and crew than many BBC shows. They were often in colour and on film and as a result carried the possibility of overseas sales and exposure in America.

There is no exact point of transition. Delgado's work for ITC adventure series was in the 1950s as much as the 1960s. In 1957 he played a safe-cracker,

Luigi, in 'Operation Big House', an episode of the series *O.S.S.*, based on the actual Office of Strategic Services during the Second World War. He appeared in the last three episodes of *Biggles*, Granada's colour adaptations of the stories about the flying ace with Neville Whiting starring. In 1961 he was a Portuguese character in 'Seawolf in Lisbon', an episode of *Knight Errant Limited*. By this point John Turner, the original star of the programme, had departed and Hugh David played the lead.

The swashbucklers did not completely disappear from his roles in the 1960s either. He gave a vigorous performance in *The Splendid Spur* on the BBC in 1960. On that occasion he was wearing his most magnificent and flamboyant costume since *The Three Musketeers*. As late as 1968 he played Monsieur Fouquet in an adaptation of *The Man in the Iron Mask*.

Nor were all of his 1960s TV roles glamorous or in colour and not all at this time were for independent companies. A small part was in *The Human Jungle* episode 'The Two-Edged Sword' as Wirral, a prisoner, on the BBC in June 1963. The prison cell and especially the prison uniform are both unusually drab for Delgado. Herbert Lom played Dr Roger Corder, a psychiatrist, but Delgado appeared in a scene with his colleague Dr Jimmy Davis, played by Michael Johnson. Delgado's performance is immaculate as an upbeat, courteous but thoroughly corrupt and villainous prisoner locked away in Wandsworth Prison. Wirral is a master hypnotist who has posed under numerous fake guises including a military man.

Delgado's scene in *The Human Jungle* lasts barely three minutes but eclipses most of the rest of the episode. The cheapness of the production is obvious; when he enters the cell, Delgado's feet echo and clatter on the wooden rostrum. But in a programme like this it's the acting that counts, and here it is two actors in close-up, and Delgado's immaculate delivery of his lines like 'My dear fellow, how else does one measure success?' when asked about hypnotising and financially exploiting someone. He's a smooth-talking confidence trickster, but momentarily a little flicker of concern flashes across his face when the psychiatrist points out Wirral's medical qualifications are fake.

Delgado's acting with voice and face is part of the performance, but then there are his hands. The hands are essential parts of a Delgado performance. Sometimes, especially when playing a Spaniard or Mexican, they flap around. Other times their movements are tightly controlled; there's the light touch on Dr Fenton's arm in *The Broken Horseshoe*, a light touch but one that stops Fenton in his tracks. His hands give depth to his characters, showing their state of mind. The fussy hotel manager in 'The Disappearance of Lady Frances Carfax' fiddles with his watch. And in *The Human Jungle* Wirral gently twirls a lit cigarette backwards and forwards in his fingers. The movement is not distracting but compelling. As the fraudster describes his manipulation of people, the cigarette twirling in his fingers is an analogue to the people he's twisted and controlled.

He was working for ATV by December 1963 with a substantial dramatic part (once again an Arab wearing a fez) in 'A Camel to Ride', which was part of the *Espionage* drama series. More black-and-white television appearances came in 1964, including for the BBC. A well-received adaptation of *Madame Bovary* starred the New Zealander Nyree Dawn Porter. The programme made the BBC sit up and notice her icy blonde beauty and she was later in their smash-hit period drama *The Forsyte Saga*. In *Bovary* Rex Tucker used Delgado as a court clerk.[325] The role was small and again he was a smaller cog in a bigger success, *The Stage*'s reviewer liking the 'general excellence' of the production.[326]

Delgado clocked up no fewer than four appearances as foreign villains in *The Third Man*, the Harry Lime series starring Michael Rennie with Jonathan Harris playing Bradford Webster, the comical sidekick. More foreign villainy means more hand gestures. As Luis Mendoza in the 1964 episode 'A Little Knowledge' Delgado emerges from the dark shadows of a sinister warehouse to confront Bradford Webster. Webster spots some stolen merchandise, but his spluttering anger about the theft turns to craven politeness when the crooks point their guns at him. 'I'm glad to see they're in safe hands,' he mutters weakly. 'Very safe hands,' replies a beaming Mendoza, with his hands splayed widely. A Spanish villain is brought to life with some little Spanish flourishes. Mendoza forces a glass of fiery cognac on Webster, and warns him: 'In Spain, Signor, a man drinks with his friend or he has no friend.'

Parts in series like *The Third Man* and *The Human Jungle* meant Delgado was part of major television successes. Several seasons of both appeared and *The Third Man* was a major co-production with Hollywood's National Telefilm Associates.

He appeared as a French policeman in *Sergeant Cork*, a high-rating ATV series. The year before, *TV Times* had profiled the show's star, John Barrie, a gruff character actor who told the interviewer James Green: 'I prefer to find my friends outside of show business,' and the interviewer reported Barrie 'regards acting as a job and not as "my art"'. Those sentiments may not have chimed one hundred per cent with Delgado, always so committed to his acting, but he would have respected Barrie's commitent to making sure he learnt his script each time.[327]

His role as Inspector Puichard in 'The Case of the Great Pearl Robbery' shows Delgado on familiar ground playing a foreign policeman, a role he had been refining since his film and television career began. Dressed in a kepi and a flamboyant uniform with braids and buttons, Delgado also has an unparalleled opportunity for some of his finest 'hand' acting. As I said, hands matter in a Delgado performance, appropriately for an actor who colleagues remember always thought deeply and intelligently about his roles. Part of that thought is how to have his hands and mannerisms as part of the performance. In *Sergeant Cork* he uses one of the characteristic Delgado gestures (also seen in *The Third Man*): hands facing outwards, thumbs touching, and all fingers splayed widely.

Then the hands go into overdrive. Someone has stolen a valuable pearl from a jeweller and the conceited Inspector Puichard has received intelligence on a suspect. His index finger points and stabs into the air as he backs William Gaunt's character across the room. The fingers count off one, two, three lumps of sugar and one hand flaps up and down as Puichard explains, 'Zis strange-looking man put ze sugar in his pocket!' The hand gestures go with florid French dialogue as Puichard reassures the visiting English policeman that the Sûreté will soon have their man, and then: '*Et voilà*, success!'

In 1964 he had a substantial role in 'Freedom!', an episode of *The Protectors* (not to be confused with the 1970s series), a monochrome series set in the office of an ex-policeman, an ex-soldier and their secretary who now provide security as the firm Souter & Shoesmith.[328] It is no surprise to find Delgado in the programme. *The Protectors* filled the schedule while *The Avengers* was on a temporary break, and the ABC team who knew Delgado used him here.

In 'Freedom!' Delgado adds another nationality to his collection, playing an Albanian who is in London with a famous composer. The episode gives Delgado a large and potent part despite playing a character who is not exactly evil, just committed to his regime and determined the composer and musician will not defect. Once again, Michael Briant's verdict is right that

Delgado did not act 'evil', he just acted determined characters who wanted to prevail. That lifts a performance out of stereotype into more interesting areas.

He may be determined but in 'Freedom!' he is also scary enough that he just has to walk through a door and characters scatter in fear. As the episode is on videotape in a studio, a lot of the impact depends on the acting rather than the production. Delgado works well in this environment and steals the scenes. In one, as a character makes a speech, Delgado watches in the background and a variety of expressions travel across his face from mild alarm when it seems the composer may say something controversial, to sardonic amusement as the Albanians embarrass a Western journalist. Small, cramped video drama needed acting of this subtlety to have any impact.

***

Recording on videotape in the early 1960s placed hideous demands on the actors to keep going no matter what, rather than stop for a retake, which was costly and difficult with the videotape. In 'Freedom!' there is a very rare instance of a fluffed line by Delgado. 'You only accept private invit… invitations at our discretion' is the slightly mangled line of dialogue, but the slip is tiny and he keeps going calmly. He's far from alone among actors on videotape in the early 1960s making a small slip and it does show that he was only human. William Hartnell and other *Doctor Who* cast members made them, as did casts in shows such as *The Avengers* when it was on tape in the Cathy Gale years. In 'The Case of the Great Pearl Robbery' the young actor David Sumner badly blows one of his lines but recovers and keeps going.

In the early 1960s the producers of ITC's *Ghost Squad* called Delgado four times to guest star in episodes. The Ghost Squad is a mysterious branch of Scotland Yard, but the show had an American star, in this case the actor Michael Quinn. Quinn's career sank almost immediately without trace but *Ghost Squad* was popular and the haunting theme music, a distinctive whistle, was well known and much imitated. One of its stars, Claire Nielsen, thought the show was hit by being the right sort of show at the right time for audiences who 'thought it was very sophisticated, very action adventure, a bit boys' own; at that time they'd started to watch American programmes like *The Naked City* and things like that. I think they were quite proud it was a kind of British version of those kind of American action series.' Time has left some of it looking quite dated. 'It looks like the school nativity play!' is Nielsen's blunt verdict on seeing the white actors dashing around in Arab headdress.[329]

In 'Death from a Distance' Delgado is one of several foreigners plotting to kill an overseas head of state in London. The visiting head of state is played by John Le Mesurier, reminding us this jobbing actor could do straight just as well as he could do comedy. Le Mesurier's career is like a mirror of Delgado's. Just as critics and viewers were sometimes surprised to find Delgado, the expert in villainy, doing comedy, Le Mesurier's frequent appearances in comedy made people sit up and notice his straight roles.

Delgado plays a man financially ruined by this corrupt ruler. Delgado's character has a weak heart and dies half way through the episode. Part of the action is out at sea, as the foreign conspirators escape from a remote island on a boat and are rescued from the rough seas by a lighthouse crew. Thankfully, in long shot on location, the people lifted from the boat by ropes and pulleys are stuntmen. In close up the scenes with Delgado are in a studio with obvious back-projection. Later on making 'The Sea Devils' for *Doctor Who* Delgado was not so lucky and a notably seasick and aquaphobic actor found himself having to perform ridiculously challenging scenes out at sea.

He was an Arab, Sheik Ben Ali, in 'The Heir Apparent' that same season. We're treated to some superb physical acting from Delgado, including leaping out of a car boot and clutching his robe, bending low, and skulking around the bushes on the film location at the Edgwarebury Hotel near Elstree. In close-up his immaculate physical acting is on show when his nimble fingers carefully open a secret compartment in a ring and tip a drug into a glass of champagne.

His part in 'Quarantine at Kavar' was larger and more dynamic. Once more in a keffiyeh and with a false moustache glued to his lip, he plays the local police chief of a small, corrupt Middle Eastern sheikdom. One blogger on television heritage sums up his part with: 'The Emir's will is enforced by his cousin and chief of police Major Syid, played by the wonderful Roger Delgado, who frequently dons an enormous pair of sunglasses.'[330] Indeed he does! They are huge and practically performing in their own right as well as making Delgado look sinister and rather cool.

The earlier episodes of *Ghost Squad* were on 35mm film but by the time 'Quarantine at Kavar' entered production the show used videotape. Behind-the-scenes photographs show the actors rehearsing and acting on the cramped set of the electronic studios with the hot lights up in the grid blazing down on them. Once again the actors were under the pressure of getting the acting done in one take. The pressure of this type of production is so hard to fathom now but it shows the iron discipline and self-control of actors who had to fight down the natural urge to stop, laugh, or falter when something went wrong.

Indeed things could go wrong, even for Delgado. In a confrontation with Ghost Squad operative Craig (Quinn) Delgado says his dialogue and spins around sharply to make a dramatic exit; his keffiyeh flicks around, adding to the effect. Perhaps between the camera rehearsal and the take, someone has moved a table on the café set where the action takes place or else Delgado is slightly off his mark, because he bangs into the corner of the table. But his composure is absolute and the action continues. Delgado shoots out his hand, quickly moves the table back into position, and strides off the set.

On set with him was the young Scottish actress Claire Nielson, later to achieve television immortality playing one of the unsatisfied guests of Fawlty Towers. But here she plays 'Porridge', the Ghost Squad's secretary. Nielson recently rewatched *Ghost Squad* and it brought back many memories of making television in the 1960s. 'It was only people who were quite powerful who could demand a retake,' she reminds me. Of the mishap with the table, 'That was not meant,' she says, 'and if you look closely you can see Michael Quinn very slightly laughing. It would just have looked ridiculous if he had not corrected it, but that was not meant to happen.' But then, 'When he did that in the rehearsal room there was no table to bang into.'[331]

Around the time Delgado made his appearances in *The Protectors* and *Ghost Squad* the actor Rupert Davies caused quite a stir among actors, television engineers, and the readers of *Television Today* when he gave an interview complaining about how television was made in Britain. He was talking specifically about the BBC and *Maigret*, in which Delgado appeared twice and which was a massive success for the BBC with over nine million viewers.[332] But generally he was talking about television drama made on videotape in studios. His comments tell us more about the conditions in which Delgado and his colleagues were acting. It makes the achievements and professionalism of television actors in the early 1960s even more amazing.

'The strain on the actor in television is greater than on anyone else. There is nothing to compare with it,' Davies told the reporter Marjorie Bilbow. He was especially peeved by what he thought was the privileged place of the technicians and their equipment on the studio floor compared to the actors. 'The practical and technical side has now got so much control that when recording we constantly have to grind to a halt simply to move the blasted cameras around.' He also was unhappy that although broadcasts were no longer typically going out live, the recording sequence was still continuous, or with the recording following the order of the story. 'When plays were transmitted live – when viewers were actually watching what you were doing in the studio – it generated an atmosphere that helped your performance. There was tremendous studio discipline.' Oddly enough, rehearsals were quite generous. The actor and writer Jeremy Burnham thinks a major feature of making 1960s television was: 'We had a two or three week rehearsal period, so that one got to know the cast.'[333] Once in the studio, however, the pressure was on, which is what Davies was complaining about.

If he read the interview with Davies, Delgado could have nodded vigorously in recognition of all these points. He'd also had the opportunity to see at first hand other actors struggling dreadfully with recording conditions. When he appeared in 'The Disappearance of Lady Frances Carfax', Douglas Wilmer played Holmes. Although Wilmer's characterisation is acclaimed as one of the best and most authentic of small-screen Sherlocks, the production of this series was stressful. Acting with Delgado was Neil Stacy playing a hotel waiter, who remembered that Wilmer 'was completely thrown if any movement crossed his eyeline during a shot, and would simply stop acting. As cameras were constantly moving around to get in position for the next scene – because, although it wasn't live, the recording was organised as if it were – Douglas interrupted proceedings quite a bit, much to the director's frustration since videotape was then very expensive and people were reluctant to cut into it.'[334]

In short, Davies was not alone in feeling the pressure of making television. He was worried about 'bad rehearsal conditions', the fact rehearsals were getting longer and longer, and the intense pressure of recording in a studio where 'you've got to get used to any readjustments of position yourself and be as familiar as possible with the set and the position of the cameras by the time you perform'. Above all Davies complained of the 'deplorable surroundings' of television, including awful dressing rooms.[335] Against descriptions like this one, the occasional slip with dialogue or bashing into a table is forgivable. In circumstances like these, Delgado and colleagues performed miracles every time they achieved a take.

***

Another black-and-white part was a 1966 episode of the immensely popular office-based drama *The Power Game*, starring Patrick Wymark. The programme emerged out of *The Plane Makers* but shifted from a factory to a world of office-based corporate plotting in the City of London. Delgado appears throughout the episode 'The Front Men', playing an Arab businessman. He has dialogue to reflect this background, including pearls of wisdom like 'The wind of the desert blows cold,' and 'The Englishman has no monopoly of integrity.' His part is there to act as a dramatic opportunity for Wymark's antihero Sir John Wilder to be scheming and clever and by the end of the episode Delgado's character, who was attempting to do some corporate wheeling and dealing, is outsmarted by Wilder.

His neat goatee beard was by now almost always in evidence, part of what was making this villainous actor a recognisable face. His scenes in *The Power Game* provide an example of another characteristic of his performances, which is what we could call 'acting while standing with your back to the other character'. Delgado is far from being the only actor to have received direction to perform in this strange manner. It presumably was a means for a director to show that a conversation was particularly significant or dramatic. However, it does come up frequently in Delgado's performances and it is a credit to him to make such a silly arrangement work. Mendoza in *Sir Francis Drake* was another one who spoke with his back turned to the other person, as does the hotel manager in *Danger Man* and Don Esteban in *The Buccaneers*.

Throughout the 1960s, his work in adventure series balanced his roles in straight, dense, intense, television drama. In 1966 he appeared in *Court Martial* as a Mafioso in the episode 'The Liberators'. *Court Martial* was set during World War Two and, with an eye for the international market, it was a series about the US armed forces' Judge Advocate General and cast two Americans, Bradford Dillman and Peter Graves, in the leads as army investigators.

Some sturdy sets at Pinewood recreate Sicily in 1944. Delgado plays Salvatore Fratuzzi, henchman to a Mafia boss played by Paul Whitsun-Jones. By now, we are getting closer to 1970 and his casting as the Master and roles like this, small but powerful parts in good quality drama, give us background to both his performance and Barry Letts' decision to cast him.

For a start, there is a type of lethal courtesy in Salvatore as he goes around the Italian countryside with his gun intimidating peasants to keep quiet and not incriminate his boss in an upcoming military trial. He appears in a farmhouse and points his shotgun straight at the neck of a fragile, elderly lady. 'One tries to respect the elderly,' he says with vicious, insincere mocking courtesy. As he leaves, having delivered a threat, he pauses at the door, bows slightly and says, 'May you grow old in peace,' again with the same venomous courtesy that in a few years' time the Master will unleash on the Home Counties. At other points in the episode, he lurks in the shadows, plants bombs and shoots at people from a window, all very Master-like behaviour!

Studio-bound drama like *Court Martial* was static and talky and needed strong actors like Delgado to carry the story. However, at the same time, this serious drama displayed the performing strengths of character actors. The director of this episode of *Court Martial* was Alvin Rakoff, a Canadian who had been successfully directing British television drama since the 1950s. Having cast Delgado, Rakoff remembers he was 'one of those actors that directors rely on'. He was the sort of actor who would 'be there, hit the marks, say the lines as they should be said, and need little help from the director'.[336]

Despite the limitations of studio recording, directors of these programmes like Alvin Rakoff could also use their resources to put the actors in visually interesting settings. The surviving recording of *Court Martial* is not in good condition, but it shows how Rakoff uses the sets to frame the action, including the well-composed shot of characters outlined by the window of a peasant's cottage. Rakoff cuts from a cloth with the sinister Mafia symbol of the white hand to a shot of the plump hand of the Mafia boss and mayor grabbing at food on his table. With so much lost from the archives, other moments like this are gone, but wordy, static drama did have visual flair as well.

Throughout the decade, producers and directors had space on television to make serious, talky and static television drama in strands like *ITV Play of the Week*, *Armchair Theatre* and *The Somerset Maugham Hour*. Delgado appeared in all of them. Drama like this, long plays often an hour and a half long and driven by character and dialogue rather than action, surely come from an age when attention spans were longer. Much of the drama came from ABC's Teddington Studios, close to Delgado's house, which Honor Blackman remembers as a 'hotbed of new television drama'.[337]

Rakoff directed Delgado twice and contributed to all the major drama strands: *ITV Play of the Week, Armchair Theatre*, and the BBC's *Play of the Month* and *Sunday-Night Theatre* among others. Like other drama directors, Rakoff was making drama for a mostly middle-class audience who by the 1950s were buying television sets in larger and larger numbers. All broadcasters wanted an audience who would be saying to each other the next day 'Did you see that thing last night?', and who were watching serious drama, which was the 'main course', as Rakoff told me, of an evening's scheduling. Some lighter programming like a musical or variety work might have been the first course.[338] The many drama strands and the commitment to serious drama needed strong actors and Delgado's career is part and parcel of the outpouring of drama in the 1950s and 1960s.

In *The Crossfire* in 1967 (for *ITV Play of the Week*) Delgado was the Muslim Dr Si Cada. French Algeria was a set inside the television studio and the director John Jacobs brought together a strong cast including Ian Hendry, Peter Wyngarde and Eric Portman. The episode survives and is heavy-going viewing. A preview in *The Stage* provided this irresistible description of a play that 'describes the horrors and dilemmas undergone by the civilian population during the war' and they didn't exaggerate.[339]

The play's content was incredibly remote from a British television audience but is from a time of television's commitment to the serious drama that audiences would sit down after 9pm to watch. *TV Times* gave wide coverage to the production, including a cover picture of Portman and Jeanette Sterke in character and comment on the comparative rarity of Eric Portman's television appearances. The 'Playbill' column by Anthony David promised viewers a play about a European physician 'caught in the crossfire between European and Moslem extremists'.[340]

Not everything survives of Delgado's television work in this time and this drama is an opportunity to see him playing a totally straight role, different from the broader performances, complete with hand-waving and eye-popping, in the stylish but light-hearted adventure series. In 1967 he had been appearing before television cameras for nearly twenty years, and the small-scale, static production of *The Crossfire* shows how much his television technique has matured. In close-up his acting, especially his facial expressions, is nuanced and controlled. The whole production is impressive and shows the care that producers and directors put into their work. The final scene, when Eric Portman's character is shot, was set in the recreation hall of the hospital. The execution interrupts the archery practice of some disabled patients shooting from their wheelchairs. To add to the realism, the director cast actual disabled people in wheelchairs and brought in an archery coach. The scene only lasts a few seconds but the team making it was determined to reach the highest levels of quality possible.

Much of Delgado's 1960s television work was in small, cramped, stressful television studios but there were the occasional opportunities to venture further afield. In 1968 Delgado was taken to Malta to play another Mafia man in *Vendetta* (with this one, *Village of Daughters* and *Court Martial*, that's at least three times his gallery of villains included the Mafia). Directing him was the BBC veteran Roger Jenkins, who remembers working with a 'very nice man', but also doing Delgado a good turn. As Jenkins tells it, Delgado came up to the director during filming and 'whispered' he was not well. To save Delgado having to run about too much during a chase scene, Jenkins was able to cleverly cut together his shots so Delgado's character seemed to be moving from behind one bush to the next, but it avoided Delgado actually having to do any running.[341] It seems typical of Delgado's private, discreet personality that he would not want to make his ill health generally known, but also typical that colleagues were happy to oblige an actor who was himself so thoroughly helpful and professional.

✳✳✳

While there was time for serious drama, many of Delgado's appearances throughout the 1960s were in more lighthearted adventure series made by the independent companies, and in succession he worked his way through parts in *The Saint*, *The Avengers*, *Virgin of the Secret Service*, *The Champions*, *Man in a Suitcase*, *The Persuaders!* and *Jason King*.

The first of Delgado's encounters with Roger Moore is *The Saint* in 1962 and 1966. We are away from both the shoddy black-and-white ITC swash-bucklers made on the Danziger treadmill and the grim ITV drama and into much more glamorous settings. In 'The Golden Journey' in 1962 he has a brief part as a Spanish hotel manager on the Costa Brava. Moore's suave, manipulative Saint, Simon Templar, has an unusual mission in this episode. His best friend is getting married but his fiancée is an appalling spoilt brat and her aunt and the Saint together scheme to teach her a lesson. Templar sneaks into her room, steals her jewels, passport and money and manages to convince the hotel manager (Delgado) that she is actually a fraud who goes around hotels pretending she is the victim of robbery and borrowing large sums of money from sympathetic men.

The Saint is just setting her up so the manager throws her out of her hotel, which forces her to join him on a gruelling hundred-mile trek through the countryside. However, the manager is taken in and Delgado goes to town on exaggerated Hispanic gestures and looks. His eyes bulge in horror when he gasps, 'But she's got one of our best rooms!' as he sighs dramatically and flicks one of his hands in agitation.

By the time Delgado reappeared in *The Saint* the original stories by Leslie Charteris had run out and the series had switched to colour. Roger Moore had also abandoned his peculiar transatlantic accent.

In 'Locate and Destroy' Delgado is a South American policeman assisting the Saint to help Israeli agents run an old Nazi to earth. Initially Captain Rodrigues is unwilling to help. The former Nazi is the richest man in the area and has the local town under his thumb. The episode was an on-set reunion with not just Roger Moore but also John Barrie from *Sergeant Cork*. Rounding out the cast was Victor Beaumont, an actor who spent almost his entire career playing Nazis.

Playing Captain Rodrigues in his military uniform with epaulettes, Delgado also looks like the South American dictator he played in a very funny commercial for Foster Grant sunglasses. Running for just one minute, the commercial is a little gem of storytelling and humour. We see a group of soldiers inside a palace; outside, a crowd is cheering but sounds impatient. On the wall hangs a portrait of their leader: it is Delgado in a pair of sunglasses.

'I wonder what can be keeping him?' asks one of the soldiers, who goes to investigate. In the bedroom next door the dictator (Delgado) is frantically searching the room. 'But my sunglasses! I can't find them; where are my glasses!' despairs the dictator while making extravagant hand gestures.

His assistant grabs a telephone and orders a search and soon soldiers are running everywhere looking for the missing sunglasses, while the dictator searches through cupboards, through papers, under the bed and everywhere else to no avail. 'Perhaps I should tell the people that His Excellency is unavoidably detained,' murmurs the second-in-command and slips out of the room. As he does so, he pulls the missing sunglasses out of his pocket, puts them on and goes onto the balcony, where in a matter of moments the crowd hails him as the new leader. Doing the commercial was a bit of extra money but also exposure for Delgado. Playing the South American dictator was of a kind with the various foreign businessmen, soldiers and politicians that the independent companies kept giving him.

Like *The Saint, The Avengers* began as a black-and-white production but the budgets grew larger and the production more lavish. Delgado spans the beginning and end of the series. He appeared in a now lost black-and-white live episode from season one with Patrick Macnee and Ian Hendry and a colour film episode from the last season made with Patrick Macnee and Linda Thorson as Tara King.

Between Delgado's two appearances, budgets got bigger, production in studio on videotape changed to film, and black and white gave way to colour. Oddly, however, the scope of *The Avengers* contracted. Earlier black-and-white episodes with Macnee starring alongside Ian Hendry, Julie Stephens and Honor Blackman were more globetrotting and had settings such as Jamaica and Greece. By the shift to film and colour, *The Avengers* stuck to England and the Home Counties. Thus Delgado's first appearance is in 'Crescent Moon', made in black and white on tape but set in the Caribbean. His second, 'Stay Tuned', is set in London and made on film and in colour.

'Crescent Moon', like almost the entirety of season one of *The Avengers*, is lost. The transmission was live but only ABC viewers in the Midlands and the North could see it.[342] A tape recording was made, a copy was available and referred to in a memo in March 1962 but there has been no sign of it since.

The demands of live television were high for the people in front of and behind the cameras. On the 3rd and 4th of February 1961 Delgado was at the studios in Teddington (near to where he and Kismet would later move when they purchased White Cottage in Park Lane). The cast and crew had two days for camera rehearsals and at 10pm on the 4th the episode went out live.[343]

Nothing survives of the episode. It is not even clear to what the crescent moon in the title refers.[344] The listings promised viewers that: 'The disappearance of a beautiful wealthy young girl involves John Steed in a trip to a warmer clime,' and another refers to 'the Caribbean Island of Pascala, where a politician's beautiful daughter has been kidnapped'.[345]

There are no prizes for guessing that Delgado was a villain and a murderer. The story was set in the Caribbean, although as Hayes, McGinley and Hayes point out, the 'Caribbean' was almost definitely inside studio 2 at

Teddington.[346] Delgado's character, Vasco, was at the centre of a complicated plot about kidnapping a girl but someone double-crossed the original kidnapper and was murdered by Vasco who then kidnapped the girl himself. To judge from surviving records, Steed questioned Vasco and Delgado would have shared screen time with Patrick Macnee.[347] Delgado and Macnee had also appeared in *The Battle of the River Plate.*

It seems the episode was not a total success. The producer Leonard White thought the episode underran, a problem with a live broadcast he thought rehearsals should have solved; and clearly the plot, whatever it may have been, was too complicated. He instructed: 'I cannot over-emphasise the importance of clarity in our presentations.'[348] Memories from the time are of a programme pulled together against the odds and against the clock, which may account for scripting and timing problems. One of the directors of the early years of *The Avengers* was Roger Jenkins, who remembered knocking together an episode during a week's frantic activity. While he might have been able to start rehearsals on a Monday, Jenkins recalled that he only 'got to block the scenes on Thursday; the rest of the time they'd spent rewriting'.[349]

December 1968 brought Delgado back to *The Avengers* and his part in 'Stay Tuned' is his most Masterish part before *Doctor Who*. Close second may be Wirral, the evil, imprisoned hypnotist in *The Human Jungle*, a charming rogue whose dialogue like 'My dear fellow' was a precursor to the Master's courtesy; but Kreer takes us even nearer to the Master.

Delgado's character Kreer is a villainous master hypnotist plotting to put a complicated and nefarious scheme into operation. His base of operation is an innocuous-looking townhouse in which he hides secret equipment and surveillance devices like a two-way mirror.

Anyone who has watched both 'The Sea Devils' and 'Stay Tuned' may find his very violent sword fight with Tara brings to mind the duel between the Master and the Doctor at the end of episode two. The difference from the fight in *Doctor Who* is that Delgado and Linda Thorson did not have stunt doubles but did the fight themselves.[350] It is superbly choreographed and edited and very violent; coming at about halfway through the episode it is a dramatic peak of the story. Thorson gets two good fights in this episode, the other being with Kate O'Mara's character. That is a fist fight whereas Tara and Kreer fight with a deadly weapon: a walking cane hiding a nasty sharp sword inside it.

Steed has been kidnapped and brainwashed and has lost three weeks' worth of memory. He regains a few scraps of memory and finds a house that seems familiar. He and Tara knock on the door and a foreign-looking man opens it, but denies all knowledge of Steed's suggestions. The man is Kreer. Later that night Tara goes back to the house and breaks in. She finds a strange room with a large mirror, a chair, and chandelier that spins around emitting gentle but eerie noises. Kreer interrupts her when he opens the door and catches her out.

At the halfway mark of the episode, Delgado stands framed in the doorway wearing a velvet smoking-jacket and monocle and entirely dominates the scene. Linda Thorson recalled Delgado's willingness to rehearse properly, unlike some other guest stars on *The Avengers*.[351] The effort pays off as he transforms a brief part into an immaculate featured performance. He swaggers slightly and flexes his narrow walking cane, his fingers gently toying with it as he shuts Tara in and menacingly asks, 'Do you like my room?'

The most Masterish moment though is not the hypnotism, not the complicated plot or the classy clothes but the vicious snarl during the fight. A wary, edgy conversation ends when Delgado suddenly bursts into action, viciously swiping Tara with his cane. Delgado's colleagues remember a warm, generous and blood-chilling man, whose enactment of villainy was so strong Katy Manning found herself almost hypnotised for real. People were amazed at the evil that could project from Delgado's lovely, kind eyes. He could change the ambience of a scene by projecting evil; when working with him the actress Damaris Hayman noticed, 'He's just very good at being a villain. He could produce a very sinister aura about himself.'[352]

However, the snarl is something else. A vicious lip curl, his face contorted in fury and his eyes flaring with insane anger, is how Delgado looks when a camera cuts into close-up of his face when fighting with Tara. We get to see that snarl again in a couple of years at the end of 'Terror of the Autons' when the Master finds his way up the gantry of a radio telescope blocked by a technician. Barry Letts' film camera cuts in close to Delgado's snarling face as his hands lunge out, grab the technician and fling him down to his death.

***

Much of his work for the independent companies was as foreign villains but there was variety, and *The Champions* cast him as a foreign good guy. *The Champions* lasted one year and thirty episodes. Its gimmick was the supernatural Tibetan powers possessed by the three agents of Nemesis, played by William Gaunt, Stuart Damon and Alexandra Bastedo. They are telepathic and superhuman.[353] As viewers and critics at the time and since point out, the series itself looked less stunning than its good-looking young cast.

Delgado is in a late episode set in the Middle East but as usual made in England with some file footage. For most of the episode Delgado is on one set, a conference room where his character is presiding over a peace conference. Delgado is an Arab, Yussef, one of many roles when he appeared with a keffiyeh wrapped around his head, although a bomb goes off in his face and blows the keffiyeh away!

He is also one of the good guys when he appears as a charming and humane South American ambassador in 'Burden of Proof' in the 1968 series *Man in a Suitcase*. Playing the diplomat, he was offering a straight version of a character type he had previously offered in 'James Bond – Where Are You?' for Harry Worth's show, but here the performance is serious. As with *Ghost Squad*, ITC brought out an American leading man, this time Richard Bradford, who punched his way through each episode playing a disgraced CIA agent and whose nervy, twitchy method acting and sexiness contrasted with the British character actors guest-starring in his show.

The main guest star of this episode was not, however, Delgado but the film star John Gregson, who like Delgado had received a Catholic education, had stints in rep and armed forces, but had then had a flourishing career as a leading man in British cinema including *Genevieve*. In *Man in a Suitcase* he plays Henry Faversham, a British advisor to the President of an unnamed South American country who has fled the country stealing almost the entirety of the government's money. It's actually an elaborate plot to force Colonel Felipe Garcia, the head of the secret police, to show his hand planning a coup against the President by stealing back the money to bribe the army into rebelling.

Delgado is the Ambassador to London for this country and is the epitome of civilisation compared to the brutal Colonel Garcia and his henchman/torturer. An unseemly brawl erupts in the lobby of the embassy when the Ambassador's chauffeur uses the racial slur 'Indio' against the half-breed Colonel and his henchman and the henchman throws him across the room.

'You're not in Capulco prison now!' says the Ambassador angrily, and shows courtly grace to Mrs Carla Faversham, who also arrives in London to try to discover what her husband is up to.

The acting weight in the episode is with Wolfe Morris. Morris specialised in sweaty, thuggish villainy, unlike his brother Aubrey who specialised in grotesque eccentrics. Morris's Colonel Garcia beats and tortures Faversham, displaying the same kind of brutal desperate evil as he did in the next decade in *The Sweeney* when he tortured and kidnapped a police driver's wife. In contrast, Delgado is coolly charming and entirely contemptuous of his visitors from the homeland. It's also a rare instance of a flat performance. Perhaps on this occasion there wasn't enough from an underwritten part to spark Delgado's creativity and the usual excitable and vivid foreignness fails to come over.

Delgado was also one of the goodies in the episode of *Randall and Hopkirk (Deceased)* called 'The Ghost who Saved the Bank at Monte Carlo'. This episode from 1969 is an example of intersecting Venn diagrams. Nicholas Courtney plays a villain, the same year that production began on season seven of *Doctor Who* with Courtney as a regular cast member. Mary Merrall plays a batty old lady, similar to her part in *The Belles of St Trinian's* when we saw her on the railway platform with Princess Fatima and Delgado as the Sultan's Aide.

We first see Delgado lurking in the background at the casino; but as Tapiro, the manager of the very posh casino, he is a suave character who speaks charmingly to the old lady. Contrary to initial expectations, he is also not one of the bad guys who are filling up the casino because the old lady has the unnatural ability to win at cards and roulette. 'I am on your side,' he insists and it turns out he is telling the truth. Delgado is also in charge of a bevy of glamorous female bodyguards, one of whom holds the bad guys at bay with her revolver.

Many of these series are 'glossy', meaning not just the glamour of the costumes, settings and women, but the fact they are on film. *Virgin of the Secret Service* was more limited, trying to recreate Edwardian imperial adventures in black and white and on videotape. Delgado guested in the episode 'The Rajah and the Suffragette' alongside the series' stars Clinton Greyn and Veronica Strong. When I asked Strong about the series, it brought back all kinds of unpleasant memories. 'I try very hard not to remember,' is her main recollection of *Virgin of the Secret Service*, as 'the whole thing was a ghastly experience'. Delgado, though, is remembered as a valuable on-set addition to a 1960s British TV series trying to evoke Edwardian India, and he displayed an unexpected and unusual talent: 'He was the only one who knew how to tie a sari; the costume department had no idea.'[354] Thinking back to Delgado's war service on the subcontinent, when he took the time and effort to learn Urdu, I also wonder if that was when he picked up his skill with the sari?

We're back to colour and glamour in 1972 in 'The Stones of Venice', an episode of *Jason King*. A successor to the colourful *Department S*, the credits are full of names of people who had been employing Delgado or working with him for years. Monty Berman, who oversaw *The Saint*, was in charge of production. A funky theme tune was provided by Laurie Johnson. The director Jeremy Summers had previously cast Delgado in *Randall and Hopkirk*.

In 'The Stones of Venice' Delgado was at the MGM-EMI studios as part of a cast with the 'Countess of Cleavage' herself, Imogen Hassall. He plays the Venetian police inspector who gets to lock Peter Wyngarde's Jason King in a cell and interrogate him. It's an arch and broad performance and the inspector is offended that King's adventure involving a kidnapped girl and jewellery robbery has been taking place without his knowledge. 'You embark on an adventure incorporating robbery, murder, espionage, and you don't say a word to me!'

Interlude
The Man of a
Thousand Voices

T HE ACTUAL MAN of a thousand voices was Lon Chaney Snr, who made the transition to the talkies shortly before his death in 1930 and whose vocal ability matched his skill with make-up.[355] Delgado may not exactly have had a thousand voices, but to play all these nationalities Delgado had the swarthy skin, goatee and piercing eyes, and the ability to switch from accent to accent.

Delgado so often performed in a foreign accent and his diversity is astonishing. Sometimes he was an Arab. Other times he was French. In a game of poker with Roger Moore in *The Persuaders!* he was a Spaniard, as he was in swashbucklers. In *Battle of the River Plate* he was Uruguayan and he was three different nationalities in turn in *Scotland Yard*. He also played Nazis and Italian criminals, Czechs and Albanians. Victor Pemberton asked Delgado to play a Chilean scientist in *The Slide* for BBC Radio and knew he was getting an actor whose 'dialect was good'.[356]

He first performed with an accent when he played a Frenchman for the Edward Nelson Company and he had studied French during his brief time at the London School of Economics. He also came from a multilingual household and grew up hearing the French and Spanish accents of his parents and their friends.

Try watching a series of his foreign-accented performances in a row. It is fascinating to see the care he put into making accents. For example, there are his roles as Laki in *Richard the Lionheart* and Hasmid in *The Mummy's Shroud*. Between them, his Arabic accent gets more exaggerated. By contrast his Spanish and Mexican accent repeats almost without change across parts as the Mexican Consul in *First Man into Space*, Pedro de Cortinez in *The Singer Not the Song* and Estoban in *The Persuaders!* Delgado's French accent gets a good workout as policemen in *Sergeant Cork* and *Maigret* and the casino manager in *Randall and Hopkirk (Deceased)*.

Some other actors had the same gift to keep an accent intact. The husky Hispanic accent Patrick Troughton used to play the evil Mexican scientist Salamander in 'The Enemy of the World', a *Doctor Who* story, was the same as the accent he had used to play an Argentinian police inspector in *The Saint* a few years earlier. For Kenneth Williams, his voices were like a rack of clothes from which he could select the 'snide' voice, the rustic Rambling Syd voice, or the wheezy American voice, amongst others.

His co-stars remember in Delgado a man who meticulously prepared his roles and absorbed himself in his parts, and that included the development of his accents. There was a great deal to distinguish between his Mexican, Spanish or French accents. Watching his posture and his mouth shows the range of his talent. For example, in *The Rivals of Sherlock Holmes* he is wheelchair-bound but also leaning back in the wheelchair when he speaks and producing the voice from the back of his mouth while keeping his chin down and restricting the movement of his top lip.

His Spanish and Hispanic accent is also the product of careful technique. He softens his plosives when speaking. The Aragonese Ambassador in *The Adventures of Robin Hood* comes out with changes to his plosives such as 'ging' for 'king'. The Spanish sea captain in *The Buccaneers* is again an accent achieved with soft plosives like 'bassenger' for 'passenger'. When saying words like 'captain' Delgado stretches his lower lip to produce 'capteyn'. To produce the 'r' sound he sometimes come out with 'err' by holding the sides of his tongue against his upper lateral teeth. Alternatively, he comes out with a rolled 'r' when the tip of his tongue is behind his top teeth.[357]

If all of that sounds rather involved, it just shows that working out an accent for a performance was a vital creative decision and a lot of work and technique. Delgado's bag of tricks as an actor had a lot in it: sword fighting, riding, use of his hands, as well as the voices. It was also vital in an era of intense drama production for the BBC and the independent companies where British actors frequently played foreign parts in European drama and directors needed to ensure there was consistency in how the actors were performing. The prolific director Alvin Rakoff is familiar with the process of actors coming up with and rehearsing with an accent, where actors would bring an accent to the director, who could then either okay it or ask for a change.[358]

For his acting, Delgado occasionally ventures into other accent territory, such as the German hotel manager Von Golling in *Danger Man* and the Gestapo man in *Long Way Home*, and his German accent is just a very light overlay over his normal voice. He tries for Patagonian in Disney's *In Search of the Castaways* and a Uruguayan in *Battle of the River Plate*.

Curiously, his weakest attempt at a foreign accent is when he is pretending to be the Greek scientist Professor Thascales in 'The Time Monster', a *Doctor Who* story. His Greek accent is very indeterminate and he is in danger of it slipping away. It comes as a relief when he stops having to pretend to be the Professor and can revert to his normal voice. For the man of many voices, was a Greek accent just a step too far?

In using an accent it was important that the intention come across right. A comedy accent like he uses as Abdul the carpet-seller in *The Sandwich Man* is fine because the film is a comedy. In serious works, it is also important that his voice not undercut the seriousness. Apart from Professor Thascales, Delgado was successful in matching the accent with the tone of the production.

Not all his co-stars were so successful. Sir Laurence Olivier played the Mahdi in *Khartoum*, in which Delgado had a small part. Time has not been kind to Olivier's efforts. 'His stab at a Sudanese accent sounds like Sebastian, the singing Caribbean crab from Disney's *The Little Mermaid*, pretending to be a Russian spy. "Oh, beylovvids!" he says to his beloved followers. "I am the Mahrhrhdi! The Exxxxpected One!"' is how the reviewer Alex von Tunzelmann eviscerates Larry's performance.[359]

Sometimes Delgado just had to be inventive. After all, who actually knows what Jews in the Holy Land sounded like in AD60? That was his part in an episode of *Paul of Tarsus* in 1960 and he had to come up with an accent to make it work. Sometimes this man of many voices did not even get to use his. Robert Rietty was an actor more often heard than seen and he dubs over Delgado's dialogue in *Khartoum*. Big, glossy films of the era dubbed the actors and most of the leading roles in the Sean Connery Bond films were dubbed over. Even well-spoken performers like Alexander Knox had their voices replaced by dubs.

The other point about Delgado's voice is how cultivated it was. While his vocal range was considerable, he rarely ventured into anything less than well-modulated tones. His impersonation of a cockney space pilot over a radio in 'Frontier in Space' is good but also a rare instance of Delgado using a working-class accent. More typical is a comment like: 'The autobiographical commentary is delivered, in impeccable English, by Roger Delgado.'[360]

His well-spoken voice, however, was no impediment to finding work throughout his career, even though 1960s stage, film and especially television has been called the age of kitchen-sink drama. *Cathy Come Home* appeared on the BBC in 1966 and followed *Up the Junction*, an instalment of the *Wednesday Play*. Frank Finlay looked back on the time as one when actors stopped trying to lose their regional accents and drama schools 'had a full-time voice coach teaching the students how to sound as if they came from up north'.[361]

But the age of kitchen-sink is far from absolute. Even Sydney Newman pointed out that the reputation of his drama for 'a lot of kitchen sinkery' was overstated and Delgado's services were required in other types of productions including the single plays.[362] He made his contribution to Newman's signature drama strand *Armchair Theatre* in the 1960 production *A Heart and a Diamond* with Joseph Furst playing the dissolute ex-King Gustavus III and was part of a plot about jewellery theft. Being posh in the 1960s did not harm his career.

Delgado's absence from kitchen-sink drama is a reminder of the sort of actor he was. There was no need for him, or no space for him, in the world of kitchen-sink. Others – Albert Finney, Richard Harris, Queenie Watts, Rachel Roberts and indeed William Hartnell – were part of that world, but Delgado stayed put in period and fantasy settings in film and television and farce on stage. By 1970 he was getting ready to play a smooth-talking villain.

Part Two
The defining role

ELGADO CONTINUED TO turn up at Elstree or Pinewood for glossy adventure series into the early 1970s including *Jason King* and *The Persuaders!* But March 1970 was a career-defining moment for Delgado. The jobbing actor is about to become a regular. The man of many voices can pack away all his different nationalities and all their funny gestures to play something totally new: an alien renegade and master villain.

His former acting colleague Barry Letts and the writer Terrance Dicks are planning the eighth season of *Doctor Who*. Chatting about it in the BBC bar, they decide they need a 'wow' factor to kick it off. They need an enemy, and bit by bit an idea forms. He will be a Time Lord, but an evil one; he'll be arrogant enough to call himself 'The Master'; and Letts knows with crystal-clear insight exactly who will play the role.

Chapter Fifteen
Creating the Master
1970-1971

T
HE MASTER MAKES his debut in the creepy, macabre 'Terror of the Autons'. The first scene is the Master leaping out of his TARDIS which is disguised as a horsebox. At the end of 'The Dæmons', six months later, the army drives the Master away in the back of a UNIT jeep into custody. In the interim, the character had appeared in all season eight stories and in almost every episode. The Master became a hit with audiences.

Viewers could have known what to expect had they paid five pence and been reading the January 2nd to 8th edition of *Radio Times*. For the *Radio Times* Pertwee, Delgado, Manning and Courtney along with Bessie, the Doctor's car, posed at Rossini's circus in a photoshoot for the magazine's cover to introduce the new season and the new regular cast joining Pertwee. Delgado's face dominated a cover that said: 'Jo Grant is the Doctor's new girl companion and she's in trouble from the start, hypnotised by the Master.' A picture of Jo has her saying in her speech bubble, 'I shall obey!' while the Master, looking menacing and tight-lipped, is saying, 'I am usually referred to as the Master'. A much smaller picture of Pertwee is saying, 'That jackanapes! All he ever does is cause trouble.'

Inside the *Radio Times* there were short interviews with Delgado, Pertwee and Letts. Given how big the picture of Delgado was on the cover and how small the picture of Pertwee, it was just as well that inside the article reported that Pertwee was 'the Leading Man rather than the Star and his approach automatically fosters "the community spirit" rather than any kind of hierarchy'.[363]

Behind the scenes the reality was quite different and Jon Pertwee was miffed. In his memoirs, the producer Barry Letts remembered that Pertwee was put out by the different sizes of the pictures.[364] The star's reaction to the *Radio Times* cover also remains fresh in Terrance Dicks' memory, and he told me: 'Pertwee was not at all pleased about this and he came to Barry and said, "Look, people are saying to me is it true you're giving it up and Roger Delgado is doing it," so we had to sort that out and calm him down.'[365]

One year into his tenure by the start of season eight, Pertwee was an authoritative figure in the rehearsal room and in the studio. One anecdote tells of him ripping out the pages of script without dialogue for the Doctor and remarking, 'It's a thin script this week.'[366] It was in these circumstances that Delgado joined *Doctor Who* to be the antagonist but where the routines of production and the scale of the lead actor's ego were set firmly in place.

By the time the January 1971 *Radio Times* cover appeared, the whole team was down in Dungeness in Kent filming for 'The Claws of Axos'. By that time, Delgado and Pertwee had been working together for months and those they were working with saw a strong professionalism between them. Timothy Combe came on board in season eight to direct 'The Mind of Evil' and had heard: 'The rumour was that Jon Pertwee felt a little bit inadequate, not being a trained actor, doing his shows and light entertainment at the BBC and things like that; and there was Roger Delgado, and I think Jon felt he wasn't a real actor like Roger was a real actor.' However, he continues: 'I never came across that; I always felt that the two of them, when they did a scene together, worked together, respected each other's ideas and it was a very, very happy show, that I directed.'[367]

It is true their careers had been very different. Pertwee had a higher star profile and higher billings, but was also 'comedian Jon Pertwee' and there was a strong variety, guitar-playing streak in his career.[368] Had Pertwee at any point ever felt upstaged, it's worth remembering that some years later the next Doctor, Tom Baker, was equally annoyed about the attention given to his small robot companion, K9, and the concern of the leading man for his leading-man status is not to be wondered at.[369]

The comments inside *Radio Times* from Delgado and the comments about his character are brief but have been influential. Here we read that the

Master is 'more than a Moriarty' and a foil to the Doctor. We also learn that Delgado thought his typecasting could be a hindrance. 'He's wary of a past history of heavily accented foreign baddies inevitably ending up in pinewood boxes.'

Delgado reminisced about having to deliver the line, 'Come in and put your feet up on the Algerian poof,' in a Midday Matinee many years earlier.[370] The article overall was a short piece suggesting that making *Doctor Who* was rather fun and there are stories about Pertwee appearing in a pub still in costume and being recognised by a fan in Morocco.

***

These comments all refer to 'Terror of the Autons' so let's backtrack slightly from its debut and its *Radio Times* cover to the steps that brought Delgado into the show and working with Pertwee and the rest of the team. Episode one aired on January 2nd 1971 and featured the debut of not only the Master but also the Doctor's new assistant Jo Grant and Captain Mike Yates. The BBC contracted Delgado by March 1970 and he was recording by September that year, but the ideas for a possible Time Lord adversary were percolating earlier.

Behind the scenes, a new level of editorial coherence was defining production. Before then, and especially during the Troughton era, the role of producer and script editor had changed hands in a way likened to a game of musical chairs between Innes Lloyd, Peter Bryant, Victor Pemberton and Derrick Sherwin. Production was rushed and exhausting with videotaping happening only weeks before broadcast.

By 1969 Troughton was desperate to leave, not only to avoid typecasting but because he found the role intolerably exhausting. The Pertwee era, barring one story and that being Pertwee's first, was entirely under the editorial control of producer Barry Letts and script editor Terrance Dicks. Their consistent tenure allowed for levels of editorial depth not previously seen. Along with the partnership of Philip Hinchcliffe and Robert Holmes, the Letts/Dicks partnership is the closest that the classic era of *Doctor Who* comes to matching the creative impact of showrunners Russell T. Davies and Steven Moffat.

Letts and Dicks had the freedom to act on their ambitions for *Doctor Who*; and their biggest plans were for the 1971 season opener, where a new adversary, a new companion, a new character Captain Yates and to an extent a new format would all come together. The new companion was Jo Grant, with Katy Manning cast in what was her second acting role.

Manning joined a show with a producer who had big ambitions. What stays in her mind from when she joined is Letts's ambition for 'taking *Doctor Who* to the next level, which is what it's always had to do. You've got to keep upping the ante, you can't just keep it plateaued.'[371]

Another cast member, John Levene, playing the UNIT soldier Sergeant John Benton, also thought the show got a lift from new cast members, especially with Delgado and Manning coming in together and having an impact as both performers and people: 'When Roger joined it was so incredible; and Katy Manning with her bubbliness, and her absolute lack of all the bullshit you get from some English and American actors, she just came in as normal and as beautifully accurate as a performer you could dream of; so suddenly we've got this core, we've Jon Pertwee, we've got Katy Manning... It suddenly turned out it was just a magnetic force that seemed to have captivated the cast of *Doctor Who* with Jon leading it with such gusto.'[372]

An energetic leading man and new cast members including a new villain combined with Barry Letts's determination to make *Doctor Who* take several steps forward. Letts, in Manning's view, showed his awareness that 'it needed to go to the next stage and it became a little edgier'. Part of the edginess was the deliciously macabre violence in 'Terror of the Autons' but also a slightly better budget for special effects. Manning also remembers a change in what some of the cast looked like, particularly the UNIT soldiers led by the Brigadier. 'When I joined *Doctor Who* many, many changes took place; they wore real uniforms... You took the Brigadier out of his banana republic paper badge hat and put them into real army uniforms.' The changes were the results of a determined producer as Letts 'fought very hard to get these things in place, he really championed the show to the next level'.[373]

By 1971 the show was growing up, getting a bit bigger, a bit more exciting, and a bit nastier. These ambitions to keep *Doctor Who* stepping up to new standards and new levels bring us to Roger Delgado. His casting remains fresh in Terrance Dicks's memory, who recalls that it all went 'like clockwork'. Season seven was finished and they were in search of the 'wow factor for the first show of the season'. Like many good ideas, this one comes from a few drinks, in this case the bar at the BBC. Terrance said to Barry, 'Look, Barry, what he needs is a Moriarty. He needs another Time Lord of equal rank and talent, but on the bad side, not the good side.' Dicks remembers Letts' response was, '"Terrific, what a great idea," and he said, "I know just the actor to play him: Roger Delgado."' [374]

Their next conversation on their new character concerned his name. Again the thought processes of the creative team are clear in Dicks's memory: 'Barry said, "What shall we call him?" and I couldn't think of anything; we talked on the spot, but next day I came in and said, "Look, I've got it: we'll call him the Master," which is analogous to the master of a Cambridge college, and also has the right tones of arrogance.' [375]

It all happened very quickly and Dicks also remembers that Delgado accepted the part with alacrity. It was a good time to get ongoing television work. From time to time the British film industry collapses and 1970 was one of those times. Nice bits of film work like that for *The Assassination Bureau* would start drying up as American companies withdrew money from British films, a move that hit directors like Basil Dearden hard. [376] Television had always given Delgado his best work and now was a good time to become absorbed in a regular TV role.

Between them, Dicks and Letts thought up the Master. Next Robert Holmes wrote the scripts for 'Terror of the Autons', which not only had to introduce the Master, Jo and Yates but also showcase the return of season seven's Autons. His brief was the Doctor's Moriarty, an idea he gave flesh to with what Letts called the Master's 'little clevernesses', or those sure signs he is an arch-criminal such as his hypnotism and 'turning people into little mannequins about six inches long'. [377]

***

Rehearsals and recording of 'Terror of the Autons' took place in September 1970 and filming began in Buckinghamshire and Bedfordshire. In the guest cast were a host of reliable character actors. Stephen Jack played the gruff Mr Farrel senior, Barbara Peake his wife, John Baskcombe (reuniting with Delgado after they appeared in *Sergeant Cork*) was the criminal showman Russell and Michael Wisher the younger and easily manipulated Farrel. The regular cast was a mixture of old and new. Pertwee, Nicholas Courtney (the Brigadier) and John Levene returned from the previous year. The young actors Katy Manning and Richard Franklin now became regulars, playing Jo and Captain Mike Yates.

Manning was very new and the set-up was daunting. 'It was lots of firsts for me; I'm meeting Jon Pertwee, I'm meeting Nick Courtney and I'm going to meet Roger Delgado and I've never been so scared in my life.' Surrounded by experienced character actors she felt 'in such awe of these people and I didn't have years of experience behind me like they did'.[378] What is equally clear was the kindness and professional generosity of her new co-stars, including Pertwee who told off a crew member for making jokes at Manning's expense when she was injured. 'Their generosity towards me was bar none.' Thinking of why colleagues universally admired and liked Delgado, she considered: 'You couldn't not: he was funny, and caring and charitable and generous, as an actor extremely generous.' Of course, Pertwee and Delgado were like father figures to her.

The first the audience sees of the Master is the confrontation between him and Lew Russell at the circus, but as usual the filming was done out of narrative sequence, and the first moments of the Master captured on film are of he and Farrel finding Jo sneaking around the plastics factory, and Jo falling under hypnotic influence. Delgado, so his co-stars found, was the sweetest and gentlest of men but once in character the kindness vanished and the evil hypnotism almost became real for Katy Manning: 'I have to tell you, the first time he looked into my eyes to hypnotise me, I nearly went under; those eyes were incredible.'[379]

With rehearsals, filming and recording completed, the Master landed on earth on January 2nd 1971 in the first seconds of episode one of 'Terror of the Autons'. In this world Delgado's impact is immediate. He leaps out of his TARDIS and spends a couple of moments looking appraisingly at the exterior, subtly indicating the Master's awareness that his TARDIS's cloaking device has worked. Within moments the audience has seen both his hypnotic ability and his violent streak. He mesmerises the thug Lew Russell and breaks into a museum.

Any performance is a combination of factors, not least the actor but also the writer giving him lines, the costume designer giving him a look, the director providing guidance and the composer giving him music. Robert Holmes's script bestowed some brilliant lines upon Delgado. After his first scene, the Master does not speak again until sixteen minutes into the episode. By then he has had a change of costume from the high-collared dark suit to a neat tweed coat and tie, posing as the businessman Colonel Masters. At this point Holmes gives the Master one of his best lines: 'The people I represent, Mr Farrel, can never get enough plastic,' he remarks apparently innocently, but the line is also an elegant reintroduction to the alien Nestene and a sign of the Master's wicked sense of humour.

His very best line comes in episode two. The Master and Farrel are coolly working out the best way to use plastic to murder thousands of people, and the latest idea is a large black plastic chair that folds in on itself and suffocates its occupant. The chair itself is quintessentially 1970s. The design is also lethal, as the assistant manager of the plastics factory shortly discovers when he sits down in the chair and it smothers him to death. Later on, speaking of the man's demise, the Master coolly explains: 'Yes, he sat down in this chair here, and just slipped away.'

The way the Master kills is also a gift for Delgado. The violence unleashed in 'Terror of the Autons' is a mixture of the subtle, the straightforward bangs and flashes of action scenes, and the freakish, with Delgado's Master as its orchestrator.[380] The Master murders Goodge by shrinking him with a weapon later called the Tissue Compression Eliminator. The Master posthumously humiliates the scientist by leaving the shrunken corpse in Goodge's own lunchbox, an appropriate end for a man whose last moments had included complaining about and then eating his lunch. Phillips's death is more ordinary but very brutal; he is blown away by a bomb and we last see his bloodied corpse lying on the ground while Jo looks away in distress. In the most horrible sequence of the serial, a plastic troll doll strangles Mr Farrel Senior to death. He falls out of view behind a sofa but to make sure the children are really traumatised the camera shows Farrel's leg twitching and jerking as the troll squeezes the life out of him, followed by an abrupt close-up on Mrs Farrel screaming.

Looking back at this collection of macabre and outlandish deaths, Katy Manning remembers the story as one with 'everything that every child could find very scary'.[381] Manning also remembers how Holmes's scripts and his methods of despatching people chimed so well with current popular culture, for the troll dolls 'were very fashionable little items for children to have then' and it was an era of 'people calling at the doors with plastic daffodils to sell their washing powders'.[382]

The renegade Time Lord is neatly dressed from head to toe in black; he even has the ability to snap his fingers while wearing black leather gloves.

Ken Trew created the patrol-collared suit in August 1970.[383] The appearance of both the Doctor and the Master prompts an interesting comparison in the study of television design by Piers Britton and Simon Baker. They look back to nineteenth-century French art to suggest that, with beard and smart clothes, the Master looked like the depiction of Mephistopheles by Eugene Delacroix, presumably the painting of Faust with Mephistopheles.[384]

There is a frisson between the Doctor and the Master because of their clothes. Towards the end of 'Terror of the Autons' the Master has the Doctor captive and is about to kill him. 'I have so few worthy opponents. When they've gone, I always miss them,' says the Master as he prepares to fire. Their clothes are a sign of that worthy rivalry. Pertwee's Doctor is the only incarnation of the classic era to dress with style and finesse. Hartnell looked like the Wizard of Oz, Troughton and Tom Baker were scruffy, and Davison, Colin Baker and Sylvester McCoy all looked eccentric. Pertwee, however, was Savile Row. The most stylish Doctor is given an adversary his intellectual *and* style equal and Pertwee's capes and lace contrasted with the Master's minimalist style. In balance against the Master's introduction in dark suit and black leather gloves, Trew added much more colour to the Doctor's outfit, introducing a claret-coloured smoking jacket and adding a bright purple satin lining to the Doctor's cape.[385] The Doctor had a style rival in a way not seen again until the confrontation between David Tennant's Doctor and the Master, dressed in an elegant red-lined overcoat when pretending to be Prime Minister Saxon.

Finally, there is the music, in this case provided by Dudley Simpson who composed the 'Master' theme heard when the Master hypnotises Russell. Simpson used the theme, described by the musicologist Emily Kausalik as 'an augmented fourth outlined over three pitches', throughout season eight to uncanny effect.[386]

***

From September 1970 when filming of 'Terror of the Autons' began to May 1971, when recording of 'The Dæmons' concluded at the Television Centre, Delgado was continuously occupied playing the Master. Across the whole of his career, it was his best run of work since his season in Leicester in 1939-1940. The continuation of the Master beyond 'Terror of the Autons' meant the role was his first continuing as opposed to one-off part since playing the

Spanish Governor in *Sir Frances Drake* in 1961 and 1962. For *Doctor Who* audiences, it meant the Doctor had his intellectual equal on the scene and things were more interesting and a lot more fun.

Chapter Sixteen
The Mind of Evil

'THE MIND OF EVIL' allows Delgado to play the Master playing Professor Emil Keller, a scientific genius who has invented the 'Keller Machine'. The machine sucks out 'negative or evil impulses' from the neural circuits in the brains of criminals incarcerated in Stangmoor Prison. Some of the story repeats what we have already seen Delgado do in 'Terror of the Autons'. There is an alias, the dupes, victims of hypnosis to be temporary assistants, and a temporary alliance with the Doctor when the Master's plot gets totally out of control. But the director Timothy Combe was ambitious, so was the writer Don Houghton and so was Delgado.

Given the material in Don Houghton's script to show the audience more, Delgado delivers the goods. Somehow, the Master has acquired a chauffeur-driven Daimler and he swanks about being chauffeur-driven, smoking massive cigars, and wearing a fur coat.

Delgado again gets some good comedy. In one scene in the limousine, sinister music is playing. Initially the viewers could think it is part of the incidental music and appropriate to the menacing character of the Master. Then the Master switches off the radio and we realise it was a music track he was listening to and clearly didn't like, in this case a track by King Crimson band members.[387] These little touches, even the fact the Master has a radio and listens to music, add to the character. You couldn't say it 'humanises' him, as he's an inhuman killer, but you get the point there's a real live personality underneath the villainy.

Delgado gets a script that marks a change of pace for him. Within seconds of 'Terror of the Autons' beginning the Master was taking direct and dynamic action in hypnotising Russell and breaking into the museum to steal the Nestene Globe. In 'The Mind of Evil' he is more a background figure and Delgado's development of the character is consequently the more fascinating. In 'Terror of the Autons' he was dynamic and immediate, but here he has spun a web. Delgado only appears sparingly in the second episode, although he is in his luxury car and by the end of the episode he has hypnotically ordered a Chinese peace-conference delegate, Captain Chin Lee, to commit a murder.

By holding back on his appearances across the first half of the six-part story, 'The Mind of Evil' gives Delgado the chance to do more with the character. Near the beginning, he gives an immaculate yet wordless performance as he changes from his disguise as a telephone engineer into his smart suit and fur coat. His hands slick back the hair from his temples, minutely adjust the tie and pocket handkerchief and then he strolls through a park to his Daimler. Off-screen we also get to know more about what the Master has been up to in the year or more since the events with the Autons. When masquerading as Professor Keller we learn from Captain Chin Lee that he was hobnobbing at an embassy function, and it creates an intriguing further impression of the Master's suaveness and social life.

By episode three what seem to have been two separate stories of a threatened world peace conference and the scientific experiments at Stangmoor Prison come together. By this point the Master has also arrived at the prison in his limousine, organised a prison riot and occupied the Prison Governor's office, installing himself comfortably behind the desk.

By inviting Delgado back for each story in season eight the producer, script editors and writers had a hitherto unprecedented chance to build character, show impact and make connections. For only his second story, Delgado was fortunate that the writer and the script editor were taking care with his character. Pik-Sen Lim, who played Captain Chin Lee, was in a good position to be aware of the scripting of the Master in the story 'The Mind of Evil' because her husband Don Houghton was writing it and working with Dicks on the character of the Master. Thinking back to the story outline and the writing, her memory was that when working on the character of the Master 'there wasn't fully a blueprint'. Instead, Houghton and Dicks were thinking 'what was the most feasible, interesting way for the both of them, the writer and the story editor, to take the character onwards.'[388]

In 'The Mind of Evil' we also get to see more of the Master and Doctor together and therefore to see Delgado and Pertwee sparking off each other. In 'Terror of the Autons' they spoke on the phone to each other in episode three but did not come face to face until episode four. In the second story the two characters and the two actors start to bounce off each other. The Doctor's insult that the Master was only a 'jackanapes' may still have been in people's minds just a few weeks later when 'The Mind of Evil' was transmitted. In only his second story, the Master gets payback for the insult and the story is gruelling for the Doctor. The mental assaults of the Keller Machine summon up the Doctor's deep fear of fire and torments him so much that one of his hearts stops.

The Master meanwhile has a good time. In a much-celebrated moment, he has the Doctor brought to him and gets to swing around slowly in a high-backed chair to face the Doctor. In another scene, the Doctor is racing around the prison while the Master waits nonchalantly in a room with one foot crossed over another and his arms crossed, waiting calmly for the Doctor's arrival.

Delgado was also well served by a production which, while not having a big budget (and as we'll see below, that caused the director major problems at the BBC), gave the Master astonishing toys to play with. The story features a great deal of location filming around Dover Castle and participation from the army. In 'The Mind of Evil' Delgado shares the screen with an actual missile that belonged to the British military and with extras who were actual soldiers. The real military hardware adds immeasurably to the authority of Delgado's performance and at one point Delgado even seems to be acting with the missile. The Master arrives at an aircraft hangar in his chauffeur-driven limousine and stands for a moment looking proudly at this stolen missile, then he nods and the crew start to get the missile in position for firing; it is as though the missile nods back to the Master as it is lowered.

The story is made beautifully. The director Timothy Combe uses resources of both film for location shooting and the videotape and vision mixer in the studio at Television Centre to give the story size and flair. On film he uses a high mounted camera to look down on the streets of London and give a sense of scale to the outdoor scenes, and the attack on Stangmoor Prison is a large-scale piece of filming to rival the military action orchestrated by Douglas Camfield in 'The Invasion' from season six and Michael Ferguson in 'The Ambassadors of Death' from season seven. The recorded studio material is also stylish and Combe does not always just cut from scene to scene. In one instance, he cross-fades from the Doctor's face to the Master's, using the studio's vision mixer to make brief allusion to the connection between the characters.

'Terror of the Autons' has gone down in history as the violent story of season eight, including the suffocating chair, the killer doll, the daffodil that suffocated Jo, and the lethal phone wire. However, 'The Mind of Evil' is surely worse. With not one but two prison riots and a full-scale military attack on a castle, it has an amazingly high death toll among the extras playing prisoners and soldiers.

The key difference, though, is Delgado. In 'Terror of the Autons' he does a great deal of the dirty work himself, with his only human allies being Farrel and Rossini. In 'The Mind of Evil' he has a whole prison full of hardened criminals to help him. Katy Manning remembers this one as the story where Jo took on a prison full of men! The story even justifies some of its death toll with the suggestion the people killed were all criminals.

The other thing 'The Mind of Evil' has is the Keller Machine itself. Initially it looks fairly innocent, although the tall cylinder, the dome and single pulsing light in the centre do suggest the appearance of a Dalek. This innocent design is also a triumph of visually realising a menace at first with subtlety and then with a horrifying and quite disgusting obviousness. When first seen, people would have to look very carefully at the Keller Machine to see that there was 'something' small and dark lurking inside. The initial appearance of there being something inside and something wrong with the Keller Machine is like a suggestion from the stories of M. R. James, in which the terrifying and grotesque are at hand but only glimpsed. At the end, though, the Doctor lifts the top of the chamber and what we see – a bloated, pulsing black 'thing' with a single eye – changes from Jamesean subtlety to something like the Trollenberg terror.

Orchestrating the action was director Timothy Combe. Like the other directors of season eight, Combe inherited and worked with the ensemble cast of the UNIT family and the Master. Combe was also already part of the scene. 'I immediately sort of fitted in,' he says. 'I just sort of knew. I'd worked, you see, with Bill Hartnell and Pat Troughton before that; I'd done the two earlier Doctors. I knew the sort of scene and the pressures that *Doctor Who* always presents to actors and directors: lack of money, lack of time usually.'[389]

One of his strongest memories of directing 'The Mind of Evil' is, sadly, its impact on his subsequent career. In short, he overspent. He was short of time and money but determined to produce a quality story and in particular to showcase the Master.

Combe directed 'The Mind of Evil' very much his way. Part of that was how he rehearsed the actors, doing so thinking of the performances before he thought about the cameras and shots. 'My style of directing put a strain on me, but I would let the actors express themselves and then I'd shoot the scene; I'd set the scene and watch them play it, then adjust it or maybe they'd have ideas, but I never put a camera on until after I'd really worked with them for a while, and then I could see how they reacted and I could pick that up. It was slightly different from a lot of directors.' [390] One of his cast members, Pik-Sen Lim, playing Captain Chin Lee, remembers Combe putting the cast through a thorough rehearsal: 'It was almost like a theatre job; we would have a rehearsal period where we came in and messed about and thrashed out all these issues and got things right.' [391] There was time to get to know fellow cast members but a lot of hard work requiring discipline.

Inheriting a cast, including Delgado, meant he was also working with actors who knew their parts, and Delgado in particular had a lot to contribute. Like many others, Combe remembers high standards, professionalism and immense talent, for 'very rarely did I give Roger any notes, because he was just spot on every time; he was a very, very good actor'. [392]

'The Mind of Evil' was only Delgado's second story and the Master's second outing on screen. Robert Holmes and Barry Letts established a lot in 'Terror of the Autons', but between them Combe and Delgado added more. For Combe, that included his determination to spend enough to make the Master look good, especially in the ensemble package of car, chauffeur, fur coat, and cigar.

The first scene where Combe directed Delgado was the location recording of Delgado in his car smoking. One thing to get right was the car, limited money notwithstanding. As Combe insists, 'If you're going to do something well, you've got to spend money on it. I can't remember the original description of the Master in his car; I thought, "We've got to have a proper car," a Bentley or a Rolls or something like that.' Unfortunately, however, 'I don't think the budget was allowed for that, probably an Austin Allegro.'

Nonetheless Combe got a Daimler limousine, one of several expensive items that he'd use including a missile, a castle, a battalion of soldiers, and a helicopter. The other thing to get right was the Master's image inside the car: 'The very first morning was trying to get him to smoke a cigar,' he recalls. Combe was clear about the type of impact he wanted to create on screen: 'I wanted to make him a sort of big boss, the master spy if you like, or that kind of James Bond character.' Delgado was a contributor as an actor thinking hard about his part: 'He had suggestions to make, quietly, very quietly, "What if I did this and what if I did that," and usually he was spot on. He was a smashing chap to work with.'[393]

The finished product shows the fruits of the thoughtful, careful approach shared by Combe and Delgado. I mentioned Delgado's immaculate little scene when the disguise of the telephone engineer comes off and the suit, coat and cigar come out. Delgado's performance for the film crew and his use of the props turns a short, silent scene into something special. He removes the mask of the telephone engineer's face and places it on a table, but at an angle whereby the eyeless mask still seems to be sitting up and looking around; the image is quite grotesque. Slightly fussy little gestures with his portable radio and his concern about his appearance come next.

The bigger picture is just as beautifully constructed. One example is the scene of the Master and Captain Chin Lee in leafy Holland Park. Combe realised that little touches added a great deal. 'I did little things in that particular scene; I wanted evil and innocence to be around, and the innocence was the kids playing in the little garden whilst all this was going on. I used two of my children who were in play school in those days, and we filmed it there; and when Pik-Sen goes and burns the thing, she's in the garden there and the children are all playing around her. Little things, little touches: it all adds on to the budget of course.'

Typical of the whole era, cast and crew battled against time and financial restraints. There is a horrifying scene in episode six when the Master gets away but runs a man down with his vehicle as he does so. The amazing scene when the Master drives the Black Maria straight into the simple-minded prisoner Barnham was achieved during 'a very frantic day' because as ever *Doctor Who*, says Combe, 'was not an easy production to work on; lack of time and particularly lack of money was a problem'.

When getting ready to film these final moments, Combe found a big plot hole. 'One of the big problems was the end, the way it was originally written, was that there'd be a massive explosion and then we cut to the next scene and the Doctor is up in London talking to the Brigadier. I said, "How are we going to get the Doctor out of that massive explosion? He hasn't got his TARDIS there." No one had thought of that, so I thought the only way of getting him out mighty sharpish was to get a helicopter in, and that put me over budget and I had to live with the reputation of being one of the directors who really overspent on *Doctor Who*; not my fault.'[394] In the end, 'Barry Letts and Terrance Dicks both said it was an absolutely brilliant production,' and Combe eventually moved on beyond his reputation for overspend and had major successes in BBC drama.

Performing with the Master

In 'Mind of Evil' Delgado was only into his second story as the Master but he hugely impressed his co-stars. One of the words that resounds through the memories of anyone who worked with him is 'professionalism'. Michael Briant, who directed him twice, remembers Delgado as a 'proper, jobbing, professional actor who thought about what he did'.[395] Thinking about what it was like working in the hectic environment of the Television Centre studio, co-star Richard Franklin reflected: 'One respects people who are very professional in their jobs; they don't waste time, they just get on with it. He was a very efficient actor.'[396] Other cast and crew members saw similar. 'Roger was so professional,' recalls Pik-Sen Lim, who shared many scenes with Delgado in 'The Mind of Evil'.[397] Interestingly, behind the scenes the villain caused much less trouble than the hero did. 'No, I never had a moment's trouble with Roger,' recalls Terrance Dicks, again thinking of his professionalism. 'It's the ones who play the heroes like Pertwee you have trouble with.'[398] Co-stars also found him charming, funny, irreverent and generous, but the impression in many people's memories is his total professionalism.

Admiration of Delgado's professionalism could extend to being in awe of him. When cast as the Chinese communist soldier and diplomat Captain Chin Lee, Pik-Sen Lim had appeared in the medical soap opera *Emergency Ward 10*, although her most famous role as a communist language student in the sitcom *Mind Your Language* was to come some years after 'The Mind of Evil'. As a relatively new actress, Lim remembers: 'I suppose I was quite in awe of him; he was the Master to me.'[399] In casting her mind back to the few weeks she spent in 1970 working with Delgado and Pertwee, her strongest memory of Delgado was his professionalism but also the way Delgado and the Master had come together in her mind. 'As far as I was concerned he was the Master; it wasn't so much that I knew Roger as I knew I'd worked with the Master.'[400]

The *Doctor Who* set was friendly but that did not necessarily mean a younger actress would have the confidence to socialise with the established cast members and the big names. Lim's memories give us an intriguing glimpse of the *Doctor Who* cast at work and rest. At work, it was all professionalism. At rest, it was clear that Pertwee was the leading man, Delgado the lead guest actor, and as such they were high-status people on set. Lim thinks Delgado 'wasn't a social butterfly'. During breaks Pik-Sen found 'he kept to himself', or else the two big stars would socialise with each other: 'I'd see him go for little conversations with Jon Pertwee, but I didn't interfere; I mean, Jon was the star of the piece and Roger was the main lead actor.' Lim found the two big stars 'would go into a corner and have their chit-chats before lunch, after lunch; I hung around mostly with Katy Manning and Fernanda Marlowe' (who was playing Corporal Bell).[401]

It's not that Delgado set out to be daunting, but younger cast members could be in awe of his professionalism and his high standards. Over forty years later, Lim remembers Delgado as an actor who makes her think of her friend Peter Cushing: one who 'shows up on time, he's perfect with his lines, never keeps people waiting, always word perfect'.[402] Lim and Delgado shared a number of scenes because in the story he has hypnotised her and made her do his evil bidding. When they filmed these scenes, Lim found she was 'just terrified that I would remember all my lines and I wouldn't have to make him do it again'.[403] A younger actor was working with a highly experienced one, one with total focus who just wanted to get on with the job: 'I certainly was hoping to get a bit of guidance from Roger, but I think he was word perfect; I aspired to be as word perfect as him so as not to hold up filming.'[404]

To a younger actress these standards may have been awe-inspiring but to directors, producers and fellow cast members, to anyone who cared about time, money, and professionalism, they were a cherished gift. This comment that Delgado was 'professional' comes freely to the lips of anyone thinking about him; often it's the first thing they said when I asked about him. He was not surrounded by unprofessionalism but there is no doubt his level of preparation made him a thoughtful, collegial person to work with.

To see why that is, let's take a brief detour for a moment from the set of 'The Mind of Evil' to Pinewood, because it shows why and how much people appreciated Roger being on time and word perfect: because it's excruciating when actors are not. Kenneth Williams (whom we've already encountered complaining that the Newquay repertory actors were not learning their lines) found himself going through hell on the set of *Carry On Follow That Camel*. The American star Phil Silvers couldn't remember his lines and Williams' diary recorded every day of the miserable experience. 'He blew on so many takes that he got humiliated and burst into tears,' said Williams of the filming on May 20th 1967. On June 1st Williams was angrier and was also using the gender-bending language he adopted for people he hated, referring to Silvers as 'she'. 'It's atrocious trying to work with P.S. Doesn't know a bloody line of the script... Today they chalked all the dialogue on a blackboard for her & she fluffed that.' By June 7[th:] 'I really hate that incompetent fool P.S.... When he came out with a line today I said "Oh! You know it? It's fantastic, how do you do it? – go to bed with a record under your pillow or something?"'[405] These comments are a hilarious mirror image of how people found working with Delgado, who arrived on set on time and with everything ready in his head. It did mean, though, that everyone else had to live up to his high standards.

Chapter Seventeen
The Claws of Axos

W HEN SEASON EIGHT began transmission on BBC One, Delgado was down near Dungeness to film location scenes for 'The Claws of Axos'. Directing him was Michael Ferguson. Like Combe, he was returning to the show from season seven, when he'd directed 'The Ambassadors of Death'.

By now, Delgado was totally in control of his character and performance. Timothy Combe hardly had to give him any notes. Michael Ferguson had the same experience and can now think of how Delgado 'had already established this characterisation of the Master, so there was little for me to concern myself in that respect'.[406] It was perhaps just as well that Delgado knew his own character as the script could not offer him too much direction. The script for 'The Claws of Axos' went through long and complex development and many changes, and writers who had not included the Master in their original outline had to find a way to make his character fit in.[407]

The final story is not one of the best loved; however, in the end the Master makes a reasonable contribution to the action in a way that is actually quite ironic given that Delgado did not enjoy doing the stunts and fighting. Ferguson included a number of strong action sequences in the location filming, some including the Master. Katy Manning and Jon Pertwee frequently did their own stunts. As soon as she started work on *Doctor Who* Manning learnt how to tumble out of a moving vehicle. Delgado on the other hand, says Manning, 'didn't like doing any of the fight sequences'.[408]

For some of the energetic scenes in 'The Claws of Axos' a stuntman took Delgado's place for some energetic moments like leaping onto a lorry.[409] Elsewhere the stuntman performed around Delgado, including Stuart Fell, who did a full backflip when shot at close range by the Master.[410]

Delgado was on set and at the centre of the action in the complex, demanding and technically challenging environment of the studio recording *Doctor Who*. Television Centre is that most fascinating of buildings that did not ever give up all its secrets. Even in its final stages of closure and abandonment it had intriguing parts of its history and structure to reveal. The television historian Roger Bunce wrote evocatively of the underground spaces powering the studios: 'It was astonishing to see all these areas in the sub-basement of which I knew nothing – huge chambers, labyrinths, ducts and rooms containing giant fans and heat exchangers. Like the engine room of a huge liner.'[411]

Up above these labyrinthine spaces were the studios. To record *Doctor Who*, Delgado was in TC3 or 4, large spaces splayed out from the concentric heart of the building. Delgado was acting at the Television Centre at a time of flourishing creativity among the casts and crews of the programmes made there. John Levene remembers the Centre as the place where he could find himself 'walking in with Mrs Slocombe from *Are You Being Served?* or John Abineri from the Mohican show or James Ellis from *Z Cars*'.[412] Katy Manning still feels the atmosphere of a place where she was 'surrounded by creativity and excitement and edgy, new, kind of dangerous new ideas'. Equally strong are her memories of the pressures of getting the episodes recorded before the studio clock reached 10pm and the lights went out and sometimes the sprinklers came on, and of the high levels of concentration needed to navigate through a complex technical environment where many of the special effects were being tried and used for the first time.

Down on the studio floor, cast and crew would be waiting, keyed up and ready to go, for a voice from the director's gallery instructing them to stand by. When recording began at 7:30pm, they would need to be focused and ready. Once under way, 'There was a lot of focus and concentration because it was "cut to film" so you had to make sure that everything that was happening, or the moment you'd done something on film, you had to follow it through in the studio.' Thinking back over the weekly experience of recording two episodes in the Television Centre, Manning remembers: 'In the studio time we had, you were really focused on the technical side of it.

We had to just nail it or not because the time had to be spent on a lot of other areas that weren't going to be so easy to work, so the actors had to be damn sure of what they were doing.'[413] The powers of concentration required were immense to ensure the performance on location film was matching what was happening in the studio and to get everything done before the lights went out.

For all the focus and concentration, the actors also had to be patient as there was a lot of hanging around. Delgado and the remainder of the cast could rehearse and record but also wait for hours while the crew achieved the special effects in the studio. Barry Letts told the interviewer Peter Griffiths how he remembered a 'waste of bloody time' trying to record the effect of the man in the lunchbox in 'Terror of the Autons' and the need to 'spend an hour or so doing a special effect which was on screen for three seconds'.[414] 'The Claws of Axos' was if anything more effects-intensive. Michael Ferguson started work on the story with an experimental session. His visual effects took in everything from model work to Colour Separation Overlay to light effects used on *Top of the Pops*.[415]

In the centre of the challenging studio environment was an actor who Ferguson remembers as a point of calmness and cooperation: 'In the hurly-burly of recording those adventures in time and space, calmness and quality such as Roger brought into the studio were always golden gifts,' he told me.[416]

By 1971 there was greater facility than there had been during the Hartnell and Troughton years to electronically edit the tape and some retakes were possible. However, Delgado was rarely anything less than word perfect. He came to the studio thoroughly prepared and ready to go. Alongside him in the TV studio was Richard Franklin playing the UNIT officer Captain Yates. During rehearsals and preparation, Franklin had noticed how Delgado's script 'unlike mine, was always incredibly neat'. No surprises there, as every-thing Delgado touched, owned or used was neat. Delgado was a trouble-free, reliable performer, traits shown in how neat he was and everything around him was.

From the way people describe him, he seems a bit like Mary Poppins in the nursery, as if he just had to walk into a room and it became tidier because of his presence. Franklin noticed the difference from himself, again thinking of Delgado's immaculate script: 'I draw little pictures and all sorts and rub things out and have new ideas and scribble all over the place, very untidy, but Roger, he'd made a clear decision about what his character was and it was sort of easy in a way; he just had to note the moves down really and I don't know whether he wrote notes the director gave him, all I could see was that every page was very clean.'[417] It was all part and parcel of a man who was 'meticulous' and it showed in everything he did, from how clean his script was to how he dressed and looked. In his mind's eye, when he thinks of Delgado, Franklin can still see 'that absolutely neat little moustache, little goatee beard, his clothes, everything, always, absolutely precise,' all part of a complete package.[418]

Meticulous preparation during rehearsals made for trouble-free performances in the studio. Again, Franklin thinks back to an actor who was a gift to directors like Michael Ferguson, who were working in tight conditions on the most complex programme made at the Television Centre. Delgado's gifts to busy, stretched directors made him in Franklin's estimate 'a director's dream'.

What were these gifts? They included: 'He always knew his lines; I'm sure he did have more than one take sometimes but his scenes always seemed to go very smoothly.' Remembering that the recording was taking place in the cavernous space of the studio, Delgado was performing in front of multiple cameras and surrounded by the complicated studio equipment, including the tangles of cables coming out of the cameras and spreading across the studio floor.

Delgado had been on TV since 1948 and did not bat an eyelid at this vast technical environment. His controlled preparation meant: 'He's one of those actors who was always facing the right camera, or looking in the right direction; the whole performance was very carefully planned,' thinks Franklin. By no means all actors have it all together so well, and: 'Some people are accident prone, they fall over the cables, they're not looking in the right direction, they don't know their lines: that wasn't Roger.'[419]

Interestingly, one suggestion that things did not always go to plan came from Pertwee, who said once that Delgado 'would go absolutely berserk with anger if he couldn't get something right'.[420] Something does not quite seem right with this reminiscence. Isn't it likelier that it was Mr Pertwee himself who would forget a line and go berserk? Surviving raw studio footage from 'Death to the Daleks' shows Pertwee going through agonies trying to get his lines out and blowing on take after take. Pertwee did have a tendency to tell stories that cast himself as the hero and displaced faults onto others.

That's in the studio. Let's backtrack to the location filming for 'Claws of Axos' down in freezing Dungeness early in 1971, where something very special happened for one member of the cast, because of the magical, generous personality of Roger Delgado. It's nothing to do with his always controlled, carefully prepared work or even his legendary professionalism, but instead the warmth of his interactions with his friends in the cast.

John Levene had been doing walk-on work for the BBC since the early 1960s and worked his way up from there. As he tells the story, 'I was a menswear salesman and then I was a monster on the Monday and then a Yeti on the Friday, and then Douglas Camfield and Barry Letts conspired behind my back to give me the part of Sgt John Benton.'[421] He'd played Benton since the end of the Troughton era, but having a part with dialogue was a different experience to being a walk-on. 'I didn't think I could act, as I'd had no stage work, no voice lessons, no theatre, no anything,' and the result in Levene's view was: 'I certainly wasn't good, so please don't humiliate me by saying "Oh yes you were" because I fucking wasn't – I was a bloke that was struggling with every line.'

But then he spoke with Delgado, a conversation that stays fresh in his memory because a photograph survives of them together on location at this time: 'You've most likely seen the famous photograph of him standing in a big coat and me with a big coat on with a high collar… that's the day or the week where he came up and said, "You know John, I've only known a couple of other people like you, who are so sensitive about the fact you think you can't act. What you don't realise, John, is the fact that you think you can't act makes you act even better in terms of the way you respond to our characters." And that was one of those days when the light went on, and I thought, "My god, Roger said that; *the* Roger Delgado has said that what I do is actually very acceptable."' Across the many intervening years Levene remembers the moment when 'Roger Delgado held my hand and said, "Don't fret, we love working with you; whatever you do, you're doing it right," and he held my hand, he put his cheek next to mine, and said, "You never have to worry again John."'[422] The photograph captures a small moment in time that still speaks across the decades.

Chapter Eighteen
Colony in Space

T HE MASTER AND the Brigadier may have been in every story, but season eight did not lack variety. 'Colony in Space' achieves variety in two ways. One is by letting the Doctor take Jo into space and the other is by holding the Master back until episode four, longer than even his delayed introduction in 'The Mind of Evil'. In 'Colony in Space' we get two alien worlds: first the Doctor's home planet (at this point, it is still unnamed), and then Uxarieus.

Doctor Who's 1970s serials are often criticised for realising alien worlds by location filming in Dorset quarries. The suggestion comes a close second to mockery of wobbly sets. To be fair, sometimes those quarries (as in 'Terror of the Autons') were actually representing quarries. But in other cases including 'Colony in Space', 'The Three Doctors', 'Frontier in Space' or even as late as 'The Greatest Show in the Galaxy' in 1988, the quarries were meant to be alien landscapes.

Director Michael Briant's choice of the Old Baal Clay Pit (in Cornwall, not Dorset) was a good choice and better than the average quarry setting for evoking an unusual and quite sinister atmosphere. Briant wanted a good location even though it was a bigger than usual effort to get the cast and crew down to Cornwall: 'I actually didn't want to film in the standard quarry. If you film in a quarry down the road from Shepherd's Bush Green, where we all worked, clearly the unit can get in their cars, drive down there, put in a couple of hours' overtime, and then drive back in the evening and that's the end of it. If you go as I did all the way to Cornwall, to the China clay quarries in Cornwall, it's an excellent location; if you do that, though, the entire unit has to get in cars, drive down there, check into a hotel, get up the next morning, go to work, go back to the hotel: you know the cost element of it is huge. So there is an element of producers with their financial hats on would rather you did it just outside London; directors like me would go, oh well, I will save money in other ways in order to be able to spend the money on a much better location.'[423]

The production of 'Colony in Space' followed the usual pattern: location work on film came first in February 1971, at the Clay Pit; recording of the rest took place in the studios at the Television Centre in March. When watching 'Colony in Space' the film sequences are generally much more successful than the studio sequences. Part of that is budget. Part of it is also the script, which had a troubled development through multiple redrafts. Nonetheless, with the script commissioned, the team had to plough on and make it work somehow. It was only later that Briant found out he had been asked to direct a difficult script: 'I didn't know this at the time, there had been about three or four attempts. There had been the original colony script, which was a lot of people running around with bows and arrows living in tents, and then onto that there got imposed something else and then something else. In those days in the BBC you weren't allowed to spend the money writing off the scripts, so whatever happened the producer had to make the script work.'

Barry Letts and Terrance Dicks put in a lot of effort to make the story work and, once on board, Briant suggested changes to some of the elements he found less than plausible: 'I looked at this tents thing and thought, come on; I'm a sci-fi fan, there is no way people are going to be living in tents. And the designer came up with the idea with these, that hexagonal shapes can make any side of a domed building and I went, "Oh really, didn't know that," and all you need to do is just import the hexagonal shapes. Hence we got all those domes, which were never in the script.'[424]

In the final version, the Doctor and Jo land on Uxarieus and find a colony of extremely middle-class English people, led by Robert Ashe (played by John Ringham). The planet (which as is normal in *Doctor Who* is a term that seems to refer to a strictly localised area rather than a whole world) also is a ripe source of duralinium, a precious mineral. The mineral is the plot's McGuffin. The unscrupulous soldiers and engineers of the Interplanetary

173

Mining Corporation want it, the colonists don't want them to have it, and the planet's native inhabitants are oblivious to its value. The Master pretends to adjudicate about access to mining rights, but he doesn't want it either and instead is after a Doomsday Weapon hidden under the ground.

It is fair to say that retrospective opinion has not been kind to 'Colony in Space', but even Briant thought: 'It was probably awful. I just didn't think I did it well enough.' A later viewing softened his opinion and after rewatching it recently he told me: 'Actually it's not bad, there's some excellent actors in there; it's not a bad show at all really.' [425]

One of these excellent actors is Delgado and the story makes us value him more. By the time he arrives in part four the story is over its worst, including incredibly laboured agrarian conversations in part one about failing crops, low yields and depleted soil. The addition of more characters and therefore more antagonists as the story moves along helps matters. Morris Perry plays Captain Dent. Throughout his career, Perry normally played callous bastards, including the Commander of the Flying Squad in *The Sweeney* and Arthur Daley's DHSS assessor in *Minder*. Here he brings a genuine nastiness to the part but also depth to a role that on paper is an underwritten villain. Dent is a swine and he lies and kills throughout, but Perry also shows a little more than the surface villainy. Once he has succeeded in his objective of cheating the colonists of their planet and sending them packing (or so he thinks) in a clapped-out spaceship, Dent is left alone for a moment in the colonists' dome and, in a moment of sudden fury, rips down their charts showing their struggling crop yields. Is the anger at least a moment of guilt? When giving his final orders to Ashe before the colonists' spaceship lifts off, Perry lingers for a moment over his farewell of 'Goodbye... Ashe,' and turns away from the video screen, as though unable to face those he has abused, terrorised and now exiled. Perry's acting is a major success for the story, especially in contrast to other bland roles.

Another success is the film sequences. The Clay Pit does look genuinely weird and the scenes there are atmospheric. The editing is tight and the scope is an expansive relief from the dreariness of the colonists' dome. In part six Michael Briant stages and shoots an excellently choreographed and truly brutal fight between a colonist (Nicholas Pennell) and an IMC guard (Terry Walsh, who orchestrated the fight) which sees them fight it out in liquid clay. The mud and the mess came courtesy of the bad weather that on other occasions was a nuisance but here added to the effect of the fight.

Looking back on filming with the mud that had fortuitously appeared, Briant sums it up thus: 'As Napoleon said, I don't want great television directors, I want lucky television directors, and in fact this was lucky.'[426]

The other success of the latter part of the story is Delgado. In this story and his next, 'The Sea Devils', Briant shows an important understanding of the gradual reveal of the appearance of monsters and villains. In 'The Sea Devils' he shows the titular monsters bit by bit: a hand creeping over the side of a boat, a figure in the shadows and behind a staircase. In 'Colony in Space' the 'Adjudicator' is first seen from the rear and a very impressive figure he is, dressed in black robes with a high collar.

Each time the Master appeared, Delgado offered something new for audiences, aided by fresh writers for each story. Robert Holmes laid the groundwork of a savage killer with a civilised veneer. The veneer stays intact in 'The Mind of Evil' when we see the Master as a figure insinuating his way into officialdom at the prison and hear of his good graces on display at an embassy party. The next story, 'The Claws of Axos', stripped away this control and made him a prisoner of another alien species.

In 'Colony in Space' Delgado's contribution is to show much more of his relationship with the Doctor; and the story comes to life in its last two episodes, which are mostly a double-hander between Pertwee and Delgado. Many people described Delgado to me as 'professional', but a different verdict was Victor Pemberton's view that he was 'imaginative'. It's not a term used much in connection with Delgado as people tend to remember control and discipline, but imagination was a vital quality when making slightly shoddy science fiction. Pemberton hammered it home: 'It's very important you use your imagination; it's that word again, imagination – use your imagination as to where you are.' That is a lesson about acting he learned from the legendary actress Gwen Ffrangcon-Davies. 'The one thing she taught over and over again: she said, "One thing is imagination. If you do not have imagination, if you cannot imagine that your character would do such a thing, to appear in such a way, or would wear such a thing, then you don't have it," and she was right.'

Indeed she was, and Delgado is calling on every ounce of his imagination in this story. Confronted with half-naked stuntmen painted green and a super-intelligent alien being that is achieved in the studio as a puppet with a mouth that moves like Miss Piggy's, he sells the audience the reality rather than the ridiculousness of the scene.

The story's director also thought Delgado's presence on set was a good thing for Pertwee and improved the star's performance. Michael Briant reminisces: 'Roger was a thoroughly professional actor; he was different from Jon Pertwee. I mean Jon was a wonderful, wonderful man, a very talented star, and I reckon that he flew by the seat of his pants; I think he did it by instinct, I think he just went out there, he would get ideas about doing things and then develop the ideas but he basically went by instinct. Roger Delgado on the other hand was an intellectual actor. Roger was somebody who thought carefully about what he did, he thought carefully about how he would present it.'[427] Briant also remembered how seriously Delgado took the part and how much he cared: 'You could never get Roger to do something untruthful to his character.'[428]

By the time Briant came on board to direct 'Colony in Space', Delgado was into his stride. Did that mean he still required direction on how to play the Master? Not in Briant's view. 'Roger had set the way he was going to play his character. Acting, directing, it's an interactive process, so Roger would come along with an idea of the way he was going to play his scene, because he was interested in his character and he saw it as the way his character would behave and react in those scripted situations, and he has to live with the way the script has been written but hopefully the script has been written with his interpretation in mind.'

Thinking back over the process of rehearsing and directing with not only Delgado but the whole cast, Briant considers: 'The players are really offering the director a melange of reactions but they find they automatically have to react to each other; provided they're good actors, provided they're truthful actors, provided they're real actors like Roger was, they will only offer you a truth of what they see as their character and the way their character would behave.'[429] That means Delgado could give Briant a carefully thought-out performance that Briant just needed to point a camera at. 'I would never for one second say that I really had any input whatsoever in the way Roger portrayed the Master. My function with an actor like that to a great extent is to present him, is to present his character to the audience in the way that he is playing his character; and provided his character is totally fitted in with the script and role, that wasn't really an effort. It was just my job to be good enough, to present him well enough.'[430]

A slow start in 'Colony in Space' gives way to genuine tension and concern. It also massively changes perceptions of the Master. His ambitions are suddenly enormous. The plan in 'Terror of the Autons', 'The Mind of Evil' and 'The Claws of Axos' was to conquer or destroy the Earth (or conquer *and* destroy the Earth). Now suddenly the plan is to control the universe and be a god. Some years later Michael Wisher playing Davros in 'Genesis of the Daleks' quivered in excitement at the thought of being 'up above the gods', but Delgado's Master gets there first. While some of Hulke's script is undoubtedly prosaic, as a writer for Delgado's character he does need credit for giving the character this epic ambition. The Master's broadcast to the 'peoples of the universe' in 'Logopolis' would not happen without Hulke getting there first.

After finding the legendary Doomsday Weapon deep underground, the Master proposes joint ownership of the weapon between him and the Doctor, an idea the Doctor rejects as 'absurd dreams of a galactic conquest':

The Master: The point is that one must rule or serve. That's a basic law of life. Why do you hesitate, Doctor? Surely it's not loyalty to the Time Lords who exiled you on one insignificant planet?

Doctor: You'll never understand, will you? I want to see the universe, not rule it.

For viewers who may have struggled through the dreary agricultural content of the earlier episodes, the scene is electrifying. Delgado delivers his dialogue in short, crisp bursts. As performers, both Delgado and Pertwee are at their very best and Pertwee's performance reaches levels of energy and drama he last delivered in 'Inferno' in 1970.[431] Delgado imbues his lines with clearly apparent savagery and, at last, the Master gets motivation.

Thinking of those moments when the two men shared scenes together, Katy Manning suggests these were 'beautifully written for the two of them' and reveal actors and characters that were contrasting but complementary: 'That's what made them such wonderful partners in the good and bad.'[432] The scene is also important for Pertwee's Doctor. Since season seven, the Doctor has been in exile, and his blue police box barely glimpsed. Jo's shock at travelling in space and time was one way to reintroduce the fact the Doctor was a traveller rather than an employee of UNIT. His argument with the Master is another way to give Pertwee's Doctor that identity back.

The amount of screen time that Delgado and Pertwee had together in 'Terror of the Autons', 'The Mind of Evil' and 'Claws of Axos' was limited. 'Colony in Space' leaves Pertwee and Delgado alone on screen together and the results are important. The most subtle is an unspoken and fleeting moment in part five. A boulder wrecks their vehicle and they set out on foot to get to the primitives' city, but as they do, the Doctor gives the Master's arm a small, affectionate, almost fatherly pat. When they reach the city the Doctor clearly enjoys showing the Master some ancient artwork and they have a perfectly rational, intelligent conversation about it. The Master for his part makes sure the Doctor escapes from a room when he throws a gas grenade at the primitives.

What about that pat on the arm? The facial expressions going with it from both Pertwee and Delgado show two actors, stuck in a Cornish quarry, pretending they are aliens on an alien planet, and sharing the moment and the screen with each other. It's a shame it is buried in a mostly disparaged story, but I'm not the first to think the little pat on the arm has real significance for both showing the acting camaraderie between Pertwee and Delgado and for being a tiny but suggestive bit of acting that brings extra life to the Master's relationship with the Doctor.

It is just as well the cast were enjoying each other's company, as the filming was miserable. Many years after the event, Michael Briant clearly recollects how unglamorous it was to make *Doctor Who*. 'On that location, during that week's filming, it was midwinter so you couldn't start filming before 9:30, ten in the morning when the light got up, and you had to finish by three in the afternoon; and during the daylight hours it either rained, or it snowed, or there was fog.'[433]

The cast and crew struggled with even the most basic bodily functions, and Briant can have the last word on this story: 'We didn't have a honey wagon, we couldn't in those days. We had a portacabin, and it was set up on the hillside; a little plastic shed, a thunder box underneath it, with the door flying open and the damn thing threatening to fall over.'[434]

178

Chapter Nineteen
The Dæmons

I s THE DÆMONS the quintessential Pertwee story? All the UNIT family
is there: the Doctor, Jo, the Brigadier, Captain Yates, Sergeant Benton
and the Master. It is set on Earth; there is an alien menace in the Home
Counties. It is quintessential in another way as being the bellwether for how
the Pertwee era comes in and out of fashion. 'The Dæmons' is a classic, then
not. It's brilliant, or it's stupid. Its effects are good or 'risible'.[435] Either way,
because it seems to sum up the era, it rises and falls with the reputation of
the whole period.

As with previous stories, it began with location filming before studio
recording on tape at the Television Centre. It also cost a bit more than
average, the location shoot was longer than average, and lurking inside the
writer's pseudonym 'Guy Leopold' were Barry Letts and a colleague, Robert
Sloman. Season eight began with Letts directing and ended with him writing.

'The Dæmons' is a timely story. At one point Miss Hawthorne, the local
white witch, announces: 'There's a Satanist cult in this village and last night
they held a sabbat.' Devil's End (or Aldbourne, the village used as the
location) is a very ordinary-looking place. The presence of a satanic cult in
such a normal-looking place was a fashionable suggestion; by then the black
magic novels of Dennis Wheatley were at the height of their popularity, and
for Wheatley they were a means to point out his belief that the suburbs of
England were full of satanic and occult activity.[436]

By the time 'The Dæmons' was broadcast in 1971, Wheatley's popular non-fiction work *The Devil and All His Works* was in print. The character of the white witch played by Damaris Hayman and Delgado's part of the Master masquerading as a Satanist masquerading as a vicar are both products of Wheatley's fiction and his public dissemination of black magic history.

In 'The Dæmons' Miss Hawthorne asks, 'Do you know when the last Witchcraft Act was repealed in this country? 1951. Why, it's as alive today as it ever was,' and the dialogue follows Wheatley's point: 'In 1951 Parliament repealed the ancient act that made witchcraft a crime'.[437] Likewise Wheatley's point about sabbats that 'those present wear uniform black robes' provides a visual cue for Magister's cult. It being broadcast on Saturday evenings on BBC One, 'The Dæmons' showed the worshippers in the black robes rather than going with Wheatley's other suggestions that Satanists strip naked and dance.[438]

At the start of the story the Master is impersonating the new vicar of Devil's End, the Reverend Mr Magister (presumably he killed the actual vicar; was Canon Smallwood shrunk down to miniature size and stuffed in a chalice?). Also towards the beginning of the story he has an argument with one of his parishioners, Miss Hawthorne, and the dialogue is not only hysterically funny but important.

> Miss Hawthorne: Vicar, have you no concern for the souls in your care?
> The Master: The soul as such is a very dated concept. Viewing the matter existentially...
> Miss Hawthorne: Existentially? Oh you're a blockhead!
> The Master: Miss Hawthorne, one moment. You're very distressed, I can see that. You know, you really are worrying unduly. There's nothing to worry about. You must believe me. You must believe me.
> Miss Hawthorne: Must believe. Oh, why should I believe you? A rationalist, existentialist priest indeed.

The argument may have gone over the heads of watching children, but the material Delgado was given in this story speaks to the care that Letts and Dicks were taking with the character; but so too were other cast members. Damaris Hayman also contributed to the development of characters and their occult associations. When preparing to film the confrontation quoted above, it seemed to Hayman that something was missing. 'I said, which didn't seem to have occurred to anyone up to then, "If he's called the Master, in occult terms that has definite status, and he's got definite powers." And I had a confrontational scene with him, and I said, "I must have some talisman, to give me strength to counter his cause," so I had an ankh; but no one seemed to have taken the title Master seriously until then.'[439]

The story works so well because Delgado plays the part of the vicar so seriously. To aid in his impersonation of the Church of England clergyman, has the Master been reading up on contemporary theology and philosophy to talk about the soul and existentialism? In 'Frontier in Space' he's reading H. G. Wells' *War of the Worlds*. While in the vicarage of Devil's End was he reading Bishop John Robinson's *Honest to God*, or Aleister Crowley's *The Book of the Law*? In this scene, Delgado is playing the Master who is playing a vicar and the layers of performance and character are remarkable. The unctuous, preachy vicar is hysterically funny and the wicked Magister suitably diabolical.

The production surrounding the character is strong. 'The Dæmons' throughout its five episodes features better-than-average special effects. Admittedly you can see the wire that sets off the fire when the Brigadier pokes his swagger stick into the heat barrier, and you can see the zip doing up Bok's (the living gargoyle) costume. However, the smoke and fire of the various explosions are well done. The effects of wind and rain are excellent and so is the ambient sound design of screeching, burbling wind effects. At the very end Miss Hawthorne points out that birds are singing again and it becomes obvious how oppressively sinister the silence in the countryside had been. The crackling, howling sound effect to manifest the heat barrier is also an excellent piece of sonic design. The final shot of the church exploding is the best model effect in the programme by that point and would be until the destruction of Harrison Chase's mansion and the Krynoid in 'The Seeds of Doom' in 1976.

The lighting is also a brilliant achievement, especially in the cavern set where weird colours and swirling incense bathe Delgado's sweaty face as he summons a devil. The story also features Christopher Barry's elegant and fluid camera movement, especially the smooth sweeps down as the camera shows the perspective of Azal the Dæmon as he temporarily shrinks and then grows as the camera swoops around Delgado.

Barry's filming work is equally a triumph. The cast and crew were on location from April 19th to April 30th, filming in the village, on nearby country lanes at Membury and at an actual ancient barrow. Aldbourne looks very pretty; it's a quintessential English village, and no wonder viewers complained when they thought the BBC really had blown up St Michael's Church. The prettiness is only layer deep; what is also special is how remarkably evil Christopher Barry and his film crew make it look. One example is the opening scene, in which the machines making wind, rain and thunder effects create a sinister opening around the church. In a small but notable touch that is a foretaste of Bok, Barry briefly shows us a close-up of a gargoyle on the roof with rain spurting out of its open mouth.

The scenes in part four around the maypole and the morris dancers are Barry's *tour de force*. For a moment, even Miss Hawthorne is taken in by the prettiness of the village green and the morris men as the villagers dance in. 'We always have the morris dancers on May Day. It's traditional,' she cheerfully tells Benton. Then Barry's camera undercuts the charm. In short, impressionistic shots we see that a child is bustled away, a worried looking woman shuts her window, the maypole dancers look oddly blank-faced. Within moments, the Fool with his bladder on the end of a stick is beating the Doctor, and soon the morris men have locked their sticks around the Doctor's throat. Next, in a confused shot from the Doctor's point of view, we see a tangle of dancers, villagers and ribbons until suddenly the maypole itself appears and it becomes clear: it's not just a maypole, it's also a stake.

Remembering that morris dancers were normally used for comic effect, as they were in *The Great St Trinian's Train Robbery* (1966) or in *Dad's Army*, the moment one of the dancers bursts into the pub and fights violently with Sergeant Benton is still shocking.

Delgado also looks as good as he ever has. He wears the dark suit, dog collar and dark-rimmed glasses very authentically, for we are after all seeing Delgado playing the Master impersonating a vicar. Even better is the red cape with Kabbalistic markings which he wears to conduct his sabbats down in the cavern. Amazingly, the amateur 8mm film that was first made available on the VHS release of the documentary *The Doctors* and is now on the DVD release of 'The Dæmons' shows him at his most cool. The silent film shows the cast and crew waiting for filming to begin. Bessie is on the village green, we see some children, other actors, and then Delgado appears in not only his incredible satanic robe but his own sunglasses, as he struts casually around Aldbourne's green waiting for his cue. Even though he is out of character and just relaxing, the effect is diabolical. Seeing him this way makes it clear why Barry Letts had not a second's doubt about who would play the Master.

***

Season eight begins with the Master leaping out of his horsebox and ends with the Doctor and Jo joining the villagers of Devil's End in dancing around the maypole. The scene is also a moment of catharsis for the Doctor, not just after that story but the whole season. Right at the beginning of season eight, Pertwee had been fretting that Delgado might overshadow him; and, watching 'The Dæmons', the critic in *The Sunday Times* thought the programme was 'rapidly becoming an upstaging contest between Jon Pertwee as the Doctor and Roger Delgado as the Master'. There's nothing wrong with that. It kept Pertwee on his toes and gave audiences a triumphantly good villain. Season eight ends on a high and 'The Dæmons' is Roger Delgado's finest moment as the Master.

***

Delgado was not in every episode of season eight but he was in every story. Delgado's professional challenge was to return in each story looking credible while picking up the pieces. Barry Letts and Terrance Dicks have in years since fallen over themselves in their rush to criticise their decision, suggesting it was overkill. Letts and Dicks are too hard on themselves, as season eight was an indisputable success. 'Terror of the Autons' had good ratings of over eight million but also a good position in the chart of the two hundred most watched programmes. That was even higher for 'The Dæmons'.[440] Their bosses at the BBC were pleased with the season.

Delgado was at the centre of this success with his confident, thoughtful performances, but writers served him well. Having Delgado on set throughout season eight was also a good thing for the performance standards, particularly Pertwee's. Pertwee's ego was big; he was after all the leading man, but Delgado was a very powerful actor with a longer and more serious acting profile. When directing his casts for *Doctor Who* Michael Briant had no doubt which of the two was the more intelligent and better prepared performer and it wasn't Pertwee: 'Once Jon got a quality actor with him, his performance would come up and he'd stop flying by the seat of his pants and actually start thinking about it and start intellectualising about it; and that's what it's like to have someone like Roger in the show: he raised it to a higher standard by his acting.'[441] Terrance Dicks also felt Pertwee knew that Delgado was a major presence on set and 'would have been a little worried by Roger's popularity'.[442] Damaris Hayman, guesting on a story and therefore coming into the situation with fresh eyes, is even crisper in her memory of the two actors: 'I don't think he and Jon Pertwee got on terribly well.' Nonetheless she feels they 'had quite a reasonable working relationship' but, like others, she noted not just the difference in standard between Pertwee and Delgado, but that 'I think Jon may have had an uncomfortable feeling in the back of his mind that Roger was actually the better actor of the two, because he was.'[443]

Delgado was also much less stress for directors. He was invariably word perfect whereas Pertwee's tendency to fly 'by the seat of his pants' meant he was part learning, part improvising, and part reading his lines from scribbled notes on the set.

For all people point to differences, there is actually a great deal in common between the two performers. They were born about a year apart and acted in the 1930s before wartime service interrupted their careers. Then there are also major differences. When he died in 1996, one of Pertwee's obituaries said he was 'born into a family so closely linked with the stage that a career in anything but show business would have been considered eccentric'. His great aunts were all actresses; his cousin Bill Pertwee was an actor and his father Roland Pertwee was a playwright, as was another relation, Michael Pertwee.[444] Delgado was born into a family where his acting career was a bizarre aberration from banking.

They were also very different actors. The same obituary for Pertwee noted his prolific activity in film, radio and stage but also vaudeville and cabaret. By the early 1950s he was famous as an all-singing, all-dancing revue and light-entertainment performer. It was even newsworthy if Pertwee made an appearance in straight theatre.[445] Meanwhile, Delgado was clocking up performance after performance in film and television. That meant, across season eight, Pertwee was making sure he lived up to the unspoken but obvious performance and professional standards of his co-star; and that meant nothing but good for the series as a whole.

Chapter Twenty
The Sea Devils

WHEN PERTWEE AND the remainder of the UNIT family assembled in September 1971 to begin rehearsing 'Day of the Daleks' they missed Delgado, and for the moment *Doctor Who* would continue without him. While the Doctor was in the 22nd century and on Peladon, what had the Master been doing? The Master was locked away in a castle prison on an island in the Solent. Delgado meanwhile was looking for work.

Delgado was feeling the effect of typecasting and of his association with *Doctor Who*. He finished 'The Dæmons' in May 1971 and would not be back in *Doctor Who* for some time. Being in season eight was regular work unknown in Delgado's career until that point. But alas by 1972 an impression had understandably formed among producers and directors that Delgado was a series regular in *Doctor Who* as much as Pertwee.

Delgado's reduced load meant he was in the third and the last stories of season nine, and in 'The Sea Devils' his character is again plotting to invade Earth. Both the writer and the director were familiar to Delgado. Malcolm Hulke provided the scripts for a six-part story and Michael Briant returned to the series to direct.

Briant has lifted his game since 'Colony in Space' but so too has Hulke. In place of dialogue that was as arid as the soil on Uxarieus, Hulke delivers a robust script with now-legendary set pieces, two strong guest roles, and enough action to sustain six parts without padding. The production is impressive, thanks to the amazing voluntary contribution made by the Royal Navy. There was a missile in 'The Mind of Evil' but now the hardware includes ships, diving equipment, big guns, a hovercraft and loads of ammunition, and it was all free of charge thanks to the Navy!

Thinking back to his budget limitations, Michael Briant pointed out: 'Don't forget our budget for an entire season is probably the budget for one episode of *Doctor Who* today.'[446] It therefore helped when manna unexpectedly dropped from heaven, as it did for Briant when he shot the impressive climax when a hovercraft sweeps the ocean for the Doctor and the Master: 'It was meant to be a tank landing craft or a smaller boat, and they went, "No, no we could get a hovercraft and we could mount a machine gun on it," and I said, "Really? And could the machine gun fire blanks?" "Oh yeah, absolutely no problem," and I went "Terrific!" because a round of ammunition cost you in those days, used to cost one pound sterling, which is a lot of money, and therefore when you were doing battle scenes, you really didn't want people pressing the trigger on an automatic weapon or a semi-automatic weapon holding it down, because you could go through thirty quid, sixty quid, in three seconds, in a blink; so the Navy giving me a hovercraft with a machine gun with hundreds and hundreds of rounds of ammunition I didn't have to pay for, was wonderful.'[447]

The Navy's contribution is one part of an impressively designed production. Around the castle grounds on the island, you get a real sense of the operation of a high-security prison, in contrast to comically insecure UNIT headquarters. As the Doctor and Jo are pursued around the island that houses the prison holding the Master and run by Colonel Trenchard (Clive Morton), Briant's camera moves over a firing range, shooting target-practice dummies; and just when you think you've seen it all, a prison guard carried on a large white horse rides majestically past. Colonel Trenchard's prison looks like a credible place to keep a master criminal.

Because of the Navy's involvement and the film work around the Solent and the Isle of Wight, a lot of 'The Sea Devils' involves the water. This element has led to one of the best-known anecdotes about Delgado. In earlier interviews both Jon Pertwee and Barry Letts insisted Delgado was terrified of water and consequently appalled by the filming he had to do on the hovercraft and in an aquatic survival suit. Pertwee called Delgado a coward, but meant it kindly, as Delgado's professionalism meant he suppressed his fear and got on with the filming.

The story of Delgado's terror during the filming is not universally accepted and Terrance Dicks has put on record that the anecdote may be exaggerated.[448] Barry Letts also wryly noted that Pertwee's stories about other people tended to star Jon Pertwee as the hero.[449] Nonetheless, Michael Briant's memory is clear. As he recalls, 'Roger was not only a trouper, he was a very, very courageous man.' Briant remembers being on the hovercraft with Delgado, Pertwee and the film crew and Delgado had an ordeal to get through: 'He was freaked out, really, really scared of the water. The way I staged the exits in the last episode, they've all gone down to the Sea Devils' world, to escape from the submarine, or they escape the Sea Devils' world wearing those survival suits which float you up to the surface and let you float around inflated.'

Accordingly, 'Dear old Roger suddenly found himself in a situation where he had to get up and get into this survival suit which inflates so you just float around, to get in that and clamber down four or five feet into the sea, and float around there when he is petrified of the water, absolutely petrified; and Jon was wonderful with him, they were really, really good friends and Jon was brilliant with him, but nonetheless I looked at Roger's face and he was ashen, with the sweat on the top lip, and really scared, genuinely scared; and God bless him, he took a deep breath and he allowed himself to be lowered down the side of the inflatable hovercraft and to float there scared rigid and then act coming out. Very, very brave man.' Katy Manning also remembers Delgado being 'the colour of fresh spinach', something she and Pertwee didn't overlook with their teasing, muttering about queasy, greasy things in Delgado's earshot. Manning believes that if you watch the film sequences carefully, he does look a bit greener than the rest of the cast, who were anyway blue with cold.[450]

Delgado's problems were not quite over as the script called for yet more aquatic action. Once more Briant, directing his film crew, saw events unfold: 'I had water scooters in that show, and there's a chase sequence involving Roger, and I needed Roger to run down the beach, get on the water scooter and set off into the sea and then stop and come back. And for him, this man who is terrified of the water, God bless him, he ran down the beach, got on the thing, came back, and I think he came ashore and if he vomited when he came ashore I don't remember, but if he did that's sort of vaguely in my memory, and all you can go is, "Thanks sunshine, thanks very much for being so brave."'[451]

In other action sequences Delgado could hold his own. In 'The Sea Devils' the audience were seeing the Master for the first time since the end of the epic narrative across all of season eight. In the meantime, Briant thought that Delgado had developed the character and could bring more to it: 'I think he allowed his character to evolve, and I can see changes, subtle changes, I think as he became more reviled or more hated; the producer's office was on the lookout for more ideas.' As an actor, Delgado had what Briant calls 'an actor's bag of tricks' including his fencing ability: 'Roger was good at his sword fighting, he'd learnt his sword fighting; Jon was the same, Jon could do sword fighting, so you ended up in "The Sea Devils" doing the sword fighting scene which evolved because they could do it and it was possible to make the scene happen and there was a realistic possibility of making it look relatively violent.'[452] It *is* violent, helped by a stuntman who covered for Delgado whose back was injured at the time, and culminates in the Master throwing a knife across the room.

Once safely back on dry land and back in the studio at Television Centre (and with Roger's stomach under control), the cast began recording the episodes. It was an on-set reunion with Clive Morton, who had played a spluttering, fulminating army officer in *Star!* and appeared in *Virgin of the Secret Service* with Delgado. Edwin Richfield had been on set with Delgado in *Village of Daughters*. Joining the cast for episode one were Declan Mulholland and Hugh Futcher, playing a pair of ill-fated caretakers on an eerie sea fort. Futcher and Delgado knew each other already from *The Sandwich Man* but did not share scenes together in 'The Sea Devils'. From time to time Futcher did see Delgado on set. As always, Delgado's rock-solid professionalism was on display and the impression Futcher has from all those years ago is, 'I admired his professionalism.'[453]

This time on the set something else really served to make his professionalism stand out. That something was Mulholland, an eccentric and rather dishevelled Irish actor. As Futcher recalls, 'On the odd occasion we saw Roger, I think he thought particularly Declan very amusing, because with the greatest respect to Declan Mulholland, most of the time when he worked he'd had a drink.'

It doesn't impact in the slightest on Mulholland's performance, which is terrific as the slobby, demented caretaker, but his on-set behaviour is poles apart from Delgado's performance; and, 'I think Roger thought this was really very amusing, because there was Roger the total professional that he was, and the idea that anybody could work and have a drink, and have maybe more than one drink...' is how Futcher thinks of the contrast. So Delgado would never have done that? 'I'm quite sure never ever,' says Futcher firmly.[454] We can imagine him with a small smile watching Mulholland, I would think without any malice but just amused, maybe a little surprised, by the contrast.

Delgado's other stand-out moment is episode one where the Master watches *The Clangers* on the television, in fact watching a very recent episode from April 1971.[455] The scene is as well remembered as that of the Sea Devils rising out of the sea. The moment lasts seconds but remains fresh in the cast and crew's memories as a demonstration of Delgado's acting brilliance. For Briant, it shows Delgado's subtlety as an actor and the shades of interpretation he managed in even a short moment: 'I used to stand in rehearsal watching Roger rehearse that sequence; I never knew whether he was thinking, "What on earth are those ridiculous creatures?" or was the Master thinking, "They've got something, maybe they're right, this is most interesting."' To keep an audience interested in the character, Delgado played the scene in a way that 'allowed his audience to decide what his opinion was'.[456] Terrance Dicks thinks back on it as 'just a kind of charming moment'.[457] Someone else who appreciated Delgado's acting in 'The Sea Devils' was the television critic James Towler, who watched the story and loved the performance of 'that "personification of evil" portrayed with such splendid style by Roger Delgado'.[458]

Chapter Twenty One
The Time Monster

'THE TIME MONSTER' was the second Master story of season nine and the final serial of the season. Like 'Colony in Space', it is a weaker story and its padding shows; but the story offers a rare glimpse of the Master at the controls of his own TARDIS. It also contains dialogue with important explanations of the character's motivations that Delgado delivers with real intensity.

'The Time Monster' is Robert Sloman's second time writing for the character. Keeping the character consistent for the actor was the responsibility of script editor Terrance Dicks, who provided a brief on the character. 'It would have come more in early discussions with the writers, but it wasn't really a problem because Roger was so well known and so clearly defined I don't think the Master was difficult to write; you knew who he was, you knew what he was like, you knew the sort of things he would do, and I think by and large everybody tackled him very well.' Likewise, Michael Briant thinks the actor's personality and presence shaped the writing: 'Roger had been cast for the Master because as an actor he reflected what people felt the script needed, so when people were writing the script they were writing for the Master which was Roger Delgado.'[459]

Sloman's script is testimony to both points, that the character was consistent and Delgado's performance and personality provided direction to writers. The Master's impeccable courtesy is present and correct. When

Jo, distraught at the thought that the Doctor is dead, tells the Master to finish her off, his reply is, 'Your word is my command. Goodbye, Miss Grant.'

The Master is also getting a bit more insane by this point. His plan to release an ancient time-eating monster onto creation appals the Doctor but excites the Master.

> The Doctor: You're risking the total destruction of the entire cosmos.
> The Master: Of course I am. All or nothing. Literally! What a glorious alternative!
> The Doctor: You're mad. Paranoid.
> The Master: Who isn't? The only difference is that I'm a little more honest than the rest.

Once again, like in 'Colony in Space', Delgado's presence on set gives a lift to Pertwee's acting and the scene shares the same intensity and crackle of their confrontation over the Doomsday Weapon. Thinking of the interplay between the Doctor and the Master, Katy Manning describes it as 'a fascinating chess game', where the two Time Lords 'were very cleverly, and very intellectually playing chess with each other'.[460]

The story also gave Pertwee the opportunity to work with Ingrid Pitt again, after they had been on stage in *A Funny Thing Happened on the Way to the Forum*.[461] But it is Delgado's scenes with Pitt that are remarkable. When the Doctor and Jo follow the Master to Atlantis, they meet King Dalios (who is more than five hundred years old) and his wife Galleia. Soon, the queen discards Dalios and the Master takes his place. For *Doctor Who* in 1972, the scenes between Delgado and Pitt are remarkably adult, not least thanks to Pitt's incredibly low-cut Atlantean frock. These scenes are also a glimpse of a mostly unseen part of Delgado's repertoire. Although decades earlier he had played the sexually awakened schoolboy in *Young Woodley* in Leicester, on the whole he did not play lovers; but here the Master sets out to seduce and succeeds. In very frank dialogue Galleia muses, 'He would not cloy upon the tongue as Hippias does.' The Master looks meaningfully at the Queen and tells her, 'Lady Queen, you are beautiful.'

Delgado was at Ealing by March in 1972 to do filming and then recorded the episodes at the Television Centre in April.[462] Although the story's reputation is not high and fans deride its special effects, Delgado does get some classy material, including the scenes where he takes over Dr Percival's office, smokes a cigar and lounges around in a leather wing chair. The

Master has been making a habit of that, as he also made himself comfortable in Farrel's office in 'Terror of the Autons', Ashe's office in 'Colony in Space' and the Prison Governor's in 'The Mind of Evil'. It is also intriguing to see different writers' takes on the character in the small touches. In 'The Time Monster' the character refers cuttingly to 'the tribal taboos of army etiquette. I find it difficult to identify with such primitive absurdities.' But in 'The Sea Devils' the Master infiltrated the naval base by dressing up as an officer, and he gave and received salutes as well as recognising a sailor's rank of chief petty officer from his uniform. Overall, there are more shades to the character appearing.

If you are a fan of the Pertwee era, it can be slightly sad to watch 'The Time Monster'. In the internal universe of *Doctor Who*, the Doctor's exile to Earth is ending. In the real world, the change to the ongoing narrative meant the ties binding together the UNIT family weakened immensely. 'The Time Monster' was the final time the Doctor, Jo, the Brigadier, the Master, Yates and Benton appeared together.

Chapter Twenty Two
Frontier in Space

A LL STORIES IN season eight, only two in season nine and now only one story in season ten featured the Master. The character comes to an end but not in the way intended. Delgado's final work for *Doctor Who* is the last three episodes of 'Frontier in Space', broadcast in June 1973.

In the real world, Delgado had a problem. He was an unqualified success as the Master, but the role had turned into something like a poisoned chalice. Terrance Dicks remembers Delgado explaining his situation: 'What we decided to do was have him in occasionally. He would pop up once or twice in a story in each season, you see, and this worked very well for a time for us; but it didn't work for Roger because eventually he came to Barry and said, "Look, I'm not being offered jobs, I'm losing jobs because people think I'm in *Doctor Who* all the time – but I'm *not* in *Doctor Who* all the time, and I'm not getting a full-time income from it." And so he said, "I think on the whole it would be better if I left."'

However, the intention was not to leave in 'Frontier in Space'. As Dicks tells the story, 'We were regretful about it, but we could completely understand his point of view; and I remember we said, "Do you want to sort of sneak away quietly or do you want to go out with a big bang?" and he said, "No, let me have a big bang and a glorious death." So we discussed very vaguely a story in which the Doctor and the Master would have to cooperate as they sometimes did, against a greater evil, and the Master sacrifices himself to save the Doctor, but that never got any more precise than early discussion.'[463]

The Pertwee era ended with 'Planet of the Spiders' but the writer Robert Sloman told the interviewer Peter Griffiths he had started a storyline 'explaining the Master was the *id* to the Doctor's *ego*'.[464] That idea sits with the philosophical and religious ideas both Sloman and Letts were keen to use in *Doctor Who* scripts, but Dicks's memory of the Master and the Doctor having to join forces fits in with the pattern of the Doctor's interactions with the Master. From 'Terror of the Autons' onwards, there would normally come a moment when they were forced to join up once things were completely out of control.

'Frontier in Space' does not give Delgado a big bang or glorious death and the end comes abruptly, but Malcolm Hulke's script does give Delgado good material. Once more the Master is in disguise and in this case it is as a Commissioner for Sirius 4. After the Doctor and Jo have landed on a cargo ship, they become caught up in a plot by the Ogrons and their (initially unseen) collaborator, the Master, to stir up a war between the Earth and the Draconian Empires.

What follows is an exciting trip across several worlds and through a dangerously volatile political situation. The make-up and costume design are excellent, including not just the Draconian masks but also the stylish ball gowns the President of Earth wafts around in while trying to stop an inter-planetary war. The sets are terrific and the studio designs cleverly match the brutalist South Bank architecture used in the location filming.

'Frontier in Space' is a series of escapes and recaptures of Jo and the Doctor together, then Jo and the Doctor separately, then Jo, the Doctor and the Master all together, but this repetition doesn't really matter when the interaction between them is so good. By episode four, events have moved on so the Doctor, Jo and the Master are all locked up together on a spaceship and the audience gets to see three characters and three actors enjoying being on the set and in the cell together.

> The Doctor: This won't be my first visit to Draconia, you know? Many years ago I spent quite some time there. I was able to help them through a period of very great difficulty.
> The Master: Displaying your usual sickening lovability, I suppose.
> Jo: So there's a good chance that they'll believe you, huh?

The Doctor: Well, it's a long time ago. Things may have changed. But I do understand the Draconian mentality, Jo. It all depends how you approach them.

Jo: So if they do believe the Doctor, you've had it.

The Master: Perhaps, Miss Grant, perhaps. But one never knows when help may be at hand. Now, if you'll excuse me, I think that this is going to be rather a long journey, so goodnight.

The Doctor: We'll wake you with a cup of tea in the morning.

The Master: Thank you.

Delgado, Manning and Pertwee act the scene beautifully as the characters bicker and lightly mock each other. It's one of many showing the irresistible appeal of Delgado's performance.

By episode six they are all together on the Ogrons' home planet. The bleak alien landscape is Beachfields Quarry in Surrey, which looks terrestrial and less alien than the china clay quarry used in 'Colony in Space'. However, director Paul Bernard uses the location well and showcases Delgado silhouetted against a cliff top looking down on the Doctor.

Location filming finished by September 12th. The recording of the studio scenes took place in Television Centre in October and November 1972, where for the very last time Delgado was on the *Doctor Who* set as the Master. Once again the Master's plot is foiled. The Doctor and his allies will be able to prevent the war between the humans and Draconians; but at the very last moment the Master appears from the shadows, shoots the Doctor, and makes his escape.

And so it ends. The Master fires the gun, the Doctor collapses and the Ogrons scatter. Paul Bernard's direction has been solid throughout, but in these last few moments the action is badly blocked, his shots fall apart and everything ends in confusion. So much so that David Maloney recorded another final scene during the next story, 'Planet of the Daleks', to bring some coherence to what had happened. Even so, it is better than the original plan that a soldier chases the Master away.

That does not mean Delgado has gone out with a whimper. The final scene is confused, but 'Frontier in Space' also contained some of Delgado's best material. If we backtrack from the abrupt ending, we get the Master at his best. His plot is neither complicated nor easily defeated. For once he is like the actual Professor Moriarty and for the first half of the story is out of sight and manipulating events from behind the scenes, using a hypnotic device to fool both human and Draconian spacemen and soldiers into believing that Draconians are attacking Earth ships and vice versa. His plans are epic and he is in alliance with the Daleks to bring about a galaxy-wide war.

That is the big picture but, at the smaller scale, Delgado gets some of his wittiest material. Hulke is writing for the character for the third time and takes the part in new directions, including some unexpected fun. Although allied with the Daleks, the Master is far from respectful and even does an impersonation of their grating electronic voices, just like children watching at home would do.

Katy Manning incidentally gets her best material as well. Some reviewers of the Pertwee-era stories have questioned the likelihood of Jo Grant being a UNIT operative based on her perceived uselessness, but far from it. In 'Frontier in Space' she successfully breaks out of the Master's captivity and resists the Master's hypnotism by filling her mind with nonsense nursery rhymes. She also gains respect at the patriarchal Draconian royal court. While her comment, 'I think it's about time that women's lib was brought to Draconia,' is a bit quaint, the Emperor of Draconia takes her seriously; and her suggestion to use an Earth police space vehicle to get from Draconia to Earth is sensible and drives forward the plot. *The Spectator* carried an opinion piece called 'Dr Who's Politics' that drew attention to Jo's useful-ness. The writer clearly had a crush on the character and the actress playing her ('my beloved Katy Manning') and thought the character was 'useful as well, able to fight and pick locks'.[465]

Manning's interactions with Delgado provide some of the highlights of the story. There is the Master's almost avuncular charm when he comes to get her out of prison and finds her sitting in depressed silence in her cell:

The Master: Penny for them, Miss Grant?
Jo: You! What are you doing here?
The Master: To coin a phrase, I've come to take you away from all this.
Jo: What are you talking about?
The Master: Well surely you don't want to spend the rest of your life in here,
    do you?

Then there is his false modesty and very evident pleasure at telling Jo how clever he is:

The Master: Believe it or not, I am a fully accredited Commissioner from the planet Sirius 4 and you and the Doctor are two dangerous criminals being handed over into my custody.

Jo: So it was you! You ordered those Ogrons to attack the ships and pretend they were Draconians.

The Master: But of course. Those lumbering idiots could never have thought up such a brilliant scheme by themselves.

As always there is the impeccable courtesy towards 'Miss Grant' and 'my dear Miss Grant' even as he taunts and torments her. Also as always, the sarcasm is close by. When the Master and Jo are about to land on the Ogrons' home planet he tells her, 'I'm afraid it's not a very comfortable place, but as the old song says: "Be it ever so humble, there's no place like home."'

***

Recording for 'Frontier in Space' finished at the Television Centre in 1972. A black-and-white behind-the-scenes photograph captures Delgado's final moments on the show. At the back of the studio Delgado, wearing his black-rimmed glasses, is waiting patiently with Pertwee for recording to start. In front of them, the floor crew are pushing the Daleks into position for a take. As usual, the actors must wait for the special effects.

In the next story the Doctor and Jo travel to Spiridon to fight the Daleks and then in the final story of season ten they return to Earth to combat a mad computer in Wales. At the end of this story, 'The Green Death', Jo leaves and in real life Katy Manning departed.

On screen, they had been the UNIT family but off screen Delgado had been part of a convivial, enjoyable group of actors, writers and production personnel. He was a private man but by no means antisocial. In some cases cast and crew lived close by, including Timothy Combe who looks back on a period when 'We had dinner parties with each other, he and his wife Kismet lived in Teddington and we lived just across in Bushy Park.'[466] Director Michael Briant remembers the social enjoyment to be had working on *Doctor Who*: 'It was a big sort of dinner-party group of Roger, and Jon and Kismet and everyone, we all ate at each other's houses.'[467] Katy Manning has memories of a group of actors who 'often went to Roger and Kismet's for dinner'.[468] One of John Levene's memories is of a special evening at the cottage in Teddington: 'One day he came up to me and said, "John, keep it quiet because I don't want lots of people round, but I want you to come round to dinner with your wife"... He had this gorgeous seventeenth- or eighteenth-century cottage, and his gorgeous wife Kismet Delgado was there; and it was just one of those absolutely magic evenings, to the point where he opened up a 35-year-old bottle of wine, which he'd only done three times before.'[469]

Delgado made a pragmatic decision to leave, but for this group of friends it was a mutually regretful one. His colleagues and co-stars have certain vivid impressions of the pleasures of working with him. One universal one is his professionalism, him being on time and knowing his lines. Another is how much he enjoyed playing the Master. You get a sense of how much he bonded with the part from the way he signed his autographs, where from 1971 onwards the flowery 'Roger Delgado' is joined by 'The Master'. As Katy Manning recalls, the era of the UNIT family was also a period of burgeoning popularity for the programme, which meant its cast coming face to face with their fans.

William Hartnell had been good at public meets-and-greets but Patrick Troughton not so much. With Pertwee and the UNIT family, the stars of *Doctor Who* were once again out and about. John Levene also remembers the public recognition that the programme attracted. 'I'd pick Jon up in the morning and then Jon would let me drive his sports car to pick Katy up. We'd pick Katy up in Chiswick, and then we'd drive all the way to Acton with those two doing all their lines in the back seat, and they were some of the most magic moments of my whole entire life... to hear those two talking in the back; and how joyous I was when the odd person down Chiswick Road or Shepherd's Bush roundabout would look up and say, "Jesus Christ, that's Jon bloody Pertwee, and there's Katy, it's John Levene driving!" Those days were so magic you could have put wings on them.'[470]

Delgado shared in this public recognition. He was playing a character who despite (or because of) his villainy was a hit with audiences. While in person colleagues found him a quiet man, he was more than able to meet and greet fans of *Doctor Who* in a customarily gentlemanly way: 'It was lovely to watch him with fans, he was really a gentleman,' says Manning, who came away having learnt 'how important it is to treat fans with respect and to nurture them'.[471]

Part Three
Other works

D ELGADO HAD A LOT in his actor's bag of tricks. His career during and briefly after *Doctor Who* is amazingly diverse. He does Shakespeare with Charlton Heston, swelters in the heat with Rex Harrison and a bunch of over-exposed extras, and plays poker with Roger Moore.

Chapter Twenty Three
During the Master

What you do in this world is a matter of no consequence. The
question is what can you make people believe you have done.
– Arthur Conan Doyle

U NSURPRISINGLY, IN 1971 Delgado made only one television appearance as something other than the Master. *The Rivals of Sherlock
Holmes* television series derived from a Penguin publication of the
same name of short stories about other Victorian detectives besides Holmes
and Watson.

The cast for this story, including Caroline John, assembled at the
Teddington studios, conveniently close to the cottage in Park Lane. Years
earlier Delgado had rehearsed *The Power and the Glory* in front of Graham
Greene. Now in June 1971 with production of *Doctor Who*'s season eight not
long completed, he sat in a room full of cigarette smoke and did the read-
through in front of Sir Hugh Greene, the programme's creative consultant
who had assembled the Penguin collection.[472]

In 'Madame Sara' (broadcast November 1971) Delgado plays a wheelchair-bound man; or is he really? The first thirty minutes of the one-off story
narrate the pursuit of the mysterious foreigner Henry Silva, sought by
Scotland Yard's Inspector Vandeleur who is investigating the strange death
of a woman, played by Caroline John. Silva seems to be a weak, pale invalid.

Investigations, however, tell a different story. Silva has used make-up and other effects to appear unwell. The part does bring inevitable comparisons with the Master as the invalid is a conniving fraud who has been manipulating events from behind the scenes, but is a less dynamic type of villain. He was 'excellent' in the part according to *The Sunday Times*.[473]

In 1972 he made a few other television appearances. While playing the Master, parts of his pre-*Doctor Who* career continued as normal including the glossy independent adventure series. 'To the Death, Baby' (an episode of *The Persuaders!*) brought Delgado face to face again with Sir Roger Moore. ATV was in full swing making its adventure series by now and the good news for Delgado was that a foreign villain was always required. Lord Grade, so *The Stage and Television Today* breathlessly reported, was spending over £8 million on his adventures.[474] He was pumping out *The Persuaders!*, *The Protectors*, *Jason King* and *Spyder's Web* with Anthony Ainley.[475] With *The Persuaders!* both the company and Delgado were on very familiar ground. As the television historian Andrew Roberts describes the show, 'In the best tradition of ITC, the duo would battle fiendish criminal masterminds of variable accents, in between squiring young ladies whose character development rarely surpassed pale lipstick and mini-skirts. Best of all, ITC's familiar stock footage of a white Jaguar Mk1 careering over a cliff was present and correct.'[476] To that list we could add Delgado, reassuringly in place as an exotic continental type.

Delgado's part, the Spanish gambler Estoban, is brief but memorable and as always he gives director Basil Dearden good value. Lord Brett Sinclair has to win a substantial sum of money and tries a poker game with Estoban. Dearden really goes to town on the scene. Delgado wears dark glasses, speaks with a fat cigar clamped in his mouth, and in one amazing close-up his dark lenses fill the screen and reflect a double view of Roger Moore's face. His Spanish accent means he is rolling his Rs. At the end of their poker game, Moore flings counterfeit money in Delgado's face, overturns the table and makes his escape, echoing the moment from 'The Mind of Evil' the year before when the Doctor did the same in the office in Stangmoor Prison.

Unfortunately the series was not a major success on American television, the network pulled the series before it ended and Delgado's episode was one of the last. That didn't matter for Moore, who from 1973 moved on to much bigger and better things.

Chapter Twenty Four
Shakespearean efforts

In all of Shakespeare's plays, no matter what tragic events occur, no
matter what rises and falls, we return to stability in the end.
– Charlton Heston

ARLIER IN HIS career Delgado appeared on stage with Paul Scofield,
the great man of the theatre and a classically trained Shakespearean
actor, in *The Power and the Glory*. Putting them side by side says a
lot about Delgado's career. There was some theatre but much more radio
broadcasting and huge amounts of film and television for Delgado. Scofield
rarely appeared on film and like many classical actors his career took a path
from younger Hamlet to aged Lear. He was steeped in Shakespeare and at
his death was hailed as 'one of the greatest Shakespearean actors of all time'
whose career was on the stage.[477]

Delgado's training was repertory not classical and, throughout more than
thirty years of acting, Shakespeare was just a tiny part of his work. While the
Edward Nelson Players gave audiences a mixture of comedy and drama,
their repertoire was drawn from the twentieth-century stage. In his post-war
theatre work there were some modern authors such as Shaw, Greene and
Maugham but not much of the classics, although one repertory production
of *The Merchant of Venice* cast him as Shylock.

Delgado doing more Renaissance theatre is an intriguing lost possibility.
It would have been fascinating to have had him in action in some of the

grimmer Elizabethan and Jacobean plays such as *The Revenger's Tragedy*, especially as so many of them have wicked Spanish characters, complex plotting and massive death counts, but his gift for playing villains was given to film and television.

Occasionally the BBC repertory players broadcast Shakespeare. Val Gielgud, related to Sir John, cast Delgado in a host of different parts, and one of Delgado's post-war jobs was playing Sir Stephen Scroop in a Third Programme broadcast of *Richard II*, with actors who at the time were big names like Lewis Casson. He was Giraldi in *Othello* in 1953 although *The Stage*'s critic gave the acting plaudits to Valentine Dyall's performance in the title role.[478]

In 1958 Delgado played in a broadcast of *Romeo and Juliet*. Rather patronisingly, Val Gielgud told an interviewer that he had 'chosen his cast almost entirely from the BBC Drama Repertory Company because its present members can, in his opinion, stand comparison with all comers in acting for the microphone.'[479] However, the Home Service broadcast bemused some listeners because of the decision to have Tchaikovsky's music playing in the background. Most of the cast were below par, according to one review, but: 'Mr Hugh Manning, the Benvolio, and Mr Roger Delgado, the Tybalt, showed the company at its most reliable.'[480] In 1969 he participated in a broadcast of *King Lear* with John Gielgud.[481]

From there Delgado and Shakespeare may have remained apart, but in 1972 Charlton Heston selected Roger along with a mostly British cast to be in *Antony and Cleopatra*. Who knows what Heston was thinking in deciding to both direct and star in a big-screen version of Shakespeare? The year before, his major success had been the science fiction *The Omega Man* and he was already a star from the 1950s and 1960s through films such as *Planet of the Apes*, but now chose to stake a claim to classical respectability.

It is less puzzling that he cast Delgado, as the two had performed together in *Khartoum*. Delgado's part had been tiny, but Heston playing General Gordon had roared 'Don't call me a liar!' in Delgado's face. Heston's cast also included Eric Porter, Julian Glover, Freddie Jones and John Castle, a sturdy collection of character performers. Heston rehearsed his cast in London but filmed in Spain. Heston described 'intense pre-location readings at a "dingy rehearsal hall near Covent Garden".'[482]

The film as a whole was not successful. Delgado and the remainder of the supporting cast escaped critical censure, which instead went to Heston as both star and director and to his choice to play Cleopatra, Hildegarde Neil. The other problem is that hardly anyone saw it. Despite a big star producing and directing, it did not receive release in the United States and had limited release in Europe. Critics despised it. Neil was called 'disastrous' and critics had fun with the asp scene, suggesting: 'Cleopatra seems to have been bitten by the asp even before the establishing shot of the messenger travelling by ship and horse from Rome to Egypt.'[483]

It is inevitable to think that some of the sarcasm was the product of British snobbery about Heston presuming to direct Shakespeare. Heston also took liberties with the script, but in later years some have been kinder about his efforts and suggested his decisions make dramatic sense. His script editing also gave more to Delgado. The part of the soothsayer is not large but Heston made it larger. After the languorous and expansive opening credits of a ship at sea, Delgado appears with bedraggled hair, a messy beard and shabby clothes. Seeing Delgado's dishevelled appearance is to be reminded how much of his career had not just been spent playing villains but well-dressed villains. As Patricia Tatspaugh says, Delgado's character is given the dialogue of another three characters, but dramatically that serves to link 'the Soothsayer with events he has foreseen: he announces to the dying Antony that Cleopatra is alive, reports Antony's death to Caesar, and speaks with Cleopatra before she applies the asp'.[484]

The result is a rare opportunity to see Delgado in a sizeable role in a big film. Although he had made many film appearances, the bigger films gave him the smallest roles. Despite its critical panning, there is no denying the film has spectacle and looks wonderful, especially compared with the sets surrounding Delgado on *Doctor Who* and some of the cardboard ITC series. After decades in the job, something new could still excite him and it's a shame the film got a critical panning. Delgado was genuinely excited about the opportunity to be in the movie. Damaris Hayman noticed his excitement about being in the film and after they'd finished making 'The Dæmons' she heard how 'he got a part in that which he was awfully excited about'.[485] Katy Manning remembers: 'He went off to some filming with Charlton Heston which he was very excited about, because we were all teasing him saying [in an American accent] "Oh, you're off to work with Chuck, honey," so we were teasing him madly.'[486]

While making *Doctor Who* kept Delgado at the Television Centre and on locations around southern England, his other work in the 1970s was giving him the opportunity to travel widely. He went to Spain not just for *Antony and Cleopatra* but also for Alvin Rakoff's *Don Quixote*, to France for *The Zoo Gang*; and, furthest afield of all, in June 1973 he made an ill-fated trip to Turkey for a small part in the French miniseries *Bell of Tibet*.

Chapter Twenty Five
Rex Harrison and Spain

Cue the goats!

W HERE TO NEXT? Delgado intended to leave *Doctor Who* in 1973 and the question would have been what he would do afterwards. Delgado sensed that directors and producers thought (wrongly) that he was permanently in *Doctor Who* and he felt this belief was costing him work and money. On a practical level, *Doctor Who* was regular money and he had bills and a mortgage to pay. Actors have a choice between saying yes to work or being unemployed. In between working with Delgado on *Randall and Hopkirk (Deceased)* and *Doctor Who* Nicholas Courtney was working as a builder's labourer.[487] Even Peter Cushing was out of work for eighteen months in the early 1960s.[488] From the money perspective, playing the Master meant Delgado knew where the next pay cheque was coming from.

The part had other positives and even broke his typecasting. While he may have been the quintessential villain, opinions vary on the extent to which Delgado was typecast as an actor. The film historian Gus Burton described him to me as 'hopelessly typecast', but Victor Pemberton thought: 'Roger was capable of presenting himself as any sort of character outside the stereotype because he had a very good speaking voice; he could speak English very well, and his dialect was very good and on top of that he was an intelligent actor.' Even if he were typecast before *Doctor Who*, playing the

Master may have been liberating. Michael Briant makes the perceptive point that playing the Master was actually a break from the type of roles, especially the foreign swashbuckling ones, that he had become so well known for before 1971: 'I think as a character actor you make your little corner, you're quite restricted to that corner, but he wasn't; the Master was not playing a swarthy Spanish courtier, it was playing the Master, a Time Lord from another universe.'[489] Playing the Master meant Delgado metaphorically packed up and put away a lot of the acting style he had been cultivating. Gone were the foreign accents, the hand flapping and the other little touches he'd used so much. The Master was a straighter, colder type of role than much of his earlier work.

Delgado's work immediately after leaving *Doctor Who* showed interesting future career directions for an actor moving on to new roles and new characterisations. *The Adventures of Don Quixote* was announced in August 1972 and eventually appeared on BBC One as a ninety-minute contribution to the *Play of the Month* at 8:15pm on January 6th 1973; it was repeated on June 19th, unwittingly scheduled to the day after his death.[490] The episode had taken him overseas to Castilla-La Mancha in Spain and the show received broadcast on CBS in April 1973, giving Delgado exposure to American audiences. The production was on film and was a lavish one (reportedly costing £200,000), not least because of the contribution made by Universal Television as a co-production.[491]

The director was the experienced Canadian Alvin Rakoff, who had been directing since the 1950s. For the last time, Delgado's name appeared in the credits alongside Paul Whitsun-Jones, who had acted with Delgado since the 1950s. Whitsun-Jones died in 1974 and his career, like Delgado's, had taken in *The Avengers*, *The Saint*, *The Persuaders!*, *Doctor Who* and many other cult productions. Rakoff had known Whitsun-Jones since the early 1950s from the early days of his career in England and the cast in general was a strong team of British character performers.

Rakoff also knew Delgado from directing him in *Court Martial*. By the time Rakoff was casting *Don Quixote*, Delgado's reign as the Master in *Doctor Who* was in full swing. He played a villainous, unpleasant role in *Don Quixote* as a member of the Black Brotherhood, but that did not mean Rakoff cast him this time because of that part or that reputation. 'I would ignore that,' he considers, thinking it a 'great mistake' to label an actor with a particular part or type of production.[492]

The location filming around a Spanish convent was hot and difficult for the cast and crew and the temperamental Sir Rex added to the stress. All of the cast were in heavy costume, including Harrison's armour and Delgado's dark monastic robes. *Radio Times* sent a reporter, Ann Leslie, out to cover the story because while a drama strand like *Play of the Month* was Delgado's natural stamping ground, Sir Rex Harrison was slumming it by appearing in a BBC television programme. Leslie found Harrison, Frank Finlay playing Sancho Panza and the rest of the cast dripping in sweat, hot, tired and beset with challenges unique to filming in Spain. Besides the heat, the cast and crew had to contend with the local priest who was appalled by the bare bosoms of the extras playing whores, and the local animals were proving hard to direct. At one point she heard the shout 'Cue the goats!' as a production assistant desperately tried to bring some order to the chaos.[493]

The shoot stays in Rakoff's memory as a very difficult one. Rakoff knew Delgado was a reliable professional but found Harrison was not the easiest actor to work with. However, steps could be taken to put the leading man in a good mood. First thing in the morning, Rakoff made damn sure that the air-conditioning was switched on in Harrison's trailer, so that Harrison would not arrive, find it off, and immediately get back into his car and return to the hotel. Having Sir Rex's wife there also helped. Nonetheless, the experience of working with Harrison was not easy for either the director or the cast.[494]

Chapter Twenty Six
Zoo Gang and Bell of Tibet

Everyone must leave something behind when he dies. A child or a
book or a painting or a house or a wall built or a pair of shoes made.
– Ray Bradbury

T HAT YEAR DELGADO travelled overseas again. He guest-starred in another independent series, appearing with John Mills and Lilli Palmer in *The Zoo Gang*. Delgado had a substantial role as Pedro, codenamed El Leon ('The Lion'), in the episode 'The Lion Hunt'.

The series was a success with audiences and a pleasure to make for its cast, including agreeable location filming in Nice. John Mills, Lilli Palmer, Brian Keith and Barry Morse are ageing French Resistance fighters. Initially the old fighters got back together to undertake slightly dodgy work to raise money for a hospital. By episode four they've diversified and, with the covert collusion of the local police, they bust Pedro out of jail by recreating one of their operations from 1944, including forged police orders, tapped phone lines, and stolen vehicles and uniforms.

Viewers watching the episode in 1974 saw an adventure filmed around the French Riviera. At the beginning a policeman catches Delgado's character, hiding beneath an exuberant wig and massive sunglasses, at an airport. The fifty-five-year-old Delgado leads a young policeman in a sprightly chase through the airport and car park, but for the remainder of the episode

Delgado is less active: sitting in a prison cell, hidden under bandages in a stolen ambulance as the Zoo Gang spirit him away, and getting locked in another cell when the Zoo Gang are double-crossed by corrupt local officials who want to relieve Pedro of over a million francs.

At the end there is a climactic gunfight in a darkened chateau, and the scenes where the four members of the Zoo Gang break El Leon out of the jail are genuinely tense. To accomplish the rescue, they've stolen a sleek black Citroën DS, police motorcycles and gendarmes' uniforms. As three members wait outside, impersonating a police escort, a fourth goes in, pretending to be a military officer come to remove the political criminal. The director Sidney Hayers makes measured, jumping zooms onto John Mills' and Lilli Palmer's faces as they wait, the jumps marking the seconds ticking away as they wait to see if the subterfuge will work. There is huge relief when the prison gate opens and El Leon walks out.

Playing El Leon, Delgado is on familiar ground as a Latino character. However, he has toned down his performance. Gone are his extravagant hand gestures and overall he is dignified and quite subdued, as if three years of the Master has changed his acting to an extent. Even though he had contributed villainous roles to the independent adventure series, his part here is more complex. If not exactly good (Pedro is a freedom fighter with presumably quite a lot of blood on his hands) he's not exactly bad either.

***

For years, when talking about Delgado's final role, people have been putting two and two together and getting five or more. *The Bell of Tibet* was apparently an incomplete comedy movie, or at least so almost all standard references on Delgado still state.[495] Apparently, it was a Turkish/French co-production and appearing in this comedy meant Delgado was 'delighted at the prospect of changing his villainous image'.[496] One source gets even weirder, claiming *Bell of Tibet* was going to be 'his first comedy film role', a claim that somehow overlooks *Sands of the Desert*, *The Road to Hong Kong*, *The Sandwich Man* or his comedy cavorting in *Harry Worth* and *Comedy Playhouse*.[497] It's hard to know where all this nonsense comes from; it's as though people were making it up as they went along. In another strange misunderstanding about this show, in 2015 there was an announcement with great fanfare that Delgado's last role had been 'found', which rather over dramatised the reality that this French-language programme was available on DVD over a decade ago.[498]

So let's get a few things straight. There is no such thing as an incomplete comedy film called *The Bell of Tibet*. There is, however, a French/German miniseries *La Cloche Tibétaine* in which Delgado appeared in a small role. All seven episodes of intense drama were well and truly completed. The whole programme was sumptuous, even lavish. Throughout his career Delgado had acted alongside some major English-language stars, Laurence Olivier, Charlton Heston and Rex Harrison being some recent ones. Now in *Bell of Tibet* he appeared with major European actors including Wolfgang Preiss, famous as Doctor Mabuse, and Karl-Otto Alberty, another one of those actors who spent most of his career playing Nazis.

Delgado played a minor role as a Spanish driver in episode four, 'L'Escadron d'Or' (The Golden Squadron), shown in France on December 23rd 1974. The programme is about an arduous trek across Asia in the 1930s and is definitely not a comedy. In the first scene of the first episode, André Citroën spells out the route for a transcontinental adventure. In part four, an eclectic group of people including a White Russian officer, a German baron, a glamorous blonde bar-room singer, a petrologist, and an archaeologist are in a saloon bar in Mongolia. At the start of the episode there's been a shootout that damages a vehicle and the Baron needs a new driver. Enter a scruffy-looking Spaniard, who's offered a glass of champagne and enthusiastically answers, '*Perfectemento*, comrade Baron!' And that's that for Delgado's contribution, with not even a close-up of him.

I must admit seeing him on the set, and with the hindsight that his death is only days away, my heart goes out to Delgado. For decades now, when he acted he could have guaranteed that he would be on set with friendly, familiar faces. Recently in Spain, it had been hot and bothersome but he was there with Paul Whitsun-Jones and Alvin Rakoff, people he had known for years. Often he had Kismet with him. On set in Turkey, he seems very alone among strangers and watching him in *Bell of Tibet* is a strangely unsettling and melancholy experience.

For many years there have been slightly different 'facts' about the catastrophe that then happened, but then there was also the 'fact' of this being a rip-roaring Turko-French incomplete comedy. On June 18th 1973 Delgado was in a car near Nevşehir, right in the heart of Turkey. He was running late apparently (on his way to the set from the airport say some sources, but that story goes with his role not being completed and he must have well and truly arrived by then) and the car turned too sharply on a corner and crashed into a ravine, killing him. After that, the details change depending on who is supplying the story.

'Dr Who star killed in crash' was the headline in the *Telegraph*, a headline Katy Manning still remembers seeing and then having to wait in horror to read the article to find out which of her friends had died. The *Telegraph*'s Ankara correspondent had some details. 'He was travelling with two Turkish film technicians when their hired car ran off the road into a ravine. One technician was killed, while the driver and the other technician were badly injured.' The report placed the blame on the driver; and, if that is the case and the driver survived, it's certainly not poetic justice. 'Police in Gulsehir, where the accident occurred, said the car ran off the road at the bend because it was going too fast.'[499] Shortly after his death a comment in *Luna Monthly* got his age wrong but told the story as: 'The 53-year-old actor was on his way to a film location at the time.'[500] Possibly *Variety* used the same source as its obituary and referred to a fifty-three-year-old 'British actor whose career spanned more than thirty years'.[501] Some suggestions include that technical crew in the car were all victims of the accident, while the actual type of crash changes from description to description, including one source saying it was a motorcycle crash.[502]

The details hardly matter when the central horrible fact is that Delgado died because of a car accident. In the registry of the deaths of British nationals who died overseas, Roger Caesar Delgado is listed and the place as Ankara in Turkey. He was fifty-five. Soon after the accident, the banal bureaucratic processes were under way. The police called around to White Cottage to inform Kismet, the British Consul in Ankara sent notification of his death back to Britain and the registrar of births, marriages and deaths received a letter from the Public Prosecutor in Gulşehir, who also sent a local death certificate to Britain. His death was registered in Britain by June 20th. By August probate was completed on his will.

As is often the case with something both unexpected and horrible, there can be confusion caused by people's distress. One uncertainty is the scale of his participation in *Bell of Tibet*. Was his role always going to be small, or was it truncated because of his death? Delgado's role is only small, but his death clearly did not bring production of *The Bell of Tibet* to a halt. Episode four is curious, however. Delgado's one scene is a long, complex and important one in which major characters are introduced. Clearly the director Michel Wyn could not omit it but Delgado is not in the scenes before or after it, and the Baron's chauffeur vanishes without trace. It's a slightly awkward narrative and this may be because of Delgado's death. We learn very little about the chauffeur. Perhaps he was a communist, as he called the Baron 'comrade'. Perhaps we would have learnt more as the episode continued.

He stays in the memories of his friends and co-stars. His remains came to Mortlake Crematorium and his ashes were scattered in its lovely grounds near the Thames and Richmond Park. The same crematorium was the final destination for a host of luminaries and Delgado keeps unlikely company with Charles Hawtrey, Tommy Cooper, Kenny Everett and Margaret and Denis Thatcher, among others sent off there.

John Levene was at the funeral. As a tribute he brought a Japanese fan which he placed on the coffin and he felt the moment deeply, realising as did others that a special man had died too soon: 'As the coffin began to go into the flames, as the whole of Roger Delgado's body was to be consumed by fire and sent to heaven, there wasn't one person in that congregation that didn't look up and say just momentarily, "With all the bad people on the earth, God, why Roger?"'[503] Terrance Dicks also remembers the funeral for its emotion and its drama especially because of Kismet's distress. He told me: 'His wife cast herself upon the coffin weeping, and it was all very emotional.' There was also the reception afterwards, which took an unexpected and poignant turn. Dicks picks up the story: 'It sort of turned into a party, with everybody chatting and reminiscing about Roger, and I remember somebody saying, "What a great party this is, what a pity Roger couldn't be here. He'd really have enjoyed it." There's an irony that happens with those things.'[504] It may be an irony but an appropriate one, given what a convivial group the UNIT family had been and the meals and dinner parties they had shared in each other's homes. Giving him one final enjoyable party seems appropriate. A close-knit group had lost one of their most cherished friends.

Members of this circle also knew it was a horrible irony that it was a car crash that claimed his life. Remember Delgado's immaculate little Mini? He enjoyed driving it and taking driving holidays. Of course, a man who was neat, controlled, punctilious and professional was also a very good and safe driver. 'He was meticulous in his driving; he was a very keen driver,' says Richard Franklin. For Damaris Hayman, his death in a car accident 'was the more poignant because he prided himself on his driving, and he had had various modifications made to his Mini to get more performance out of it'.[505]

Putting his careful driving together with the accident that claimed his life, Franklin also still has fresh in his mind a sadly ironic moment that happened when he and Delgado were on location filming *Doctor Who*. 'He and I were filming and we were supposed to be on location the following morning, and having done a day's filming Roger and I went into the hotel; and the first assistant came in, running in, they were always in a hurry, he gave us our call for the following morning and then he ran out again. And then suddenly Roger followed him out, ran out, and caught him up, outside the glass doors and I saw them talking for a moment or two; and having just been given our call for six o'clock in the morning – you always get very early calls in filming – I then saw Roger come back in to the hotel and he came up to me and said, "I hope you don't mind, Richard, but I've asked for the call to be at 5:30." And I said, "No, 5:30, six, it's all horrible, I don't mind at all; but why?" and he said, "Well, I don't like these film drivers to be in a rush."'[506] It is a very dark irony. So is the fact that this neat, controlled, organised life should end in such a messy, chaotic and disorganised way.

After the accident, his colleagues reached out to Roger's widow. Michael Briant was a near neighbour after Kismet was left alone at the house in Teddington. 'I remember after Roger died Kismet lived around the corner from me and I used to go there quite often.'[507] He also cast her in an episode of *Dixon of Dock Green*, and Barry Letts used her voice talents as one of the spiders in 'Planet of the Spiders', meaning there was still a Delgado in the credits of season eleven.[508] Other colleagues were distraught at his death. Thinking back across the decades his *Avengers* co-star Linda Thorson thought, 'He was far too young to leave the planet.'[509]

Colleagues tried to help. The voice actor Robert Rietty wrote to the *Stage* in July 1973. He had known Delgado for decades and had produced *The Rising Sun* at the International Theatre in 1953 with Delgado in the cast.[510] 'The sudden tragic death of Roger in a car accident in Turkey has deprived the profession of an exceptionally talented actor, and his colleagues of one of the kindest of friends who never begrudged or envied others their success. He possessed a charm and courtesy which made his presence particularly noticeable and welcome in any company.' Now Rietty wanted to repay that kindness and established a fund to help Kismet: 'May I through your columns ask my colleagues who are in a position to do so, to send a contribution to the Roger Delgado fund.'[511] As it turned out, Kismet desperately needed money.

The saddest news came the next year when the *Telegraph*'s reporter Gerald Bartlett championed Kismet, who was struggling on multiple fronts. Besides the trauma of losing her husband and having to pay to repatriate his body, she was out of work, out of money, and trapped in an acrimonious legal battle with Telecip, which was making *Bell of Tibet*, trying to get some compensation out of them. 'Mrs Kismet Delgado, widow of Roger Delgado, "The Master" in BBC Television's "Dr. Who" is having to live on social security.' Bartlett's report was accompanied by a striking photograph of the attractive and dark-haired Kismet, dressed impeccably and pictured in the garden in Teddington, and quoted her saying: 'I am not quite destitute but I desperately need some sort of compensation. The French film company have behaved monstrously.'[512] It was almost another year until, in February 1975: 'The French social security authorities accepted yesterday that the death was an "industrial accident."' It seems more than a little insulting that they agreed to pay her £8 a week.[513] There is a happier ending though. Kismet made a new life with the actor William Marlowe and they married in 1979. Marlowe of course had been on set with Delgado in 'The Mind of Evil'.

***

Delgado had played characters of all kinds, but the cremation at Mortlake brings home how he lived most of his life in the same small part of the world. If you cross Chiswick Bridge over the Thames from Mortlake you come to Chiswick. Keep walking and, before too long, you'll be in Woodstock Road.

Afterlife

T
ELLING THE STORY of someone's life also includes the afterlife or aftermath of that life. Delgado died in 1973. But that is not an ending. Such a busy actor naturally had works in the pipeline, including radio work. *The Zoo Gang* received broadcast on May 3rd 1974. 'There's a poignant touch to tonight's *Zoo Gang*,' said the television page in the *Glasgow Herald* for that day; 'It's the last appearance of Roger Delgado, one of those TV faces you kept seeing in a variety of villainous roles.' Continuing that idea, it says of his part in *Zoo Gang*: 'Inevitably he plays a man on the run from the police.'[514] The comments are interesting but not unexpected for what they say about the sort of actor people thought he was. With the broadcast of *The Zoo Gang* in May 1974 and *Bell of Tibet* in December, that was that for original performances.

Who can say what he would have done next, except to say that there would always have been work for a professional, versatile actor. It's not hard to picture his career in the 1970s continuing with appearances in programmes like *The Protectors* or to imagine him appearing alongside the enormous cast of character actors like Kevin Stoney in the BBC's *I, Claudius*. Directors always wanted him. Timothy Combe had wanted to use him later in the 1970s and, 'When I went on to do other things at the BBC I did ask for his availability, but I was never very lucky; he was an actor that was in demand.'[515]

In the absence of original performances, television repeats showed a range of films Delgado had appeared in such as the Hammers *Stranglers of*

216

Bombay and *The Mummy's Shroud*, which appeared on ITV in 1978.[516] The television schedules could unwittingly bring familiar names together. On one occasion, a repeat of his appearance in *Sea Fury* was followed by an episode of *Worzel Gummidge* with Jon Pertwee.

Repeats kept his name alive. The *Glasgow Herald* columnist Jack McLean wrote a piece in October 1981 on 'British thrillers' and amidst some jottings on the pleasures of rising from bed late in the day and working from home, Delgado suddenly gets mention eight years after his death. 'My colleagues will be unaware of this, but there are daytime movies. Most of them are in black and white, and are British thrillers in which Roger Delgado is stabbed to death with an oriental dagger in a Belgravia flat. Delgado never seemed to cease being stabbed to death with oriental daggers in Belgravia flats. His murder is always solved, in every movie, by a Canadian in a white crew-cut and a Humphrey Bogart raincoat.'[517] The plot description actually sounds more like what happens in Delgado's second appearance in *The Avengers* or could be a confused jumble of his 1950s B movies like *The Mark of the Phoenix*. But the comic exaggeration is a sign that Delgado was still remembered as a particular type of actor in a particular type of production.

But at the time of his death, there were some people pointing out that Delgado was much more than a screen villain. *The Times*'s obituary of June 20th 1973 noted his 'vivid portrayal' of the Master.[518] On June 26th a former colleague of Delgado, writing as 'A.V.' added another obituary, which said: 'It would be a tragedy if the passing of Roger Delgado should be noted mainly because of his success as a "villain".' A.V. went on: 'His television performances threaten to overshadow the work of an actor of breadth and sensitivity in other spheres, with a range well beyond the television stereotype.'[519] The two obituaries in the same paper are in thought-provoking dialogue. The first is much in line with McLean's comments on British thrillers, the other a rare insistence that there was much more to Delgado than screen villainy.

Over forty years since his death, memories of Delgado remain fresh in the minds of colleagues. Approaching Delgado in terms of his career, his relationships and his personality, one particular comparison comes to mind, and that is with the saintly Peter Cushing (1913-1994). Like Delgado, the lean, gaunt Cushing was a prolific (in fact more prolific) actor, especially in genre work like *The Avengers* and of course Hammer horror; *Doctor Who* is a further common factor between them.[520]

217

The ultimate point of comparison is that there seems to be not a single negative recollection or anecdote about them on record. That comes as no surprise to Terrance Dicks: 'This is in accordance with a theory of mine which is the people who play the villains are extremely nice; Boris Karloff was very charming, and Peter Cushing, and Christopher Lee,' he says of not just the high regard colleagues held Delgado in but how much they loved him and found him a joy to work with.[521]

To place that fact in the wider history of *Doctor Who* is nothing less than incredible. The recollections of co-stars and production personnel about William Hartnell, Patrick Troughton and Jon Pertwee have left ample testimony of committed and professional actors who were inspiring to work with but also very difficult personalities and sometimes strained working relationships. There are also quirks and oddities like Patrick Troughton urinating his way across the golf courses of Britain.

Other people in the *Doctor Who* fold have their controversies. The recent biography of *Doctor Who*'s first producer, Verity Lambert, by Richard Marson is a story of high ambition and achievement but is also full of dramas and bitch fights along with scandals like rigged voting at the BAFTAs and Lambert's ability to make implacable enemies.[522] People queue up to say how impossible Tom Baker was, and memoirs and interviews recalling behind-the-scenes dysfunction, screaming matches, and personality clashes are how we remember the 1980s. Even in the revived series, there are rumours and half-truths of clashes between Russell T. Davies, the showrunner, and Christopher Eccleston, the actor he cast as the Doctor in 2005.

For Delgado the testimony is entirely different and the personality and actions of a man entirely loved and respected emerge from what people thought of him. Like Cushing, the interest in Delgado's career is the distinction between the warmth people found in him as a person and his casting as a villain.

The warmth of friends' and colleagues' memories lifts to an extent the sombre feeling that surrounds the Turkish car accident in 1973. His co-star Katy Manning has strongly emotional memories of 'the nicest man in the world', of someone who was 'gentle, didn't like fighting or violence, but always played bad guys'.[523] Stephen Thorne, Azal in 'The Dæmons', remembers a man who was 'knowledgeable, witty, and a pleasure to work with'.[524] For the director Michael Ferguson, Delgado's calm, friendly professionalism in a frantic television studio was a 'golden gift'.[525] The actor Hugh Futcher remembers it was 'always a pleasure to come into contact with him'.[526] These views are of a kind for anyone who knew Delgado. Some worked with him briefly, long ago on a fast-paced production treadmill, but still the memory sticks. Brian Blessed recalls a 'nice man and a great actor' from their brief time on the set of *Randall and Hopkirk (Deceased)*.[527] Blessed's wife Hildegard Neil shared a set with Delgado on Charlton Heston's Shakespeare, remembering 'a lovely actor, a lovely human being'.[528] Adding to these tributes, Damaris Hayman found him 'one of the nicest, kindest people I think I've worked with'.[529] Many actors have facility in portraying villainy, but not all do so with such total insistence from colleagues that they performed the villainy from a starting point of an entirely lovable personality.

***

However, it is villainy that has kept his name alive and his most famous character remains an ongoing concern in the new *Doctor Who*. Delgado's actual performances as the Master were available on VHS from the 1980s onwards and all his stories are now available on DVD. From the 1980s Delgado's face was on *Doctor Who* merchandise.[530] As for the rest of his career, not everything survives. His theatre roles are accessed from reviews, programmes and theatre archives but a great deal of his television work is missing from the archives. That is not just his appearances on live television in the late 1940s and early 1950s, although there are massive archival gaps here. Even appearances as late as *Vendetta* in 1968 and *Codename* from 1970 are missing from the BBC archives. The BBC's haphazard approach to preserving its output has cut a swathe through his television appearances. Even his *Doctor Who* stories are a mishmash of some original colour videotapes, 16mm black-and-white film prints, and North American Betamax videos.[531]

While we can rewatch his stories, in deeper ways his character has lived on. The character of the Master was not off the screen for very long after 'Frontier in Space' finished transmission. To start with, it did seem Delgado was irreplaceable. After Tom Baker replaced Jon Pertwee, Baker gave an interview to Philippa Toomey in *The Times* discussing the programme and Toomey commented: 'The Doctor had a Moriarty figure in his life in The Master, a Time Lord like himself, who was a worthy adversary.' The interview was in January 1976; Delgado by then was remembered for his villainous roles: 'The liturgy asks that we shall be delivered from the glamour of evil, and the Master certainly had it. Roger Delgado, who played the Master with great panache, was killed in a car accident in 1973, and has proved irreplaceable.'[532] The allusion to the glamour of evil from the Roman Catholic liturgy is unusual and is a nice touch. Had Toomey watched 'The Dæmons' and seen the gorgeously attired Mr Magister?

Later that year Delgado was no longer irreplaceable. 'The producer of Dr Who had a problem. The Doctor's most effective adversary was the Master. But tragically Roger Delgado, the actor who played him, had been killed in a car crash.' So reported the television pages in *The Sunday Times*. Channelling a type of Dick Barton language, the article continued: 'With one bound, they had the answer: let a new actor (Peter Pratt) play the part, but keep him in a mask to hide his identity at the same time as adding to the creepiness.'[533] But it is the reason for putting the mask on Pratt, as explained by the *Doctor Who* production office in *The Sunday Times* report, which stands out: 'They could have made the Master change faces, as they have several times with Dr W himself, but this might strain even the innocent viewer's credulity.'[534] Why would that be? Could viewers not accept seeing another actor in the part besides Delgado?

The character therefore returned, in a story again by Robert Holmes, in 'The Deadly Assassin' in 1976 facing Tom Baker's Doctor. Then he was back in 1980 in 'The Keeper of Traken'. In 'Assassin' the fact Delgado was no longer around was disguised by turning the Master into a decomposing nightmare. Heavy make-up covered the actor Peter Pratt, including tubes pumping liquid to make his face look living but rotten.[535] The change not only accommodated the fact a new actor was in the role but also brought the character into line with the heavily Gothicised themes and imagery in the programme in 1976.

The story, by showing another actor could play the Master, would change *Doctor Who* forever. Robert Holmes thought one function of his script was to give the Master 'several fresh leases of life. He is now set up ready to appear in some totally new guise should any future script editor wish to bring the character back into the series.'[536] Holmes's comments are important, as the 'new guise' means in effect an actor who is not Roger Delgado, and does not need to be Roger Delgado.

Holmes was spot on that later production teams would want the Master back. As his predecessor as script editor says of his own creation, 'The

Master is a good idea and a useful character.'[537] Once it became possible to have the Master without Roger Delgado, there was no reason not to have him around. In 'Traken' the producers took a similar approach and make-up covered Geoffrey Beevers to look like he was rotting away. At the end, the decrepit Master snatches a new body and gets a new look, but the costume and make-up decisions about Anthony Ainley's appearance in the role followed the Delgado template. As Consul Tremas undergoes his appalling transformation, his long grey locks shorten and his beard darkens into a tidy goatee.

Ainley, a superb actor, brought his own abilities to play the role and the 1980s revival of the Master was an undoubted success.[538] But Ainley's appearance each time created a space throughout the 1980s that was a visual reminder of Roger Delgado. Karen Louise Hollis's biography of Ainley included the 'before' and 'after' shots of Ainley to reveal the process of making him up to look the part of the Master and an obligatory aspect was the goatee beard, as well as dark clothing and black leather gloves.

Replacing a highly successful actor in his own part is unenviable. Someone who knows that better than most is Terrance Dicks, who script-edited every episode Delgado was in but also wrote for the Ainley incarnation in 'The Five Doctors' (1983). In Dicks's view, 'Following Roger Delgado, you're really on a hiding to nothing you know, very difficult. Anthony Ainley did it and played him as a very similar character. Anthony was good in his own right; I used him quite a lot in the anniversary show I wrote called "The Five Doctors", and Ant was very good in it you see, but he wasn't Delgado; that was the only thing, for all of them – they weren't Roger Delgado. Which of course they couldn't help.'[539]

Both the Ainley Master and *Doctor Who* vanished from television screens together in 1989. To attempt to bring back the show in a US co-production in 1996, the adversary chosen was the Master, with the American actor Eric Roberts cast. Roberts has since commented on his awareness that his interpretation of the character differed markedly to Ainley and Delgado. However, at the very start of the movie an 'Old Master' appeared being sentenced to death and was played by Gordon Tipple. Although barely visible on screen, this Master wore the dark suit and goatee established by Delgado as the still standard look until the appearance of Eric Roberts.[540]

Although the 1996 revival was a dead end in terms of television production, the show returned as a British programme in 2005, but then the

Master had to wait some time for revival. In the meantime, Delgado's impact in the role resurfaced in the unexpected context of a comedy one-off. *The Curse of Fatal Death* (1999) starred Rowan Atkinson, Hugh Grant, Richard E. Grant, Jim Broadbent and Joanna Lumley as the Doctor but also Jonathan Pryce as the Master. Dressed in black and with a goatee beard, the resemblance to Delgado was striking. Pryce himself realised the similarity.[541]

The producer and head writer of the post-2005 revived show, Russell T. Davies, expressed ambivalent feelings about the character. He clarified them by bringing the Master back, doing so as the villain in a major end-of-season storyline. In 'Utopia' the Doctor has met the elderly and benign Professor Yana, who wears a fob watch and chain. Opening the watch releases Time Lord DNA that floods back and the Master is reborn.

In 'Utopia' a familiar voice is heard: 'Destroy him! And you will give your power to me!' as the enigmatic 'Professor Yana', played by Derek Jacobi, suddenly and dangerously recovers all his memories. For a brief wonderful moment Delgado's performance is heard again as the Master's memories come tumbling out. Like Mr Magister, Sir Gilles Estram or later on Missy, the Master was hiding in plain sight and the audience and the Doctor realise in the same moment of time that the kindly old Professor is not what or who he seems.

We only get a brief glimpse of Derek Jacobi in character as the Master, but the change from the benevolent Professor Yana to the evil Master is extraordinary. It is a testament to Jacobi's acting ability but also to the acting template laid down by Delgado. For one thing, with his memories restored, Yana/the Master recalls that the correct way to address young females is 'my dear': 'Not to worry, my dear. As one door closes, another must open,' he says in mock reassurance to his young assistant Chantho. The Master promptly uses an electrical cable to murder Chantho. In dramatic terms, the act connects across the decades with Delgado's ability to act the Master's vicious and spiteful side.

Since Yana, the character template brought to life by Delgado remains constant, despite what may seem to have been drastic external changes, including the later casting of Michelle Gomez as a female regeneration of the Master calling herself Missy.

What was the Delgado template? One is that the Master is often a lot of fun to be around. Pertwee's Doctor in particular could be quite stodgy, given to preaching and moralising. In contrast, the Master was just a lot more fun.

It's a relief when he turns up in Jo Grant's cell in 'Frontier in Space' and lets her out, telling her she can go with him or stay in the cell, asking, 'Do you really wish to vegetate in this hole for the rest of your natural?' The same dynamic plays out decades later when Missy and Clara team up as temporary allies to enter the Dalek city on Skaro and rescue the Doctor. On their way, their banter brings back memories of Jo and the Master:

> Missy: He's trapped at the heart of the Dalek Empire. He's a prisoner of the creatures who hate him most in the universe. Between us and him is everything the deadliest race in all of history can throw at us. We, on the other hand, have a pointy stick. How do we start?
> Clara: We assume we're going to win.
> Missy: Oh. Pity, really. I was actually quite peckish.
> Clara: Can I have a stick too?
> Missy: Make your own stick.

Part of the fun with the Master is his disguises, both disguising himself as other people and disguising other people as him. In just his first story he infiltrates UNIT headquarters disguised as a telephone technician. Come 'World Enough and Time', the Master was cavorting around as 'Mr Razer'. There is some brief explanation for why the Master is in hiding under a mask, but mostly you get the sense he's doing it because it's such fun.

Another part of the Delgado template is that the fun veneer cracks. He may be fun, but he is also lethal company. In 'Terror of the Autons', the most shocking moment comes towards the very end. The Master escapes from UNIT and runs up the steps of the radio telescope. Blocking his path is a nameless technician and the Master grabs him and flings him down to his death. Barry Letts, directing, gives us a sudden close-up on the Master's face snarling in fury as he flings the technician from a great height.

In the next story something as sudden and vicious happens again. Making a getaway at the end of 'The Mind of Evil' the Master steals a van and drives off, but in doing so runs down the mentally disabled character Barnham. Again, the director lets us see the horror up close and the camera closes in on the Master's face through the windscreen as he makes the split-second decision to keep driving and run the man down. The casual and even thoughtless sadism is the trademark established by Delgado that continues to shape the scripts given to later performers. Ainley's Master remorselessly killed those who were in his way or who had been of short-lived value. In order to demonstrate that she has not turned 'good' in any way, Missy deliberately kills several UNIT operatives at the start of the 2015 episode 'The Magician's Apprentice'. One of them, she casually notes, was obviously a new father to judge from stains on his clothes.

On a lighter note, another characteristic is that the Master enjoys playing dress-ups. Any incarnation of the Master could have delivered Eric Roberts' line 'I always dress for the occasion,' but again it is part of the Delgado template. He dresses up frequently and clearly enjoys the formality of impersonating the Adjudicator, a judicial officer, in 'Colony in Space'. In 'The Dæmons' the Master has quietly murdered Canon Smallwood but has also stolen the Canon's clerical dog-collar, which he wears throughout the story, along with the clerical cassock, but best of all he's also acquired the luridly red satanic gown. In 'The Sea Devils' he has a dressing gown in black and silver and gets to dress up as a naval officer. By 'Frontier in Space' he is impersonating 'a fully accredited Commissioner from the planet Sirius 4' with an ornate uniform to go with it.

Ainley's incarnation of the Master wore a more elaborate velvet costume including a tailcoat and high collar, and Eric Roberts wore leather and heavy Time Lord robes. John Simm had flashes of good taste, including a red-satin-lined overcoat. Finally, Missy played by Michelle Gomez has stretched but continued the template. Her Edwardian blouse, skirts, cameo and brooch may bring to mind Mary Poppins, but they continue the propensity to dress up that all the Masters have shared.

Indeed, 'Missy', underneath what Terrance Dicks calls the 'surface' change of the gender switch, brings not just the Master but Delgado back to life in ways the actor may have appreciated.[542] 'Roger would have loved it,' is Katy Manning's firm judgment on the new Master. She told me: 'Everyone said to me, "What would Roger think of this?" and I said I don't really know, but knowing him as well as I did, I know how much he would have appreciated it.'

What he would appreciate, in Katy Manning's view, all these years later is that the Master still is Delgado: 'It's Roger, in the same way as for the Doctor you have to take William Hartnell as the template.'[543] The Master is a member of the Doctor's own race; he is one of the Time Lords. Like the Doctor he has eschewed the common Time Lord policy of non-interference, but unlike the Doctor he does not explore the universe but plots its conquest. If he cannot always scheme to have the whole universe, his ambition may just be to conquer the Earth and enslave or destroy its inhabitants. These were his goals in his first story and they remain so now.

Katy Manning has watched the Mistress and thinks, 'There's a similarity in so many ways,' including the understanding both actors have: 'The most menacing people are the quietest and the calmest.' In character as Missy, Gomez can be loud and bonkers, but her scariest moment may be whispering in a character's ear, 'I'm going to kill you,' a threat she promptly follows through on. 'If you think of *The Godfather*, the quieter you say something like that to someone, the scarier it is,' says Manning by way of comparison.[544] Manning sees another resemblance as well between the first Master and the most recent: 'He has that wonderful Spanish look, which also belongs to Michelle Gomez. Look at their faces, beautiful, aquiline Spanish. They could be related.'[545]

Michelle Gomez has also thought about appearances and told the journalist Kathryn Williams: 'I did go back and look at past Masters, particularly Roger Delgado, and I hope there are a few similarities there. He had the brilliant eyebrow arch, and was also quite comedic and quite fun.'[546] It was a nice touch that Gomez, in costume, appeared in a short video for World Book Day reading a text called *World Domination*. 'I like to read something light,' she says, holding it up; on the back is a picture of the author: it's Delgado.[547]

***

Born in Whitechapel, killed in Turkey, in between there are hundreds of performances in all mediums, great success, and professional respect from colleagues. As an actor we've see him working alongside stars and character actors of the status of Rex Harrison, Julie Andrews, Dirk Bogarde, Christopher Lee, Peter Cushing, Patrick Macnee, André Morrell, Laurence Olivier, Charlton Heston and Oliver Reed. He also built a career that would be impossible today as his commonest part, his typecasting, was as an exotic, foreign and normally villainous character.

Delgado's professional life lets us see a much wider history of the experiences of working and acting in film and television in post-war Britain. Simply put, Delgado seemed to be in everything. Obviously that's an exaggeration and there's plenty of film and television he wasn't in. On the other hand, there was a strong possibility that someone switching on their television any time from the early 1950s to the early 1970s would see Delgado in a drama or comedy. Tara King knocks on a door in *The Avengers* and Delgado opens it. Don Quixote gets into trouble with the Holy Brotherhood, and it's Delgado under the monk's hood. Someone listening to the wireless in the early 1950s would most definitely have had a good chance of hearing Delgado, especially any religious broadcasting.

Comedy, drama, horror, science fiction, BBC and ITV, Pinewood, Bray, Shepperton, Merton: Roger was everywhere. His career is a time capsule of the world of production around him which found him indispensable, both typecast and versatile. His life was a non-stop trip through decades of ceaseless work where he barely seemed to draw breath.

The Master was never going to be the climax of his career, but a tragically early death means Delgado's best and most notable role was his last. He was an intelligent, thoughtful man and perceptive enough to know that he would be remembered for the Master. Delgado indeed is not usually but universally known as the Master.

Bibliography

Periodicals, newspapers and trade papers

Banbury Express
The British Medical Journal
The Cornishman
Doctor Who Magazine
Evening Express
Evening News
Glasgow Herald
The Guardian
Illustrated London News
The Leicester Mercury
London Gazette
London Hospital Gazette
Luna Monthly
Manchester Evening News
The Manchester Guardian
The Medical Directory
Museums Journal
Northern Daily Mail
The Northern Whig and Belfast Post
Nottingham Evening Post
Nottingham Journal

The Observer
Plays and Players
Radio Times
Royal Leamington Spa Courier and Warwickshire Standard
Rugby Advertiser
The Scotsman
The Spectator
The Stage and Television Today
The Standard
The Sunday Times
Sunderland Echo
The Telegraph
Theatre World
The Times
Variety
The Vaughanian
Warwick and Warwickshire Advertiser
The West Australia
Western Morning News
Yorkshire Post and Leeds Mercury

Books and articles

Ainsworth, John (ed), *Doctor Who: The Complete History Stories 58-60*, Panini Magazines.

Baker, Phil, *The Devil is a Gentleman: The Life and Times of Dennis Wheatley*, Dedalus, 2009.

Banham, Martin, *The Cambridge Guide to Theatre*, Cambridge University Press, 1995.

Bowden, Geoff, *Intimate Memories: The History of the Intimate Theatre, Palmers Green*, The Badger Press, 2006.

Briant, Michael E., *Who is Michael E. Briant?*, Classic TV Press, 2012.

Briggs, Asa, *The History of Broadcasting in the United Kingdom Volume IV: Sound and Vision*, Oxford University Press, 1979.

Britton, Piers D. and Barker, Simon J., *Reading between designs: visual imagery and the generation of meaning in* The Avengers, The Prisoner, *and* Doctor Who, University of Texas Press, 2003.

Brook, Peter, *Threads of Time: A Memoir*, Methuen, 1998.

Brown, Karen E., *The Yeats Circle: Verbal and Visual Relations in Ireland, 1880-1939*, Routledge, 2011.

Burton, Alan and O'Sullivan, Tim, *The Cinema of Basil Dearden and Michael Relph*, Edinburgh University Press, 2009.

Cabell, Craig, *The Doctors Who's Who: The Story Behind Every Face of the Iconic Time Lord*, John Blake Publishing, 2011.

Carney, Jessica, *Who's There? The Life and Career of William Hartnell*, Fantom Films, 2013.

Chapman, James, *Swashbucklers: the Costume Adventure Series*, Oxford University Press, 2015.

Chibnall, Stephen and McFarlane, Brian, *The British 'B' Film*, Palgrave Macmillan, 2009.

Clapham, Mark, Robson, Eddie and Smith, Jim, *Who's Next: An Unofficial and Unauthorised Guide to Doctor Who*, Virgin Books, 2005.

Cochrane, Claire, *Twentieth-Century British Theatre: Industry, Art and Empire*, Cambridge University Press, 2011.

Cody, Gabrielle H. and Sprinchorn, Evert, eds. *The Columbia Encyclopedia of Modern Drama*. Columbia University Press, 2007.

Cook, John R., 'Adapting telefantasy: the *Doctor Who and the Daleks* films', in I. Q. Hunter, *British Science Fiction Cinema*, Routledge, 1999.

Cooke, Lez, *British Television Drama: A History*, British Film Institute, 2003.

Cotter, Robert Michael Bobb, *Ingrid Pitt, Queen of Horror: The Complete Career*, McFarland, 2010.

Crang, Jeremy A., *The British Army and the People's War, 1939-1945*, Manchester University Press, 2000.

Dahrendorf, Ralf, *LSE: A History of the London School of Economics and Political Science, 1895-1995*, Oxford University Press, 1995.

Dixon, Wheeler Winston, *The Charm of Evil: The Life and Films of Terence Fisher*, Scarecrow Press, 1991.

D'Monte, Rebecca, *British Theatre and Performance 1900-1950*, Bloomsbury Methuen, 2015.

Donnelley, Paul, *Fade to Black*, Omnibus Books, 2010.

Elliott, Malcolm, *Victorian Leicester*, Phillimore, 1979.

Eyles, Allen, *The Granada Theatres*, Cinema Theatre Association, 1998.

Giddings, R. and Selby, K., *The Classic Serial on Television and Radio*, Palgrave Macmillan, 2001.

Goodwin, Cliff, *Sid James: a biography*, Virgin Books, 2001.

Hayes, Alan, McGinlay, Richard, and Hayes, Alys, *Two Against the Underworld: the Collected Unauthorised Guide to the Avengers Series 1*, Lulu, 2015.

Hesse, Beatrix, *The English Crime Play in the Twentieth Century*, Palgrave Macmillan, 2015.

Howe, David J., Stammers, Mark and Walker, Stephen James, *Doctor Who: The Eighties*, Virgin Publishing, 1996.

Huckvale, David, *Ancient Egypt in the Popular Imagination: Building a Fantasy in Film, Literature, Music and Art*, McFarland 2012.

Jacobs, Jason, *The Intimate Screen: Early British Television Drama*, Clarendon Press, 2000.

James, Lawrence, *The Rise and Fall of the British Empire*, Abacus, 1994.

Jacobs, Jason, *The Intimate Screen: Early British Television Drama*, Clarendon Press, 2000.

Johnson, Tom and Miller, Mark A., *The Christopher Lee Filmography: All Theatrical Releases, 1948-2003*, McFarland, 2009.

Jones, Matthew, 'Far from swinging London: memories of non-urban cinemagoing in 1960s Britain', in Judith Thissen and Clemens Zimmermann, *Cinema Beyond the City: Small-Town and Rural Film Culture in Europe*, Palgrave, 2016.

Kabatchnik, Amnon, *Blood on the Stage, 1950-1975: Milestone Plays of Crime, Mystery, and Detection*, Scarecrow Press, 2011.

Kausalik, Emily, *Time Signatures: Music and Sound in Doctor Who (1963–89, 1996, 2005–)*, University of Texas PhD.

Keaney, Michael F., *British Film Noir Guide*, McFarland, 2008.

Kistler, Alan, *Doctor Who: A History*, Rowman and Littlefield, 2013.

Kustow, Michael, *Peter Brook: A Biography*, A&C Black, 2013.

Lee, Christopher, *Tall, Dark and Gruesome*, Victor Gallancz, 1997.

Letts, Barry, *Who and Me: The Memoir of* Doctor Who *Producer Barry Letts, 1925-2009*, Fantom Films, 2009.

Lewis, Roger, *Charles Hawtrey 1914-1988: The Man Who Was Private Widdle*, Faber and Faber, 2001.

Lord, Cliff, Lord, Chris, and Watson, Graham, *Royal Corps of Signals: Unit Histories of the Corps (1920-2001) and its antecedents*, Helion and Company, 2011.

Mank, Gregory William, *Hollywood Cauldron: Thirteen Horror Films from the Genre's Golden Age*, McFarland and Company, 1994.

Marson, Richard, *Drama and Delight: The Life of Verity Lambert*, Miwk Publishing, 2015.

Miller, David, *Peter Cushing: A Life in Film*, Titan Books, 2013.

Mitchell, R. J. and Leys, M. D. R., *A History of London Life*, Pelican Books, 1963.

Molesworth, Richard, *Robert Holmes: A Life in Writing*, Telos Publishing, 2013.

More, Kenneth, *More or Less*, Coronet Books, 1979.

Murphy, William Michael, *Prodigal Father: The Life of John Butler Yeats (1839-1922)*, Syracuse University Press, 2001.

Neibaur, James L., *The Bob Hope Films*, McFarland and Company, 2004.

Newman, Kim, *Quatermass and the Pit*, BFI Film Classics, Palgrave Macmillan, 2014.

Nicoll, Alardyce, *English Drama, 1900-1930: The Beginnings of the Modern Period*. Cambridge University Press, 1973.

Panayi, Panikos, *Immigration, Ethnicity and Racism in Britain, 1815-1945*, Manchester University Press, 1994.

Parrill, Sue and Robison, William B., *The Tudors on Film and Television*, McFarland, 2013.

Perera, S. S. and Muthiah, S., *The Janashakthi Book of Sri Lanka Cricket, 1832-1996*, Janashakthi Insurance, 1999.

Pixley, Andrew, *The Quatermass Experiment/Quatermass II/Quatermass and the Pit Viewing Notes*, BBC, 2005.

Porter, Roy, *London: a Social History*, Penguin Books, 1996.

Rattray Taylor, Gordon, *The Great Evolution Mystery*, Harper and Row, 1983.

Reid, Beryl, *So Much Love: an Autobiography*, Arrow, 1984.

Reid, John Howard, *Cinemascope 3: Hollywood Takes the Plunge*, Lulu, 2006.

Reid, John Howard, *Success in the Cinema: Money-Making Movies and Critics' Choices*, Lulu, 2007.

Richards, Sandra, *Rise of the English Actress*, Springer, 1993.

Rogers, Dave, *The Complete Avengers*, Boxtree, 1989.

Rothwell, Kenneth S. and Melzer, Annabelle Henkin, *Shakespeare on Screen: An International Filmography and Videography*, Neal-Schuman Publishers, 1990.

Rowell, George, Jackson, Anthony and Jackson, Tony, *The Repertory Movement: A History of Regional Theatre in Britain*, Cambridge University Press, 1984.

Sanderson, Michael, *From Irving to Olivier: A Social History of the Acting Profession*, St Martin's Press, 1984.

Sexton, Max and Cook, Malcolm, *Adapting Science Fiction to Television: Small Screen, Expanded Universe*, Rowman and Littlefield, 2015.

Spence, Lyndsy, *Margaret Lockwood: Queen of the Silver Screen*, Fantom Films, 2016.

Tatspaugh, Patricia, 'The tragedies of love on film', in Russell Jackson (ed), *The Cambridge Companion to Shakespeare on Film*, Cambridge University Press, 2000.

Vahimagi, Tise, *British Television: An Illustrated Guide*, Oxford University Press, 1994.

Waller, John H., *Gordon of Khartoum: The Saga of a Victorian Hero*, Atheneum, 1988.

Wearing, J. P., *The London Stage 1950-1959: A Calendar of Productions, Performers, and Personnel*, Rowman and Littlefield, 2014.

White, Leonard, *Armchair Theatre: The Lost Years*, Kelly Publications, 2003.

Williams, Kenneth, *The Kenneth Williams Diaries*, ed. Russell Davies, HarperCollins, 1993.

Wheatley, Dennis, *The Devil and All His Works*, Arrow Books, 1971.

Wheatley, Helen, 'Putting the Mystery back into *Armchair Theatre*', *Journal of British Cinema and Television*, May 2009, vo. 1, no. 2, pp. 197-210.

Wright, Adrian, *A Tanner's Worth of Tune: Rediscovering the Post-War British Musical*, Boydell Press, 2010.

Zucker, Carole, *In the Company of Actors: Reflections on the Craft of Acting*, Psychology Press, 1999.

Notes

[1] Interview June 27th 2016

[2] Porter, *London: a Social History*, p.169

[3] Mitchell and Leys, *History of London Life*, pp.271, 276

[4] http://www.warpedfactor.com/2014/06/doctor-who-roger-delgado-original-master.html

[5] *London Hospital Gazette*, no.197, March 1918, p.56

[6] *The British Medical Journal*, volume 1, part 2, 1907, p.1346

[7] I owe this information to Richard Meunier, Deputy Archivist/Curator, Royal London Hospital Archives & Museum, Barts Health NHS Trust.

[8] I am grateful to María Paola González Sepúlveda of the School of Languages and Linguistics at the University of Melbourne for advice on Spanish naming customs.

[9] I am grateful to Dr Beatriz Carbajal for this information.

[10] Karen E. Brown, *The Yeats Circle*, p.164

[11] Murphy, *Prodigal Father*, p.117

[12] *Birmingham Post*, December 23rd 1940, p.1

[13] R. R. Kenefeck, *A Talk to Parents of New Boys*, p.8

[14] Interview July 19th 2016

[15] *The Vaughanian* 1934, p.3

[16] *The Vaughanian* 1934, p.38

[17] *Lancashire Daily Post*, June 9th 1904, p.2

[18] Paul Donnelley, *Fade to Black*, p.204

[19] *41 Lothbury 1834-1984*, p.2

[20] *41 Lothbury 1834-1984*, p.10

[21] I owe this information to the archivists of the Royal Bank of Scotland.

[22] I owe this information to the archivists of the Royal Bank of Scotland.

[23] For example, look at the entry for Delgado on the British Film Institute website, the Metacritic site and any of his obituaries.

[24] Dahrendorf, *LSE*, p.142

[25] Dahrendorf, *LSE*, p.142

[26] I owe this information to the archivists of the Royal Bank of Scotland.

[27] I am grateful to Richard Temple of the Senate House Library, University of London, for this information.

[28] I owe this information to the archivists of the London School of Economics, especially Sue Donnelly.

[29] I am grateful to Anna Towlson of the LSE Library for this point.

[30] *The Telegraph*, August 23rd 2016, http://www.telegraph.co.uk/films/0/alastair-sim-our-greatest-comic-actor/

[31] Miller, *Peter Cushing: A Life in Film*, p.12

[32] Sanderson, *From Irving to Olivier*, pp.4, 246

[33] http://www.screenonline.org.uk/film/id/1170549/

[34] Letts, *Who and Me*, p.6

[35] Elliott, *Victorian Leicester*, p.18

[36] http://www.arthurlloyd.co.uk/LeicesterTheatres/TheatreRoyalLeicester.htm

[37] https://www.youtube.com/watch?v=ykqeFptGqYI

[38] http://www.arthurlloyd.co.uk/LeicesterTheatres/TheatreRoyalLeicester.htm

[39] http://www.arthurlloyd.co.uk/LeicesterTheatres/TheatreRoyalLeicester.htm

[40] http://www.arthurlloyd.co.uk/WatfordPalaceTheatre.htm

[41] *The Times*, March 1st 1938, p.14; *The Stage*, January 23rd 1939, p.13

[42] *The Standard*, May 28th 1938, p.3

[43] *The Standard*, July 16th 1938, p.3

[44] *The Standard*, July 25th 1938, p.3; July 30th 1938, p.3

[45] Goodwin, *Sid James*, p.41

[46] More, *More or Less*, p.76

[47] Reid, *So Much Love*, p.18

[48] Williams, *Diaries*, p.12

[49] Williams, *Diaries*, pp.28-30

[50] Williams, *Diaries*, p.29

[51] Sanderson, *From Irving to Olivier*, p.236

[52] *The Stage and Television Today*, November 5th 1970, p.12

[53] Interview November 18th 2016

[54] *Leicester Mercury*, April 18th 1939, p.17

[55] *The Stage*, April 29th 1939, p.7

[56] Nicoll, *English Drama, 1900-1930*, p.416

[57] *Leicester Mercury*, May 2nd 1939, p.21

[58] *Leicester Mercury*, May 30th 1939, p.4

[59] *Leicester Mercury*, June 13th 1939, p.15

[60] *Leicester Mercury*, June 27th 1939, p.17

[61] *Leicester Mercury*, July 4th 1939, p.11

[62] Cody and Sprinchorn, *The Columbia Encyclopedia of Modern Drama*, p.1417

[63] *Leicester Mercury*, July 11th 1939, p.3

[64] *The Stage*, July 13th 1939, p.7

[65] *Leicester Mercury*, July 18th 1939, p.4

[66] *Leicester Mercury*, August 22nd 1939, p.15

[67] *Express and Advertiser*, September 11th 1929, p.4

[68] *Leicester Mercury*, August 29th 1939, p.153

[69] *Leicester Mercury*, October 10th 1939, p.9

[70] *The Stage*, October 12th 1939, p.9

[71] *The Stage*, August 24th 1939, p.2

[72] *Leicester Mercury*, November 28th 1939, p.6

[73] *The Stage*, November 30th 1939, p.2

[74] *The Stage*, December 7th 1939, p.4

[75] *Leicester Mercury*, December 12th 1939, p.9

[76] *Leicester Mercury*, December 12th 1939, p.9

[77] *Leicester Mercury*, December 27th 1939, p.9

[78] *Leicester Mercury*, December 27th 1939, p.9

[79] *Leicester Mercury* December 19th 1939, p.13

[80] *The Stage*, January 4th 1940. I am grateful to Matthew Lloyd for this reference.

[81] *Theatre World* volumes 33 and 34, 1940, p.66

[82] Interview June 30th 2016

[83] Interview November 18th 2016

[84] I am grateful to Martin Skipworth of the Royal Signals Museum for this point.

[85] *Second Supplement to the London Gazette of Tuesday, the 16th of September, 1941*, September 19th 1941, p.5410

[86] Crang, *The British Army*, p.24

[87] Lord, Lord and Watson, *Royal Corps of Signals: Unit Histories of the Corps (1920-2001)*, p.372

[88] Cecil, '1941-1945 Eastern Travels Part 2'

[89] http://archive.spectator.co.uk/article/18th-august-1950/5/-army-form-b199a-revised-1949-is-a

[90] http://www.kabristan.org.uk/kabristan-indexes/sri-lanka-indexes/139-sri-lanka-formerly-ceylon-births-baptisms-indexes/ceylon-births-baptisms-sri-lanka-kandy/ceylon-births-baptisms-sri-lanka-kandy-1901-1927/1932-kandy-st-paul-s-church-births-baptisms-marriages-1901-1927-a

[91] *The Scotsman*, July 25th 1921, p.9

[92] *The Scotsman*, June 10th 1944, p.6

[93] Perera and Muthiah, *The Janashakthi Book of Sri Lanka Cricket, 1832-1996*, p.281

[94] All genealogical information from 'Genealogy of the Family of Anthonisz of Ceylon', compiled by D. V. Altendorff.

[95] Interview June 26th 2016

[96] Philip MacDonald, 'More than a Moriarty', *Doctor Who Magazine*, 311, 2001, p.20

[97] Kitsiri Malalgoda, *Buddhism in Sinhalese Society, 1750-1900*, p.96

[98] Interview September 29th 2016

[99] Interview September 29th 2016

[100] *The Cornishman*, August 21st 1947, p.8

[101] *The Stage*, July 17th 1947, p.9

[102] *Nottingham Evening Post*, November 1st 1947, p.3

[103] *Nottingham Evening Post*, November 4th 1947, p.3

[104] *Nottingham Journal*, November 4th 1947, p.4

[105] *Western Morning News*, December 9th 1947, p.5

[106] *Nottingham Evening Post*, February 28th 1948, p.3

[107] *The Guardian*, December 4th 2007,
https://www.theguardian.com/news/2007/dec/04/guardianobituaries.television

[108] *Sunderland Echo*, March 20th 1948, p.3

[109] Eyles, *The Granada Theatres*, p.140

[110] *Rugby Advertiser*, April 6th 1948, p.3

[111] Rowell, Jackson and Jackson, *The Repertory Movement: A History of Regional Theatre in Britain*, p.81

[112] Rowell, Jackson and Jackson, *The Repertory Movement*, p.193

[113] Cochrane, *Twentieth-Century British Theatre: Industry, Art and Empire*, p.168

[114] *Royal Leamington Spa Courier and Warwickshire Standard*, February 18th 1948

[115] *Warwick and Warwickshire Advertiser* February 4th 1949, p.3

[116] *Royal Leamington Spa Courier and Warwickshire Standard*, February 4th 1949, p.6

[117] *Warwick and Warwickshire Advertiser* April 3rd 1949, p.3

[118] *Royal Leamington Spa Courier and Warwickshire Standard*, April 8th 1949

[119] *The Stage*, May 26th 1949, p.9

[120] Zucker, *In the Company of Actors: Reflections on the Craft of Acting*, p.19

[121] Banham, *The Cambridge Guide to Theatre*, p.627

[122] *Live from The Intimate Theatre*, https://screenplaystv.wordpress.com/2012/02/15/live-from-the-intimate-theatre-1946-1949-part-1/

[123] Sanderson, *From Irving to Olivier*, p.276

[124] Spence, *Margaret Lockwood: Queen of the Silver Screen*, p.124

[125] Jacobs, *The Intimate Screen*, p.14

[126] D'Monte, *British Theatre and Performance 1900-1950*,
https://books.google.com.au/books?id=M4KKBgAAQBAJ&pg=PT198&lpg=PT198&dq=Geoff+Bowden+theatre&source=bl&ots=jmCdjqfmYw&sig=OFjJ_hCqXj75FevvLqzvXU2FxKg&hl=en&sa=X&ved=0ahUKEwi3krfPjYnPAhXLPD4KHflRBc0Q6AEIKzAD#v=onepage&q=Geoff%20Bowden%20theatre&f=false

[127] Bowden, *Intimate Memories*, p. 78

[128] *The Times*, January 6th 1948, p.6; *Radio Times*, issue 1290, 1948, p.27

[129] Hesse, *The English Crime Play in the Twentieth Century*,
https://books.google.com.au/books?id=Ua2hCgAAQBAJ&pg=PT192&lpg=PT192&dq=Beatrix+Hesse,+The+English+Crime+Play+in+the+Twentieth+Century&source=bl&ots=VTFr3hFX5-&sig=kdT1qPWQ7LXCld6F8h6cc26fyCs&hl=en&sa=X&ved=0ahUKEwjyobmIoL3PAhVGqJQKHUToDloQ6AEIMzAE#v=onepage&q=distinguished&f=false

[130] http://www.doollee.com/PlaywrightsP/parish-james.html#95538

[131] Bowden, *Intimate Memories*, p. 70

[132] Bowden, *Intimate Memories*, p. 75

[133] Interview July 19th 2016

[134] *The West Australia*, June 9th 1949, p.2

135 Interview November 18th 2016

136 *Radio Times* issue 1652, 1955, p.38

137 *Radio Times* issue 1516, 1952, p.47

138 Sexton and Cook, *Adapting Science Fiction to Television*, p.44

139 *The Times*, December 1st 1958, p.14

140 *The Times*, December 1st 1958, p.14

141 *The Times*, December 1st 1958, p.14

142 BFI Screenonline: White Falcon, http://www.screenonline.org.uk/tv/id/1218638/index.html

143 Briggs, *History of Broadcasting*, p.918

144 Pixley, *Viewing notes*, p.21

145 Pixley, *Viewing notes*, p.22

146 http://ohyesrogerdelgado.tumblr.com/page/3

147 *Evening News*, October 22nd 1955, p.4

148 Pixley, *Viewing notes*, p.

149 *The Spectator*, February 17th 1956, p.8

150 *The Yorkshire Post and Leeds Mercury*, November 14th 1955, p.5

151 Carney, *Who's There*, p.169

152 Pixley, *Viewing Notes*, p.25

153 BFI Screenonline: White Falcon, http://www.screenonline.org.uk/tv/id/1218638/

154 Parrill and Robison, *The Tudors on Film and Television*, p.298

155 BFI Screenonline: Cold Light, http://www.screenonline.org.uk/tv/id/1218604/index.html

156 *The Observer*, December 15th 1957, p.10

157 *The Times*, December 9th 1957, p.12

158 *The Stage*, January 14th 1960, p.20

159 *The Spectator*, January 22nd 1960, p.18

160 *The Stage and Television Today*, May 26th 1966, p.11

161 *The Stage and Television Today*, September 22nd 1960, p.10

162 Interview July 19th 2016

163 Interview June 26th 2016

164 *The Stage*, January 31st 1957, p.12

165 *The Times*, January 28th 1957, p.12

166 Chibnall and McFarlane, *The British 'B' Film*, p.191

167 Interview September 29th 2016

168 Reid, *Success in the Cinema*, p.100

169 http://www.britishclassiccomedy.co.uk/the-belles-of-st-trinians-1954

170 http://www.dvdcompare.net/review.php?rid=2769

171 What follows is courtesy of a conversation with Dr Matthew Jones about his research into cinemagoing in the 1950s and 1960s. For more see Jones, 'Far from swinging London: memories of non-urban cinemagoing in 1960s Britain'.

172 https://noirencyclopedia.wordpress.com/2013/12/10/mark-of-the-phoenix-1958/

173 *Portsmouth Evening News*, October 18th 1952, p.7

174 *Daily Telegraph*, March 26th 1957, p.11

175 *Museums Journal*, vol.66, p.246

176 *Radio Times*, August 9th 1962

[177] Olga Rattray Taylor, Foreword to Gordon Rattray Taylor, *The Great Evolution Mystery*, 1983

[178] Interview September 29th 2016

[179] Interview September 29th 2016

[180] http://www.bbc.com/news/entertainment-arts-23398206

[181] Interview September 29th 2016

[182] Interview September 29th 2016

[183] Lee, *Tall, Dark and Gruesome*, p.192

[184] *The Observer*, April 13th 1975

[185] https://www.theguardian.com/stage/2003/jul/09/theatre.samanthaellis

[186] *The Stage*, November 29th 1951, p.7

[187] *The Stage*, August 2nd 1951, p.7

[188] *The Stage*, May 10th 1951, p.7

[189] *Manchester Guardian*, May 12th 1952, p.5

[190] *The Stage*, May 29th 1952, p.7

[191] *The Yorkshire Post and Leeds Mercury*, October 9th 1953, p.4

[192] *Glasgow Herald*, March 23rd 1956,
https://news.google.com/newspapers?nid=2507&dat=19560323&id=2GlAAAAAIBAJ&sjid=X5UMAAAAIBAJ&pg=3601,2772514&hl=en

[193] *The Stage and Television Today*, January 27th 1966, p.11

[194] Interview September 29th 2016

[195] Interview July 19th 2016

[196] Johnson and Del Vecchio, *Hammer Films: An Exhaustive Filmography*, p.99

[197] *The Telegraph*, November 25th 2011

[198] Keaney, *British Film Noir Guide*, p.198

[199] Johnson and Del Vecchio, *Hammer Films*, p.169

[200] *The Times*, December 7th 1959, p.14

[201] James, *Rise and Fall*, p.221

[202] Dixon, *The Charm of Evil*, p.391

[203] Interview September 29th 2016

[204] Johnson and Del Vecchio, *Hammer Films*, p.185

[205] http://www.latimes.com/entertainment/herocomplex/la-et-hc-christopher-lee-christopher-lee-dies-saruman-peter-jackson-20150611-htmlstory.html

[206] Johnson and Del Vecchio, *Hammer Films*, p.285

[207] Huckvale, *Ancient Egypt in the Popular Imagination*, p.43

[208] *The Times*, May 18th 1967, p.8

[209] *Evening Express*, December 31st 1955, p.6

[210] *The Northern Whig and Belfast Post*, November 11th 1955, p.3

[211] *The Banbury Advertiser*, February 1st 1956, p.2

[212] *Evening Express*, April 20th 1955, p.3

[213] Johnson and Miller, *The Christopher Lee Filmography: All Theatrical Releases, 1948-2003*, p.55

[214] https://www.theguardian.com/film/2011/mar/24/dirk-bogarde-singer-not-song

[215] Reid, *Cinemascope 3: Hollywood Takes the Plunge*, p.226

[216] https://www.theguardian.com/film/2011/mar/24/dirk-bogarde-singer-not-song

[217] http://www.screenonline.org.uk/film/id/508279/synopsis.html

[218] *Variety*, March 11th 1964

[219] Neibaur, *The Bob Hope Films*, p.138

[220] Neibaur, *The Bob Hope Films*, p.138

[221] *Illustrated London News*, March 31st 1962, p.514

[222] Interview August 11th 2016

[223] Interview August 11th 2016

[224] Interview August 11th 2016

[225] Interview August 11th 2016

[226] *Variety*, April 21st 1965

[227] *The Times*, March 25th 1971, p.18

[228] *The Times*, March 25th 1971, p.18

[229] *The Stage and Television Today*, October 4th 1962, p.14

[230] *Variety*, February 27th 1963

[231] https://h2g2.com/edited_entry/A2430181

[232] Pers.com

[233] Pers.com

[234] *The Stage and Television Today*, February 25th 1965, p.10

[235] http://archive.spectator.co.uk/article/10th-june-1966/18/cinema

[236] Lewis, *Charles Hawtrey 1914-1988: The Man Who Was Private Widdle*, p.17

[237] *The Times*, January 9th 1966, p.8

[238] Waller, *Gordon of Khartoum*, p.302

[239] *The Stage and Television Today*, May 9th 1968, p.12

[240] Pers.com

[241] *The Guardian*, March 21st 1969, p.8

[242] *Illustrated London News*, March 29th 1969, p.31

[243] *Star! A Robert Wise Film*, National Publishers, 1968; Richards, *Rise of the English Actress*, p.145

[244] *The Stage*, September 24th 1953, p.12

[245] *The Stage*, January 21st 1954, p.10

[246] *The Stage*, April 28th 1955, p.8

[247] Helfer and Loney, *Peter Brook*, p.77

[248] *The Stage,* March 1956, p.4

[249] *The Times*, February 24th 1956, p.7

[250] *The Power and the Glory* programme

[251] Wearing, *The London Stage*, p.423

[252] *The Times*, April 6th 1956, p.3

[253] *Theatre World*, May 1956, pp.9, 34

[254] Brook, *Threads of Time*, pp.32-33

[255] Brook, *Threads of Time*, p.33

[256] Kustow, *Peter Brook*, p.96

[257] Brook, *Threads of Time*, p.34

[258] Gardner, 'Paul Scofield', *The Guardian*, March 20th 2008, https://www.theguardian.com/film/2008/mar/20/2

[259] *The Times*, April 6th 1956, p.3

[260] *The Stage*, April 12th 1956, p.9

[261] Quoted in Custow, *Peter Brook*, p.89

[262] *Theatre World*, April 1956, p.8

[263] *The Stage*, March 26th 1959, p.6

[264] *The Guardian*, December 16th 1959

[265] *Manchester Guardian*, April 15th 1959, p.7

[266] *Manchester Guardian*, April 15th 1959, p.7

[267] *The Stage*, April 16th 1959, p.18

[268] *The Stage*, July 30th 1964, p.12

[269] *The Spectator*, January 5th 1962, p.28

[270] *The Stage*, March 3rd 1962, p.5

[271] *The Stage*, November 30th 1961, p.3

[272] *The Stage*, January 11th 1962, p.3

[273] *Daily Mail*, July 6th 2008, http://www.dailymail.co.uk/femail/article-1032365/Why-Charlie-Drake-left-just-5-000-5m-blew-women-horses-fast-cars.html

[274] Wright, *A Tanner's Worth of Tune*, p.131

[275] http://www.overthefootlights.co.uk/1962-1963.pdf

[276] *The Stage*, May 9th 1963, p.14

[277] *The Stage*, June 20th 1963, p.10

[278] *The Stage*, July 21st 1963, p.15

[279] *The Times*, July 4th 1963, p.16

[280] *The Stage*, September 3rd 1964, p.1

[281] http://www.express.co.uk/news/obituaries/704378/brian-rix-1924-2016-died-august-20-aged-92-crusading-comic-actor-campaigner

[282] *Theatre World*, November 1964, p.27

[283] *Plays and Players*, December 1964, p.42

[284] *Plays and Players*, December 1964, p.43

[285] *Theatre World*, November 1964, p.30

[286] Interview July 19th 2016

[287] Donnelley, *Fade to Black*, p.204

[288] *Plays and Players*, May 1967, p.17

[289] *Plays and Players*, May 1967, p.17

[290] *The Stage and Television Today*, March 9th 1967, p.15

[291] *The Stage Year Book 1968*, 37th Edition, p.245

[292] Interview June 27th 2016

[293] *The Times*, November 25th 1954, p.5

[294] *Northern Daily Mail*, November 29th 1954, p.6

[295] Vahimagi, *British Television*, p.45; Kabatchnik, *Blood on the Stage*, p.217

[296] Vahimagi, *British Television*, p.35

[297] Interview June 26th 2016

[298] Williams, *Diaries*, p.137

[299] Williams, *Diaries*, p.427

[300] 'Richard Greene, TV's Robin Hood, dies', http://articles.latimes.com/1985-06-02/local/me-15028_1_fan-club

[301] John Kelly, *Roger Delgado: The Master*, DVD Extra on 'Frontier in Space', 2010

302 http://www.screenonline.org.uk/tv/id/1136160/

303 *The Stage and Television Today*, April 13th 1961, p.10

304 *The Stage and Television Today*, May 28th 1961, p.11

305 *The Stage and Television Today*, September 14th 1961, p.10

306 Interview June 27th 2016

307 Interview June 26th 2016

308 Interview June 26th 2016

309 Chapman, *Swashbucklers*, p.90

310 Chapman, *Swashbucklers*, p.91

311 Interview June 26th 2016

312 Interview August 8th 2016

313 *The Guardian*, October 12th 2009, https://www.theguardian.com/tv-and-radio/2009/oct/12/barry-letts-obituary

314 *The Telegraph*, August 31st 1958, p.8

315 *The Stage and Television Today*, March 3rd 1960, pp.2 and 11

316 Interview June 26th 2016

317 Chapman, *Swashbucklers*, p.93

318 Andrew Pixley, 'DWM Archive: Terror of the Autons', *Doctor Who Magazine*, no.311, p.31

319 Kelly, *Roger Delgado*

320 Interview August 8th 2016

321 Interview August 8th 2016

322 I am grateful to Sheena Harold and members of the Teddington Society for this information.

323 Interview June 30th 2016

324 Theatre programme

325 Giddings and Selby, *The Classic Serial on Television and Radio*, p.45

326 *The Stage and Television Today*, April 30th 1964, p.12

327 *TV Times*, 28th July-3rd August 1963

328 *The Stage and Television Today*, February 27th 1964, p.9

329 Interview November 18th 2016

330 http://tvminus50.blogspot.com.au/2013/06/saturday-1-june-1963.html

331 Interview November 18th 2016

332 *The Stage and Television Today*, October 12th 1963, p.9

333 Pers.com via email, July 9th 2017

334 Pers.com via email, July 6th 2017

335 *The Stage and Television Today*, September 12th, p.10 and October 17th 1963, p.10

336 Interview September 12th 2016

337 Foreword to Leonard White, *Armchair Theatre: The Lost Years*

338 Interview September 12th 2016

339 *The Stage and Television Today*, January 26th 1967, p.12

340 *TV Times*, February 4th-February 10th 1967

341 Interview August 11th 2017

342 Hayes, McGinley and Hayes, *Two Against the Underworld*, p.143

343 Hayes, McGinley and Hayes, *Two Against the Underworld*, p.143

[344] Hayes, McGinley and Hayes, *Two Against the Underworld*, p.143

[345] *Manchester Evening News*, February 4th 1961, p.7, http://deadline.theavengers.tv/keel-005-CrescentMoon.htm

[346] Hayes, McGinley and Hayes, *Two Against the Underworld*, p.145

[347] Rogers, *The Complete Avengers*, p.20

[348] Hayes, McGinley and Hayes, *Two Against the Underworld*, p.144

[349] Interview August 11th 2017

[350] http://www.dissolute.com.au/the-avengers-tv-series/series-6/620-stay-tuned.html

[351] Interviewed by John Kelly for his documentary on Roger Delgado

[352] Interview July 14th 2017

[353] Hayward, 'Alexandra Bastedo obituary', *The Guardian*, January 14th 2014

[354] Pers.com, August 15th 2017

[355] Gregory William Mank, *Hollywood Cauldron*, p.56

[356] Interview September 29th 2016

[357] For these points on accents, I am deeply indebted to Carolyn Butler White, who watched a number of Delgado's performances for me.

[358] Interview September 12th 2016

[359] *The Guardian*, November 12th 2009, https://www.theguardian.com/film/2009/nov/12/khartoum-reel-history

[360] *The Telegraph*, February 11th 1973, p.40

[361] http://www.telegraph.co.uk/news/obituaries/12134279/Frank-Finlay-actor-obituary.html

[362] Newman quoted in Wheatley, 'Putting the mystery back into *Armchair Theatre*', p.197

[363] *Radio Times*, issue 2461, 1971

[364] Letts, *Who and Me*, p.126

[365] Interview June 27th 2016

[366] http://tomsalinsky.co.uk/blog/index.php/2014/09/01/

[367] Interview July 12th 2016

[368] *The Stage and Television Today*, June 14th 1962, p.9

[369] *Radio Times Return of the Time Lord Souvenir*, 1996, p.10

[370] *Radio Times*, issue 2461, 1971

[371] Interview July 19th 2016

[372] Interview September 1st 2016

[373] Interview July 19th 2016

[374] Interview June 27th 2016

[375] Interview June 27th 2016

[376] Burton and O'Sullivan, *The Cinema of Basil Dearden and Michael Relph*, p.315

[377] Molesworth, *Robert Holmes*, p.138

[378] Interview July 19th 2016

[379] Interview July 19th 2016

[380] Letts, *Who and Me*, p.148

[381] Interview July 19th 2016

[382] Interview July 19th 2016

[383] Andrew Pixley, 'DWM Archive: Terror of the Autons', *Doctor Who Magazine*, no.311, p.30

[384] Britton and Barker, *Reading between Designs*, p.174

[385] Britton and Barker, *Reading between Designs*, p.174

386 Kausalik, *Time Signatures*, p.160

387 Kausalik, *Time Signatures*, p.161

388 Interview June 30th 2016

389 Interview July 12th 2016

390 Interview July 12th 2016

391 Interview June 30th 2016

392 Interview July 12th 2016

393 Interview July 12th 2016

394 Interview July 12th 2016

395 Interview June 26th 2016

396 Interview August 8th 2016

397 Interview June 30th 2016

398 Interview June 27th 2016

399 Interview June 30th 2016

400 Interview June 30th 2016

401 Interview June 30th 2016

402 Interview June 30th 2016

403 Interview June 30th 2016

404 Interview June 30th 2016

405 Williams, *Diaries*, pp.305-306

406 Pers.com

407 Alan Barnes, 'Fact of Fiction: The Claws of Axos', *Doctor Who Magazine*, 432, 2011, p.51

408 Interview July 19th 2016

409 Andrew Pixley, 'DWM Archive: The Claws of Axos', *Doctor Who Magazine*, 264, 1998, p.33

410 Barnes, 'Fact of Fiction', p.55

411 http://www.tvstudiohistory.co.uk/tv%20centre%20history.htm

412 Interview September 1st 2016

413 Interview July 19th 2016

414 'Beyond the Fringe', *Doctor Who Magazine*, 270, p.10

415 Pixley, 'DWM Archive', p.32

416 Pers.com

417 Interview August 8th 2016

418 Interview August 8th 2016

419 Interview August 8th 2016

420 Kistler, *Doctor Who: A History*, p.91

421 Interview September 1st 2016

422 Interview September 1st 2016

423 Interview June 26th 2016

424 Interview June 26th 2016

425 Interview June 26th 2016

426 Interview June 26th 2016

427 Interview June 26th 2016

428 Interview June 26th 2016

429 Interview June 26th 2016

430 Interview June 26th 2016

[431] Clapham, Robson and Smith, *Who's Next*, p.134

[432] Interview July 19th 2016

[433] Interview June 26th 2016

[434] Interview June 26th 2016

[435] http://www.bbc.co.uk/doctorwho/classic/episodeguide/daemons/detail.shtml

[436] Baker, *The Devil is a Gentleman*, p.514

[437] Wheatley, *The Devil and All His Works*, p.285

[438] Wheatley, *The Devil and All His Works*, p.285

[439] Interview July 14th 2016

[440] Letts, *Who and Me*, p.148

[441] Interview June 26th 2016

[442] Interview June 27th 2016

[443] Interview July 14th 2017

[444] *The Times*, May 21st 1996

[445] *The Stage*, January 24th 1957, p.12

[446] Interview June 26th 2016

[447] Interview June 26th 2016

[448] In Jon Kelly's biography on the DVD release of 'Frontier in Space'. See also http://www.bbc.co.uk/doctorwho/classic/episodeguide/seadevils/detail.shtml

[449] Letts, *Who and Me*, p.79

[450] Interview July 19th 2016

[451] Interview June 26th 2016

[452] Interview June 26th 2016

[453] Interview August 11th 2016

[454] Interview August 11th 2016

[455] 'Fact of Fiction: The Sea Devils', *Doctor Who Magazine*, 465, 2013, p.55

[456] Interview June 26th 2016

[457] Interview June 27th 2016

[458] *The Stage and Television Today*, March 30th 1972, p.11

[459] Interview June 26th 2016

[460] Interview July 19th 2016

[461] Cotter, *Ingrid Pitt, Queen of Horror: The Complete Career*, p.168

[462] Andrew Pixley, 'The Time Monster', *Doctor Who Magazine*, 268, pp.19-21

[463] Interview June 27th 2016

[464] Peter Griffiths, 'Are you receiving me?', *Doctor Who Magazine*, 276, 1999, p.9

[465] *The Spectator*, May 25th 1973, p.4

[466] Interview July 12th 2016

[467] Interview June 26th 2016

[468] Interview July 19th 2016

[469] Interview September 1st 2016

[470] Interview September 1st 2016

[471] Interview July 19th 2016

[472] *The Stage and Television Today*, June 17th 1971, p.12

[473] *The Sunday Times*, October 31st 1971, p.52

[474] *The Stage and Television Today*, May 6th 1971, p.11

[475] *The Stage and Television Today*, July 1st 1971, p.12

[476] http://www.screenonline.org.uk/tv/id/537703/index.html

[477] https://www.theguardian.com/film/2008/mar/20/2

[478] *The Stage*, December 3rd 1953, p.10

[479] *The Times*, November 18th 1958, p.13

[480] *The Times*, November 18th 1958, p.13

[481] *The Stage*, October 2nd 1969, p.17

[482] Rothwell and Melzer, *Shakespeare on Screen*, p.28

[483] Rothwell and Melzer, *Shakespeare on Screen*, p.29

[484] Tatspaugh, 'The tragedies of love on film', pp.154-155

[485] Interview July 14th 2017

[486] Interview July 19th 2016

[487] Andrew Pixley, 'The DWM Archive: Terror of the Autons', *Doctor Who Magazine*, no.311

[488] Miller, *Peter Cushing*, p.111

[489] Interview June 26th 2016

[490] *The Times*, August 16th 1972, p.14

[491] *The Sunday Times*, 7th January 1973, p.48

[492] Interview September 12th 2016

[493] *Radio Times*, issue 2565, 1973, p.56

[494] Interview September 12th 2016

[495] http://dweveryday.blogspot.com.au/2011/10/343-frontier-in-space-episode-six.html; Philip MacDonald, 'More than a Moriarty', *Doctor Who Magazine*, 311, 2001, p.25; Jonathan Rigby, 'Past Master', *The Essential Doctor Who Series – The Master*, Panini, 2015, p.25

[496] https://h2g2.com/edited_entry/A2430181

[497] Cabell, *The Doctors Who's Who: The Story Behind Every Face of the Iconic Time Lord*, https://books.google.com.au/books?id=nbpkAgAAQBAJ&pg=PT55&lpg=PT55 &dq=kismet+delgado&source=bl&ots=MonnkmF6Bg &sig=uB67NinOOnl7sRvAncDWx_O0SBs&hl=en&sa=X &ved=0ahUKEwjwj_WympPQAhXJFZQKHTyKADQ4HhDoAQgZMAA#v=onepage &q=kismet%20delgado&f=false

[498] http://kasterborous.com/2015/05/roger-delgados-last-appearance-found/; http://doctorwhocastandcrew.blogspot.com.au/2014/05/frontier-in-space.html?m=1

[499] *The Telegraph*, 20th June 1973, p.19

[500] *Luna Monthly*, Issues 32-49, p.2

[501] *Variety*, 27th June 1973

[502] https://h2g2.com/edited_entry/A2430181; Emily Herbert, *Matt Smith: The Biography*, https://books.google.com.au/books?id=9aD_AQAAQBAJ&pg=PT24&lpg=PT24 &dq=roger+delgado+biography&source=bl&ots=4cgZziCc0d &sig=gOi8OkjCOW4fS2xScFiExf8p0u4&hl=en&sa=X &ved=0ahUKEwjt3s-1uoTQAhVMHpQKHWf_CCQ4FBDoAQgZMAA#v=onepage &q=roger%20delgado%20biography&f=false

[503] Interview September 1st 2016

[504] Interview June 27th 2016

[505] Interview July 14th 2017

[506] Interview August 8th 2016

[507] Interview June 26th 2016

[508] Briant, *Who is Michael E. Briant?*, p.86

[509] Pers.com

[510] *The Stage*, September 10th 1953, p.8

[511] *The Stage*, July 12th 1973, p.21

[512] *The Telegraph*, March 31st 1974, p.4

[513] *The Telegraph*, February 20th 1975, p.17

[514] *Glasgow Herald*, May 3rd 1974

[515] Interview July 12th 2016

[516] *The Guardian*, September 22nd 1978, p.20

[517] *Glasgow Herald*, October 2nd 1981

[518] *The Times*, June 20th 1973, p.20

[519] *The Times*, June 26th 1973, p.18

[520] Cook, 'Adapting telefantasy', p.119

[521] Interview June 27th 2016

[522] Marson, *Drama and Delight*, p.284

[523] Interview July 19th 2016

[524] Pers.com

[525] Pers.com

[526] Interview August 11th 2016

[527] Pers.com via Stephen Gittins at AIM, July 10th 2017

[528] Pers.com via Stephen Gittins at AIM, March 7th 2017

[529] Interview July 14th 2017

[530] Howe, Stammers and Walker, *Doctor Who: The Eighties*, p.168

[531] Ainsworth (ed), *Doctor Who: The Complete History Stories 58-60*, p.80

[532] *The Times*, January 3rd 1976

[533] *The Sunday Times*, October 24th 1976, p.52

[534] *The Sunday Times*, October 24th 1976, p.52

[535] 'The Fact of Fiction', *Doctor Who Magazine*, 332, p.27

[536] Molesworth, *Robert Holmes*, p.283

[537] Interview June 27th 2016

[538] *The Times*, June 15th 2004, p.30

[539] Interview June 27th 2016

[540] Simon Guerrier, 'Snake Eyes!', *Doctor Who Magazine*, 497, 2016, p.43

[541] Alan Barnes, 'Can you still love me in my new body', *Doctor Who Magazine*, 278, 1999, p.11

[542] Interview June 27th 2016

[543] Interview July 19th 2016

[544] Interview July 19th 2016

[545] Interview July 19th 2016

[546] http://www.walesonline.co.uk/whats-on/film-news/doctor-whos-missy-scary-actress-10041645

[547] https://twitter.com/bbcdoctorwho/status/573486957432602625/video/1